Performance Management in Health Care

Improving patient outcomes: an integrated approach

Edited by

**Jan Walburg, Helen Bevan,
John Wilderspin and Karin Lemmens**

 Routledge
Taylor & Francis Group

LONDON AND NEW YORK

First published 2006
by Routledge
2 Park Square, Milton Park, Abingdon, Oxon OX14 4RN

Simultaneously published in the USA and Canada
by Routledge
270 Madison Ave, New York, NY 10016

Routledge is an imprint of the Taylor & Francis Group

© 2006 Jan Walburg, Helen Bevan, John Wilderspin and Karin
Lemmens

Typeset in Perpetua and Bell Gothic
by Book Now Ltd
Printed and bound in Great Britain
by Antony Rowe Ltd, Chippenham, Wiltshire

British Library Cataloguing in Publication Data
A catalogue record for this book is available from the British Library

Library of Congress Cataloging in Publication Data
A catalog record for this book has been requested

ISBN10: 0–415–32397–5 (hbk)
0–415–32398–3 (pbk)

ISBN13: 9–78–0–415–32397–0 (hbk)
9–78–0–415–32398–7 (pbk)

Contents

CONTENTS

Illustrations

FIGURES

TABLES

Contributors

Phil Glanfield was previously Director of the Performance Development Team and is now an Independent Organisation Consultant, NHS Modernisation Agency, UK.

Robbert Huijsman is Professor of Integrated Care Management and Director of Education at the Erasmus Medical Centre, Institute of Health Policy and Management, Rotterdam, The Netherlands.

Richard Lendon is Clinical Lead at the NHS Modernisation Agency, UK.

Wim Schellekens is CEO of the CBO, Dutch Institute for Healthcare Improvement, Utrecht, The Netherlands.

Astrid van Dijk is Manager of Research at the Dr Leo Kannerhuis Centre for Austism in Doorwerth, The Netherlands, and Development Researcher at the Amsterdam Institute of Addication Research, Amsterdam, The Netherlands.

Foreword

If you pause and think of our health services, the chances are that you will think of service and people rather than structure and processes. Health care pervades the media and often our personal lives. Mention of it captures attention and makes the audience linger. We respect its practitioners and voluntarily put our lives in their hands.

At the same time, health services across the developed world face increasing pressures: an ageing population, constantly improving medical technologies, and ever-higher expectations from more consumerist societies. Simply increasing expenditure on healthcare is not an option, so alternative strategies must be pursued.

Central to this challenge is the need to improve the performance of our health-care organisations. Borrowing initially from industrial and commercial models, health service leaders have become far more sophisticated in the way they manage their organisations, searching for greater efficiency and 'payback' on the investment they receive.

This performance management approach has brought some dividends, and a more structured way of addressing the complex challenges of providing modern healthcare. However, all too often 'performance' has been construed very narrowly in terms of financial targets or increased efficiency, and not in terms that are meaningful to patients, or to healthcare professionals.

This book addresses that challenge head on. It explores how performance management was introduced into health services, and sets out the prerequisites for a high-performing health care organisation. Crucially, it addresses how performance can be improved at the level of the clinical team, in terms of the outcome and experience of individual patients.

Drawing on the experience of the authors in the UK and Dutch health system, it sets out how 'best practice' techniques can be applied to make a real and sustainable difference to the outcomes of healthcare. The book argues that a focus on performance and outcomes should be at the heart of clinical practice. It also poses questions as to how the theory and practice of performance improvement can be further developed for the benefit of patients. These are important issues that all those of us involved in leading and developing health services should be considering.

Professor Aidan Halligan
Deputy Chief Medical Officer for England
Director, Healthcare Quality and Standards Directorate

Series preface

In almost all Western countries, health care is in a state of radical transformation. How can we meet the needs and demands of increasingly empowered 'consumers', contain costs, incorporate 'evidence based' modes of working, and re-motivate health care professionals – and all at the same time? The health care systems in Western countries are usually compared and contrasted along their axes of difference: nationalized versus fully market-driven; tax-based versus insurance-based financing; 'gatekeeping' general practitioners versus self-referral to hospital care. Yet, with the exception perhaps of the USA, these health care systems are struggling in strikingly similar ways to achieve the optimal balance between market incentives and government controls; and between professional self-regulation and explicit accountability to patients and payers. It has become clear that simple solutions will not work: neither 'the market' nor 'state control' offers the complete answer to the challenges that face us. Equally, neither 'professional self-regulation' nor 'paying for performance' offers the simple recipe that will heal our health care systems' woes.

New models of health policy and health management are needed throughout the Western world, including a shift from a downstream preoccupation with health care services to an upstream focus on the health of communities and its improve-ment, tackling the widening 'health gap' between social groups; novel conceptions of organising integrated care and chronic disease management; new approaches to performance management; innovative and realistic information management; effective human resource management; new models for managing clinical work; and so forth. These new models and approaches need to be theoretically sound, empirically based, and speak to professionals and patients and the problems facing them.

There is a great and urgent need for leadership in health and health care, and the many managers and professionals who end up in health management roles cur-rently lack a well-defined series of textbooks to equip them with the requisite knowledge and insights derived from experience and research. We do not need more management hype, or yet another management fad or fashion that is unthinkingly applied to health care. These days more than ever, however, we do need to learn from each other's experiences and mistakes, and we need to be able to communicate and build upon 'best practices' developed elsewhere.

The *Routledge Health Management Series* aims to meet these needs by providing health care managers with the theoretical knowledge, practical insights and concrete examples they require in today's rapidly changing health care environment, including experiences from adjacent fields (e.g. business, service industry, and so forth) where relevant. The series has a strong international orientation, comparing related developments and drawing on examples from different countries. The series is aimed at Masters students, other postgraduate students and also at experienced managers providing them with an up-to-date overview of the latest developments in their particular field(s) of interest. The books in the series contain a balanced mix of theoretical backgrounds and starting points on the one hand, and practice-oriented advice and guidance on the other in order to show how these theoretical concepts might be applied to concrete management challenges. Finally, each book pays explicit attention to the 'practitioner perspective': each book contains direct accounts or case studies, often written by practitioners, of the relevance (or otherwise) to them of the issues presented.

Prof. Dr. Marc Berg, MD, PhD
Prof. Dr. Robbert Huijsman, MBA, PhD
Prof. Dr. David J. Hunter, MA, PhD, HonFPHM, FRCP(Edin.)
Prof. Dr. John Øvretveit, PhD

Chapter 1

Introduction

The challenge of performance improvement in health care

Jan Walburg, Helen Bevan, John Wilderspin and Karin Lemmens

KEY POINTS OF THIS CHAPTER

■ Why existing approaches to quality improvement, in isolation, will not deliver sustained performance improvement

■ The need for an integrated approach to the application of quality of care tools

■ The potential of outcome management in healthcare

INTRODUCTION

Health care organisations are busy with efforts to improve the quality of care on a number of fronts. Many institutions are conducting 'improvement projects'. Typically these involve the formation of a team around a specific problem and then using the Plan-Do-Study-Act (PDSA) cycle to make changes (Langley *et al*. 1966). Other institutions are applying the principles of quality management and frequently make use of the European Foundation for Quality Management (EFQM) Excellence Model. These quality improvement measures are currently applied at the corporate level of the organisation.

In addition, various professional groups are involved in active efforts to improve the quality of work carried out by their professions through training programmes, registration schemes and the development of evidence-based guidelines and protocols. Similarly, the health care sector is very active with respect to quality certification. Numerous hospitals and healthcare organisations now participate in an accreditation trajectory, for example. Other institutions are investing in certification with the aid of the International Standard Organisation (ISO) system which has been specially adapted in a number of cases for use within the field of health care.

Despite all these efforts, a huge gap exists between the potential for quality improvement in health care and the reality. Health care systems are characterised by variation in clinical care, lack of responsiveness to users' needs, waste, delays and financial challenge (Institute of Medicine 2001). Current quality improvement efforts are typically not delivering enough change, at a fast enough rate. What stands out most is the difficulty of implementation and the fact that efforts to improve the quality of care tend to remain at the level of the organisation and thus receive insufficient expression at the point where clinicians actually treat patients. Part of the background to this book is the all-too-common scenario of 'undershoot' in corporate quality programmes. Although no studies comprehensively document the outcomes of large-scale quality programmes in health care, experts agree that most organisations are left with disappointing results (Bate *et al*. 2004). The current top-down quality systems are mostly oriented towards systems and processes, which means that the efforts of the relevant professionals and the efforts of organisational leaders are not sufficiently attuned to each other and thus inadequate.

What we need is corporate quality improvement strategy aimed at concrete results in terms of patient care. At the same time, there are risks when clinical teams embark on a myriad of grass roots local improvement projects if such projects are not aligned with the goals and priorities of the corporate organisation. A situation can be created where clinical teams work on one quality agenda and corporate leaders focus on a completely different set of priorities. Opportunities to spread best practice on outcome improvement and organisational learning are diminished (Bate *et al*. 2004). This must be based on the intrinsic motivation of individuals and teams, with the professionals and corporate leaders largely in agreement. Current practices typically do not come close to meeting these requirements. When we look at managers, we see that they often devote considerable effort to the implementation of quality systems. At the same time, however, their own management systems are often exclusively aimed at operational management and finances. Operational management and finances are the predominant topics used for accountability in annual reports.

The result of this is that the social environment (society) may look favourably upon a health care organisation which reports staying within its budget while meeting productivity targets but hardly be enthusiastic about the organisation. Such an approach can lead to confusion within the organisation as well. That is, the corporate leaders say that they are going to implement quality policy but act on the basis of productivity and financial figures. An orientation towards financial data is, of course, critically important in the management of a care organisation. However from the point of view of most of society, it misses the point because the performance of the organisation in the area of care is of primary importance.

2

When we look at treatment providers, we see that they generally already have their hands full with the conduct of their daily clinical work. They may, at times, attempt to improve the way they work on the basis of the guidelines provided by professional groups and on the basis of certification and accreditation schemes. But the implications of these efforts for the outcomes of the care process are not yet really known. Care professionals typically receive no systematic reporting with regard to their outcomes. And if they do receive such feedback, it typically involves a very high level of aggregation which makes it impossible to understand or interpret clinical performance at the level of the individual care giver or clinical team. Feedback may be provided with regard to patient satisfaction, for example, but only at the level of the organisation.

The purpose and significance of the care professional's work lie predominantly in the treatment of the individual patient and his or her reaction to treatment. A professional can therefore be inspired by being given direct insight into the results of his or her diagnostic and treatment efforts. Declining team results or evidence that a team is performing less well when compared to another team may be very disturbing and indeed downright unacceptable. However, when the care results are later seen to improve, the provision of such feedback constitutes a real source of satisfaction.

We can conclude that the many instruments available to measure and improve the quality of care only gain their significance and really become a part of the normal functioning of the care organisation when their impact on the care results becomes clearly visible to the treatment provider, the patient and the corporate leader. While the manager and the care professional typically have their own distinct objectives, with the one aimed at organisation and the other at content, focusing their orientation towards the continual improvement of care outcomes can provide a shared objective. We are therefore of the opinion that the isolated application of quality of care 'tools' in the form of projects, certification or models such as the EFQM has had its day. We believe that the tools must not only be applied in an integrated manner but also clearly directed at the outcomes of the care given to patients.

Support for the integrated application of quality of care tools comes from a comprehensive review of the literature on the influence of various instruments on the quality of care. When Grol (2001) reviewed the use of a number of strategies such as professional guidelines, professional development, feedback with regard to care results, increased involvement of the patient and total quality management to improve the quality of care, he came to the conclusion that the different methods were only partially successful. When it comes to improving the quality of care, Grol concludes that integrated methods applied to the care process itself appear to be most effective. Care outcomes improve when guidelines are carefully implemented, care professionals are intensively but personally educated and the care organisation applies quality of care policy on a broad basis. Quality of care policy aimed at the improvement of actual care results also appears to be of critical importance.

We describe this as 'outcome management' in the book, and it is based on the two principles:

- the integrated application of quality of care principles, and
- a strong and consistent orientation towards the improvement of actual care results.

We define outcome management here as the continual improvement of outcomes for the best possible care processes.

In this book we also talk in terms of 'performance improvement'. This is based on the premise that performance management in health care has traditionally focused on finances and operational management. As such, it has been of little relevance either to clinical professionals, or to the users of health services. Taking the disciplines of performance management, but relating them to the outcomes of care, seems much more relevant to both clinicians and users. This must be applied in a way which leads to continuous improvement in outcome for patients, hence performance improvement.

The design of the book is based on a staged approach to factors of importance for the realisation of outcome management and performance improvement. The first four chapters provide an introduction to learning in organisations, which is the foundation stone for improved outcomes (Chapter 2), to the model for outcome management (Chapter 3) and to the steps that healthcare leaders can take to create the organisational conditions for performance improvement to flourish (Chapter 4). The building blocks for outcome management are then described in the following ten chapters:

- the importance and impact of effective teamworking for performance improvement (Chapter 5);
- how performance can be improved by focusing on processes and systems (Chapter 6);
- how to define 'outcome of treatment' in multiple dimensions (Chapter 7)
- the importance of patient characteristics as variables in the outcomes of care (Chapter 8);
- benchmarking as a mechanism for comparing our own results to those of other teams (Chapter 9);
- effective mechanisms for feeding back data in ways that will lead to action (Chapter 10);
- how outcome management and performance improvement can contribute to a holistic disease management perspective (Chapter 11);
- issues pertaining to the public disclosure of performance outcomes (Chapter 12);

- actions to strengthen the scientific value of outcome measurement (Chapter 13);
- a summary of the major themes covered by the book and potential future directions (Chapter 14).

In the various chapters in this book, the different components of a model of outcome management are considered. The aim of doing this is to provide support for the efforts of teams and institutions to attain better care results. With the conscientious introduction of outcome management, health care can gradually develop a focus on the continual improvement of care results.

Teams receive information with regard to their results and can then compare this information to the results of others. Competition is no longer a question of who has the most beds or the largest care region but who attains the best results. Healthcare professionals are therefore supported in their natural predisposition to provide the best possible care for patients. With outcome management, care organisations can also contribute to the substantive scientific development of clinical disciplines on the basis of hand-on experience and not just research conducted within the artificial context of double-blind clinical trials. Finally, patients and society can be more thoroughly informed of the results of care with the widespread introduction of outcome management.

CONCLUSION

This book is an international cooperation between Dutch and British authors. Our healthcare systems are very different; one is social insurance based, the other is tax based. The structures and stakeholders are hard to compare. Yet we face many of the same problems and recognise the potential for outcome management in healthcare, whatever the national or cultural context.

There is a need for systematic, integrated approaches to improving the quality of care. Such approaches need to help corporate leaders deliver corporate goals at a strategic level. They also need to engage individual clinicians and clinical teams in the continuous improvement of their care and, in doing so, liberate the natural energy and creativity of the healthcare workforce.

The principles in this book can help your improvement journey whether you are an individual clinician, or student of healthcare or a corporate leader.

DISCUSSION QUESTIONS

1 To what extent is your existing approach to quality improvement delivering the results you require in the timescales you require?

2 What are the opportunities to develop a more integrated approach to the quality of care?

3 Which of the topics covered by the chapters in this book seem most relevant to your local situation?

REFERENCES

Bate, P., Bevan, H. and Robert, G. (2004) *Towards a million change agents: a review of the social movements literature – implications for large-scale change in the NHS*. NHS Modernisation Agency www.modern.nhs.uk

Grol, R. (2001) Improving the quality of medical care: building bridges among professional pride, payer, profit and patient satisfaction. *Journal of the American Medical Association*, 286(20): 2578–2585.

Institute of Medicine (2001) Crossing the quality chasm: a new health system for the 21st century. Washington, DC: National Academy Press.

Langley, G., Nolan, K., Nolan, T. and Provost, L. (1966) *The Improvement Guide: a practical approach to enhancing organisational performance*. San Francisco, CA: Jossey-Bass.

Part I

Background and principles of performance management

Chapter 2

The learning organisation in the health care sector

Jan Walburg

KEY POINTS OF THIS CHAPTER

- What organisational learning means in the healthcare sector
- Learning organisation and performance improvement
- Using information and knowledge to improve

INTRODUCTION

Outcome management is about improving outcomes of health care. The goal of outcome management is to support employees in learning from their work experience by letting them know about the outcomes of their care processes and to continuously improve the results of the care. Learning is at the centre here. In this chapter we will consult the existing knowledge about organisational learning. In doing so we hope to discover principles that promote learning in order to strengthen the delivery of outcome management.

LEARNING IN HEALTH CARE ORGANISATIONS

Health care organisations offer a multitude of opportunities for learning, opportunities which are capitalised on in outcome management (see Figure 2.1).

- *Learning from science.* The care processes are designed and modernised with taking evidence-based, cost-effective treatment methods into account.

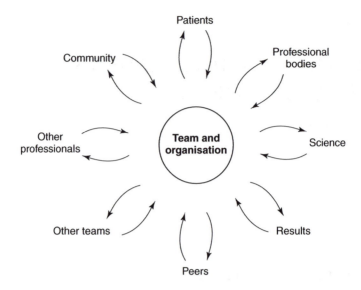

Figure 2.1 *Learning processes in outcome management.*

- *Learning from results.* The care team is regularly informed about care process outcomes in terms of clinical results, the quality of learning, patients' appraisal and costs.
- *Learning from peers.* Care processes are designed in an integrated manner, taking into account the input of different disciplines. Furthermore, the team works in a multidisciplinary framework.
- *Learning from other teams.* The results of one team are compared with the results of other teams involved in comparable health care processes. The site of best health care process is visited and the care process studied.
- *Learning from other professionals.* The teams receive current information about the results of their work and on that basis can adapt their work method to examine whether the results have improved.
- *Learning from the community (social environment).* The organisation makes information available to the community and enters into a dialogue.
- *Learning from patients.* Patients are involved in goal-setting, the implementation of treatment and treatment evaluation.
- *Learning from professional bodies.* Outcome management is about improving outcomes of health care. Closely related to learning from science. Care processes incorporate professional guidelines and protocols.

Before defining the principles of outcome management, to explore in depth what precisely is meant by learning and how organisational learning can be encouraged.

KNOWLEDGE AND LEARNING

A health care organisation consists of professionals who use their knowledge to prevent medical problems, to treat patients with medical problems and to take care of patients with chronic problems. The knowledge they have changes, is updated and expanded, which is why health care professionals have to enrich their knowledge in a way which allows them to better achieve their treatment goals. Professionals – both at individual and at team level – thus learn continuously from the experiences of others outlined in literature and other forms of knowledge dissemination, but, above all, from their own experiences.

Professionals in health care work with their hands, their head and (not to forget!) their heart. Working with their head entails putting to use the knowledge stored in their brain. This knowledge is acquired in a learning process; knowledge and learning representing the key words that we will explore in more detail. To this end we will use the observations of Weggeman *et al.* (1997).

We differentiate between three concepts:

- *Data* are symbolic representations of figures, quantities, variables or facts.
- *Information* is attributing meaning to data; using data such that they take on meaning, for example by means of data comparison.
- *Knowledge* is what enables a person to fulfil a certain task by selecting, interpreting and assessing information.

Applied to health care: we have *data* about the number of infections that occur with a certain medical intervention. These data are categorised over time such that a trend becomes visible. The trend is then compared with the national average and this process generates *information*. Based on that information we make statements such as 'the number of infections decreases in the course of time' and 'the number of infections is lower than the national average'. This is *knowledge*: it is applied when decisions are made regarding an adaptation of the health care process, and is a rather linear representation of what is, in fact, a cyclic process.

In other words, knowledge (staying with Weggeman) is the capacity that enables a person to perform a certain task.

- *Knowledge* (K) is the result of information (I). Knowledge, on the one hand, is a matter of explicit and established knowledge concerning a certain task and, on the other hand, involves experience, skills and attitudes (ESA), also referred to as implicit knowledge, which is not laid down in words or numbers, but exists in an implicit or subconscious way. Knowledge thus is a resultant of both explicit and implicit knowledge, and can be reflected in a formula: $K = I (ESA)$.
- *Explicit knowledge* is a theory, procedure or protocol, transferable through

education and obtainable through study. A fundamental characteristic of explicit knowledge is that it can be tested.
- *Implicit knowledge* is attained from experiences, skills and attitudes; it is transferred through demonstration and acquired through imitation and experimentation.

Learning is going through a process that enriches existing implicit or explicit knowledge. Hence learning is the development of knowledge. The input of learning is knowledge, but so is the output: enriched knowledge.

Learning thus entails converting new knowledge or external knowledge in order to continuously adapt existing knowledge and improve its suitability for (in our case) performing care and treatment tasks. The knowledge creation process also entails that something is added to the knowledge domain with existing components in new combinations.

The components 'information' and 'experiences, skills and attitudes' thus are updated, for example by a new theory, through broadening of one's experience, the adaptation of skills and change in attitudes.

Nonaka and Takeuchi (1995), using these forms of knowledge, arrive at four forms of learning (see Table 2.1).

- *Socialisation:* e.g. learning how to dance or, translated to health care, acquiring surgical skills. Another person is needed for these activities, i.e., the activity cannot be performed alone.
- *Externalisation:* documenting experience in the form of language, e.g. in care protocols or clinical paths, or the certification of care processes.
- *Internalisation:* capturing knowledge tacitly, for example the (virtually intuitive) routines of nursing staff and physicians.
- *Combination:* e.g. the development of knowledge which comes about when the knowledge of an illness is combined with the knowledge of prevention, as is the case in disease management. Or when the knowledge and the experience of nursing staff are combined with the knowledge of the physician, as is the case in teams.

Two concepts are mentioned in Table 2.1 that require some additional clarification: empirical learning and rational learning. *Empirical learning* means acquiring knowledge through experience, such as learning how to walk or how to ride a bicycle. *Rational learning* is enriching one's knowledge through the transfer of existing knowledge, e.g. learning arithmetic. In health care, both forms of learning exist: acquiring experience through work and the development of knowledge based on a thorough knowledge of the human anatomy and its diseases.

The major source of knowledge in health care, according to the words of Nonaka and Takeuch (1995), is *implicit knowledge*. Normally the management of the

Table 2.1 *The four learning processes*

	To implicit knowledge	To explicit knowledge
From implicit knowledge	*1 Socialisation*	*2 Externalisation*
	■ copy from others, imitate ■ create supervisor–apprentice–student relationships ■ learn through *trial and error* (form of empirical learning; not possible at individual basis)	■ express in words what has become clear through socialisation, dialogue or reflection on one's own actions ■ express implicit knowledge in explicit concepts (metaphors, analogies, models, hypotheses, theories) (empirical and rational learning; can be done individually and in teams)
From explicit knowledge	*3 Internalisation*	*4 Combination*
	■ *learning by doing* ■ expands the operational efficiency of thinking and doing ■ integrate socialisation, externalisation and combination of experiences in the individual *tacit knowledge* base (empirical and rational learning; not possible in teams)	■ studying ■ reconfigure existing knowledge by sorting, categorising, linking, etc. ■ find *New Combinations* ■ create knowledge systems by combining existing *bodies of knowledge* (form of rational learning; is possible individually and in teams)

institution will activate that source by seeing to it that the 'wheel' of the four learning processes is continuously followed through, thereby constantly generating new implicit knowledge of a higher quality. Outcome management intends to systematise this stimulation (see Table 2.2).

ORGANISATIONAL LEARNING

In organisations, learning processes take place at different levels. First, learning at the individual level. Each health care professional has gathered a certain amount of

Table 2.2 Learning processes in outcome management

	To implicit knowledge	To explicit knowledge
From implicit knowledge	1 *Socialisation* ■ continuous learning ■ learning through doing	2 *Externalisation* ■ protocols ■ guidelines ■ clinical guidelines ■ quality assurance ■ transfer of knowledge
From explicit knowledge	4 *Internalisation* ■ experimental learning ■ learning through doing	3 *Combination* ■ multidisciplinary teams ■ working in health care chains ■ information on results ■ benchmarking ■ transfer of knowledge

knowledge through education and experience keeps that professional know-how up-to-date and expands upon it. Learning at individual level manifests itself in terms of an improved professional work method and improved individual treatment results.

Second, learning takes place at team or group level. Here, a number of health workers who collaborate in a care process develop collective knowledge, skills and competences. This is not so much a matter of the total sum of knowledge of the individual knowledge, but markedly the *collectiveness* of knowledge and skills acquired in the process of collaboration of the team members and the mutually reinforcing competences. Learning at team or group level expresses itself in the improvement of the results in a particular process under the team's responsibility.

Third, learning at organisational level. At the centre of organisational learning is the knowledge which is required and developed in order to be able to collectively implement the mission of the organisation. Learning is directed at the realisation of the organisation's goals. This includes improving the quality of the organisation's overall functioning and developing new services and products. Learning is expressed in the improvement of the performance of the organisation as a whole.

Organisational learning hence relates to creating knowledge about learning processes at individual, group and organisational level. Creating awareness in the context of health care aims to provide patients and others involved with increasingly better services. In other words: 'organisational learning relates to the experience-based improvement of the implementation of the goals of the organisation' (Argyris 2000).

It is striking that most authors always define or describe 'learning' in a positive sense, as though learning automatically assumes improvement. Naturally learning processes can exist which lessen the performance of individuals, teams and organ-isations. As least as interesting is the phenomenon 'unlearning' in health care organisations. It is a regular occurrence that work methods, having once crept in, are difficult to get rid of, even if it was demonstrated that another, new method works better. For example:

- not adopting a service providing attitude, because this supposedly does not befit a health care organisation;
- not cooperating with other teams because a team is judged only by its own performance;
- an organisation not operating in a market-oriented way because its culture is product-oriented, with the aim to manufacture increasingly better products from the perspective of the professionals and not from the perspective of the patient.

Swierenga and Wierdsma (1990) give several examples of organisations in which learning is goal-oriented but not effective, such as the teaching organisation and the didactic organisation. A teaching organisation generally has a pioneering char-acter, with the strategy intuitively geared to the short term, the structure infor-mal and the culture characterised by the power of a few. Learning in these organisations goes well, but only into one direction. The didactic organisation usu-ally is a stable bureaucracy, with a defensive strategy, the structure very hierarchic with many formal rules, and the culture rational, efficient and conflict avoiding. These organisations do not learn well. Incidentally, it does not take much effort to recognise the didactic culture in many health care organisations.

Organisational learning (described in more non-normative terms) is the occur-rence of behaviour changes under the influence of knowledge. We have termed the more ideological form of organisational learning 'the learning organisation'.

Organisational learning in its simple form is if an error is detected and subse-quently corrected. Argyris (2000) refers to this process as *single-loop* learning. This form of learning does not change the organisation nor the principle of the health care process. An assessment is made whether the health care process met the applicable standard, and if it did not, adaptations are made. Many quality improve-ment projects can be called single-loop learning. *Double-loop learning* involves changing the underlying principles. The term covers e.g. *business process re-engineer-ing*. Double-loop learning thus is about 'why': why do we deliver this care process in that particular way? Why do we collaborate in that particular manner? In order to achieve more fundamental and sweeping changes.

A third 'loop' must be added to the two loops of Argyris: *triple-loop learning* (Swierenga and Wierdsma, 1990). Triple-loop learning is when the principles upon which the organisation is based are put into question: do we or do we not want to provide health care on a commercial basis? Do we want to design our organisation initially such that it is a very pleasant place for our professionals or do we design our organisation with the focus on the patient?

These three forms of learning can be summarised in a diagram (see Figure 2.2).

In somewhat simplistic terms one could equate single-loop learning to improvement, double-loop learning to amendment and triple-loop learning to development (Swieringa and Wierdsma, 1990). This gives us enough building blocks to examine the learning organisation.

THE LEARNING ORGANISATION

'The learning organisation' is a management philosophy whose application has not been systematically studied, yet it still holds great attraction for many managers. The reason is that many managers are very aware of the fact that an organisation can develop only if it learns from the daily interactions with the community, the clients, the staff, the suppliers and others involved.

Peter Senge from the United States is the most renowned champion of the visions on which the learning organisation is based. He distinguishes between five 'disciplines' with which a learning organisation can develop (Senge, 1992):

- systems thinking
- personal mastery
- mental models
- building shared vision
- team learning.

1   *Systems thinking.* An organisation, but also the interaction of an organisation with the environment, is made up of systems with interdependent components. Both an individual and an organisation are part of such a system, hence making it difficult to see that system. Nonetheless, if one wants to solve problems, the system must be made visible, as problems rarely occur in merely one of the system's components, but are embedded in the total system. The

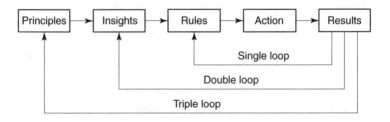

Figure 2.2 *Different forms of learning.*

development of thinking in terms of processes in the health care field is an example of systems thinking, as is thinking in health care chains and disease management.

2   *Personal mastery.* Individuals develop their personal skills and knowledge in an organisation. This is a purposive development as the consequence of someone's personal goals. The strongest basis is created when the goals of the organisation and individual goals match. In the health care field there is a strong dependence on the specialist know-how of the individual professional. A health care organisation 'fails or succeeds' with this know-how and will have to nurture and develop it.

3   *Mental models.* Employees capture their vision of the organisation in a mental model. These are the internal and usually implicit assumptions and generalisations about the organisation. The environment is then perceived from these mental models. This bears the risk that – should the community impel the organisation to change – it will still continue on from the existing mental model. In order to accomplish change, the mental models too will have to adapt. In the health care field, we also see mental models that are being challenged, for example:
    – the professional autonomy is challenged by the management which wants to be involved in the thought process about the content of the work;
    – the idea of the monopoly position is challenged by commercial health care providers;
    – the idea of being untouchable is challenged by the community, which wants health care organisations to be made to account for their actions;
    – the idea of autonomy is challenged by the chain concept.

4   *Building shared vision.* An organisation needs a mission and a vision which create unity and coherence between the activities of the organisation's components. The vision will have to be shared in one way or another by the employees of the organisation: they must be able to identify with such a mission and vision. The shared vision must also prevent that teams or individuals do not attune their own mission and goals sufficiently to those of the organisation.

5   *Team learning.* In most organisations people work in teams on one common process. In order to be able to improve that process, cooperation and synergy between individual team members is a prerequisite.

OUTCOME MANAGEMENT AND THE LEARNING ORGANISATION

Many of the principles of the learning organisation can be recognised in outcome management. We indicate how aspects of outcome management can be grouped under these principles.

17

Systems thinking in outcome management is stimulated by:

- the cooperation of different disciplines;
- the cooperation of teams in health care chains;
- thinking in terms of processes;
- stakeholder involvement;
- coherence between the mission of the organisation and the mission of the team and the individual in a shared mission.

Personal mastery is stimulated by:

- drawing up development plans for every employee;
- stimulating professional training in relation to team performance;
- continuous learning at the workplace.

Adjusting mental models is stimulated by:

- intensive interaction between the management and teams;
- active involvement of stakeholders including patients;
- development based on results and not based on ideology and dogma;
- accounting to and dialogue with the community.

Building shared vision is the starting point for outcome management. It is further strengthened by:

- negotiations between the management and teams about the team's mission and vision;
- negotiations between the team leader and individual team members about their personal vision and mission: this not only *creates* an organisation mission through dialogue, but also *strengthens* it over time.

Team learning is reinforced by:

- helping a team to create a mission and a vision in alignment with the organisation's overal mission;
- stimulating the formation of teams and explicitly supporting teams in their development;
- feedback of information on results at team level;
- giving the team a certain degree of autonomy concerning the responsibility for the care process;
- making team roles (more) explicit.

CONCLUSION

We can argue that outcome management is an operationalisation of the principles of the learning organisation, applied to health care (see Figure 2.3).

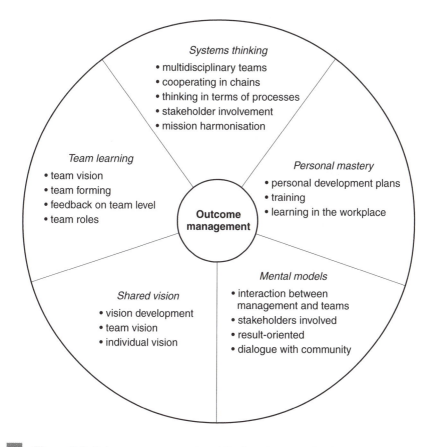

Figure 2.3 *Outcome management and the learning organisation.*

DISCUSSION QUESTIONS

1   Is my team or organisation capitalising on the learning opportunities that are available?
2   Are we creating the conditions that enable learning processes to take place?
3   We are encouraging the key learning processes that are necessary for effective outcome management (socialisation, externalisation, internalisation, combination)?
4   Do we have opportunities for learning at individual, team and organisational level?
5   Are we using single-loop, double-loop or triple-loop learning?
6   Does our strategy or plan for outcomes management build on the components of the learning organisation adjusting mental models, shared vision, team learning?
7   Where we identify gaps in our learning strategy, what steps can we take to fill them?

REFERENCES

Argyris, C. (2000) *On organisational learning*. Oxford: Blackwell Business.

Nonaka, I. and Takeuchi, H. (1995) *The knowledge creating company: how Japanese companies create the dynamics of innovation*. New York: Oxford University Press.

Senge, P.M. (1992) *De vijfde discipline: de kunst en praktijk van de lerende organisatie*. Schiedam: Scriptum.

Swierenga, J. and Wierdsma, A.F.M. (1990) *Op weg naar een lerende organisatie*. Groningen: Wolters Noordhof.

Weggeman, M.C.D.P., Cornelissen, V.B.J., Fisscher, O.A.M. *et al.* (1997) *Kennismanagement. Reeks: HRM in de praktijk, afl. 8*. Deventer: Kluwer Bedrijfswetenschappen.

Chapter 3

Principles of performance management

Jan Walburg

KEY POINTS OF THIS CHAPTER

- A history of outcome management
- The elements of an effective outcome management system
- Outcome management compared with other quality improvement approaches
- The evidence for outcome management

INTRODUCTION

In a learning organisation, people acquire information and insights that enable them to develop their knowledge and skills. Knowledge and insights are obtained at work by reflecting on the results of our work, and identifying ways to improve these results. This chapter examines how a health care organisation can organise and arrange the work in ways that maximise the opportunities for learning and improvement. We present a model for outcome management that builds on 'outcome thinking' in health care.

THE DEVELOPMENT OF OUTCOME MANAGEMENT IN HEALTH CARE

Florence Nightingale not only is famous for her exemplary dedication to her patients, but also was the person who introduced outcome indicators to health care. During the Crimean War, she collected figures on wounded soldiers who subsequently died. She compared the mortality rate with the medical care these wounded soldiers had received. Nightingale discovered that effective nursing reduced the mortality rate among wounded soldiers from 32 per cent to 2 per cent. After she had broken down her research in more detail, she was able to demonstrate that health care outcomes were related to hygiene. This created interest in the quality of care in hospitals.

In 1914, Dr Codman, a surgeon, made an important next step. He believed that the outcomes of clinical care was the only thing that really counted in the assessment of a hospital. By measuring results, it would be possible to detect where errors occurred and subsequently prevent them from reoccurring. In particular, Codman concentrated on the indicator 'hospital mortality', differentiating between unavoidable and avoidable deaths. He believed the latter to be connected to the quality of the provision of care. As a result of his critique of the existing system, Codman was expelled from the medical profession and founded his own hospital: The End Result Hospital.

As the twentieth century progressed, many hospitals in the United States and in Europe continued to use outcome indicators. However, it was not a simple case of cause and effect. It was recognised that care outcomes depended heavily on factors other than the actual care provided. These included factors such as the severity of the medical problem, the condition of the patient, age and gender, etc. The healthcare quality improvement movement thus did not continue to focus on outcome indicators. Increasingly, the orientation towards structure and process characteristics developed. Between 1940 and 1970 the Joint Commission on Accreditation of Healthcare Organisations (JCAHO) in the United States emphasised structure standards above all else. Increasingly more indicators were used as measurable elements of care which give indications about quality, these are in fact exclusively process indicators.

Three events in the 1980s returned the focus once again to outcomes. For one, an article published in the *New York Times* in 1986 listed the mortality rate of hospitals in the United States. Consequently, the JCAHO in 1987 launched the *Agenda for Change*, aimed at clinical and organisational outcome measurements. The second set of events came in the form of publications of John Wennberg about the large regional differences in health care outcomes. The third issue came from Avedis Donabedian, who, in the 1980s, made a clear differentiation between three aspects of health care: *structure* (the available resources needed to provide care), *process* (the degree to which professionals comply with applicable guidelines) and *outcomes* (the change in a patient's health after treatment). As a consequence, a different definition can be applied to quality of care: 'the extent to which care processes raise the chance on patient-desired outcomes and reduce the likelihood of undesirable outcomes, given the present state of medical knowledge' (Des Harnais and McLaughlin, 1994).

Since that time outcome orientation is the predominant quality direction movement in the United States, with the Joint Commission leading the way. What we see is that the drivers of the outcome orientation are largely external: the interest of the public payers and the government in outcomes linked with the need for cost reduction, increased competition and the developments in the field of data collection and processing.

Health care organisations are following this trend. However, there is not a track record of success, in converting outcome orientation into internal management systems. Forms of outcome management have developed only in dribs and drabs in the field of somatic care (Nelson *et al*. 1998) and in the mental health sector (Joint Commission 1998; Lyons *et al*. 1997). The practice of publishing care outcomes, adjusted to account for *case-mix,* by hospital and even by specialist is becoming increasingly widespread, particularly through the Internet. Health care presently is still largely oriented towards process and structure and most health care organisations try to substantiate their quality policy through certification and accreditation. Several care organisations introduced the EFQM, but often without including clinical outcomes in the business results.

A MODEL FOR OUTCOME MANAGEMENT IN HEALTH CARE

A further trend since the early 1980s has been the application of business concepts of 'performance management' to health care. Performance management is the use of interrelated strategies to improve the performance of individuals, teams and organisations. It enables organisational leaders to monitor and respond to how the organisation delivers its goals. The performance management system will involve measuring progress against a series of performance indicators. We have already identified the fact that the primary concern in health care is the prevention, diagnosis and treatment of illness. Consequently that is what performance management in a care organisation will have to be geared at. The traditional limitation of the planning and control department to financial and production parameters must be removed so that the department will also be involved in a thorough and reliable measurement of care results. Performance management in health care thus relates especially to care outcomes, which is why we use the term 'outcome management'.

Through outcome management we want to achieve the continuous improvement of care outcomes from the best care processes possible, making the most efficient use of resources. The core of outcome management is giving clinical teams feedback and information about the outcomes of their care processes so that they can improve them. The relevant questions are (Joint Commission, 1998) as follows:

- ■ What are the outcomes for the individual patient who undergoes treatment? Which processes contribute to these outcomes?

- What are the outcomes for a certain population and which processes contribute to these outcomes?
- What are the outcomes for the individual patient who undergoes treatment, and which processes contribute to these outcomes?
- What are the outcomes for a certain population and which processes contribute to these outcomes?
- What are the outcomes for a certain group of patients who share certain characteristics (e.g. age, comorbidity, health condition), and which processes contribute to these outcomes?
- What are the outcomes connected with a certain treatment or approach, and what are the contributing processes?

The elements of outcome management are:

- the patient
- the care team
- the care process
- the outcomes.

These elements combined form a clinical microsystem. A clinical microsystem is defined as:

> A small group of people who regularly work together to provide care to a certain patient sub-population. The system has clinical and business-related objectives, interlinked processes and a similar information environment and it sees to it that outcomes are produced. Microsystems develop over time and are often embedded in larger organisations. They are complex, self-adaptive systems and perform the primary tasks that ensue from the central objectives, meet the needs of the employees and maintain themselves as clinical units.
>
> (Nelson *et al*. 2002)

The connection between these elements is reflected in Figure 3.1.

Patients enter a care process in a certain state of health. This state of health changes (preferably improves) or stabilises under the influence of a treatment professional or a team of professionals in charge of the treatment. The change in the patient's health is determined in terms of care outcomes. We shall deal with the various elements of clinical microsystems in more detail.

- *Patient*. In order to begin treatment, insight into the health of the patient is needed. This insight is also needed to assess the outcomes. Countless factors influence the results of the care process, e.g. the severity of the illness, gen-

Figure 3.1 *First feedback cycle: the clinical microsystem.*

der, age, the physical condition and the social background. This is also referred to as the *case-mix*, which is established ahead of treatment and which differs for each care process and each patient. This allows the analysis of differences in outcomes in their relation to patient characteristics.

■ *Care team*. In health care different professionals work together in an interdependent relationship with a common goal: the recovery of the patient. That is what makes them a team. In order to be able to function as a team, a number of organisational and socio-psychological factors must be met, such as clear responsibility for the care process, a shared insight into and vision of that process, cooperation, joint evaluation of the results and experiencing an environment in which the results of the care can be safely discussed. The care team is responsible for the implementation and improvement of the care process and thus is the entity which receives the information about the results of that care process.

■ *Care process*. The care process is the intervention carried out by the team in order to accomplish an improvement in the patient's health. The care process is regulated by a number of professional guidelines. In the context of outcome management it is important that the care process is documented, for example, in a flow chart, making it possible to connect the results with a certain process phase or component. Documentation can also be developed through protocols or clinical pathways. The care process can be assured through certification or accreditation.

■ *Outcomes*. Outcomes are patient characteristics that can change as a result of treatment. Outcomes must indicate the immediate consequences of an intervention, but also the consequences in the longer term, especially where patients have long-term conditions and diseases.

There is a difference between outcomes that are part of a certain clinical picture (illness-specific clinical outcomes) and outcomes that are more general in nature, for instance, relating to life quality. Additional aspects which are important in evaluating the results of a care process are its assessment by the patient and the costs of the process. An outcome quadrant can be developed based on these factors. They will vary per illness and per patient (see Figure 3.2).

25

Figure 3.2 *Outcome quadrant.*

Outcomes, in all four areas of the quadrant, in their interrelated connection, related to patient characteristics, are fed back to the care team. To make the outcomes more significant they can be compared with a norm in the form of a previously formulated goal. However, it is also possible to compare or benchmark the outcomes with the results of other teams responsible for implementing a comparable care process. The outcomes are subsequently collected in a central databank, allowing the team to compare its results with those of other teams and to conduct an analysis of care processes that produce better outcomes. The results of the best performing teams can form a standard goal which all teams might aspire or seek to move beyond. That is what we refer to as the second feedback cycle (see Figure 3.3).

Hence outcomes can be supplied by more teams and compared with the outcomes of other teams with the help of the central databank (see Figure 3.4).

A third feedback cycle is created on account of the fact that the data in the central databank can systematically be consulted by experts to conduct meta-analyses of the results. These meta-analyses can lead to the adaptation of guidelines for specific patient groups or specific settings in which treatment takes place. This is how outcome management contributes to the development of a particular specialist field (see Figure 3.5).

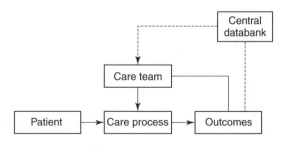

Figure 3.3 *Second feedback cycle.*

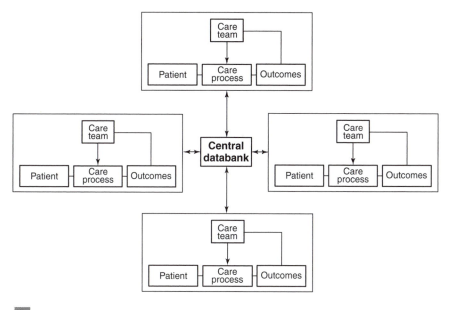

Figure 3.4 *Clinical benchmarking of outcomes.*

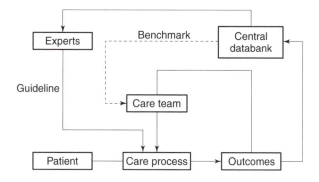

Figure 3.5 *Third feedback cycle.*

Outcome management is principally geared at organisations and teams that provide care and improve and assess their results with the help of outcome management. An organisation/team may decide to publish their results in one form or another for the benefit of the patients, financial sponsors or commessiary. The reactions on the outcomes that will come from these stakeholders create the fourth feedback cycle (see Figure 3.6).

Although there is a need to create an environment where a safe and 'unthreatened' discussion of results can take place between health care professionals, it is

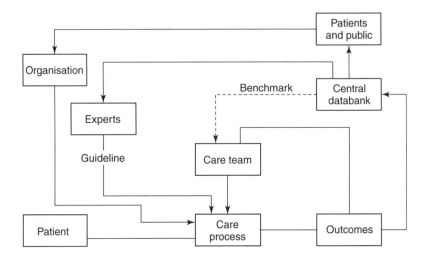

Figure 3.6 *Fourth feedback cycle: the community.*

virtually impossible to disregard the interest of other stakeholders in these outcomes. They too could be involved in a dialogue which ensures that such that their involvement leads to an improvement of the care process. With sponsors, for example, the financial consequences of qualitative better care could be discussed; with the wider system, the funding of preventive care; with patient organisations the outcomes of the patient assessment research, and with scientists the need for additional scientific know-how.

OUTCOME MANAGEMENT AND QUALITY MANAGEMENT

Outcome management should be regarded as a form of quality management. After all, what matters is the continuous improvement of the organisation's performance. Outcome management should be positioned in conjunction with commonly used quality models.

Quality improvement on a project-by-project basis

A quality project is a temporary, structured and team-oriented activity. Often a time limited project team is formed, bringing together people from across the organisation. It is aimed at the improvement of this activity. Quality improvement on a project-by-project basis may involve the identification of a specific problem in service delivery, with a team using the Plan-Do-Study-Act cycle to find the solution. The search for the solution might take place by carefully mapping the process, measuring process characteristics, analysing the cause of problems, brainstorming about and weighing possibilities for improvement, implementing the desired change and objectively determining the improvement; after which the next cycle can begin.

The same principles are used in outcome management where team orientation, measurement focus and applying the PDSA cycle are concerned. The difference lies in the organisation-wide application of outcome management, care teams instead of ad-hoc teams and the continual character of the improvement actions that refer to all aspects of care. Outcome management applies all principles of the project-by-project based improvement in a wider framework.

Quality assurance through accreditation and certification

Quality assurance aims to systematise and document the operational processes. As basis for documenting these processes, many care organisations use the ISO certification scheme, which – in its modern and revised version – aims more than ever at improving and designing the PDSA cycles for various subjects.

Accreditation involves an external review to establish the extent to which the organisation meets the rules and standards of its own sector. In a certification process this review is performed by external, independent inspectors.

In outcome management too, it is important that processes are documented in order to facilitate a stable delivery and the comparison of processes with one another, and this is where certification or accreditation comes in very appropriately. Moreover, the new generation of ISO-based certification schemes is considerably more outcome-oriented, including the PDSA-cycle.

Integral quality models such as the EFQM Excellence Model

The European Foundation for Quality Management Excellence Model is a widely used framework for quality. It enables organisations to self-assess their performance. Organisations that utilise the EFQM Excellence Model seek to maximise their results in the four key areas of performance, customers, people and society. They do this through the enabling factors of leadership driving policy and strategy, delivered through people, partnership resources and processes. For professionals, it often is too abstract a model with too small a connection to the primary process. It is striking that clinical results nowadays are rarely included in the business results, which focus more on financial and management indicators than on outcome indicators.

Outcome management has the same organisation-wide ambition of achieving continuous improvement and focuses much more on care results. A good combination might be if the organisation were to take the EFQM model as basis, working out elements with the help of outcome management principles that are more connected with the delivery of the care.

Professional quality improvement

Clinical professionals have their own tradition of quality improvement, particularly based on education, professional registration and inter-collegial peer-review. These activities are often initiated by scientific associations, sponsored by the various professional groups. In outcome management the care professional and the clinical team take centre stage. The clinical team receive information about their outcomes and they decide which improvements are possible and what is required in terms of know-how and skills. Outcome management is enhanced when care professionals invest deeply in their own development. This investment is determined on the one hand by what professional groups deem necessary, and on the other by the shortcomings encountered during the delivery of the care. Table 3.1 summarises the similarities and differences once more.

The conclusion is that outcome management can easily be combined with traditional quality systems and that both are mutually reinforcing. The integration of the various models from outcome management takes place in the contribution by the quality systems to the improvement of the care results.

Table 3.1 *Outcome management and quality systems*

	Similarity	Difference
Project by project	■ structured ■ team oriented ■ based on objective measurements	■ scope and impact ■ ad-hoc team instead of care team ■ continuous instead of incidental
Quality assurance	■ process documentation ■ application of PDSA-cycle ■ review of standards	■ particularly focused at care results instead of processes ■ review of results
EFQM Excellence Model	■ continuous improvement ■ organisation wide	■ managers and especially top management oriented instead of aimed at professionals ■ focus on business results instead of focus on care process results
Professional quality	■ education, training, testing	■ especially process oriented instead of outcome oriented

THE IMPLEMENTATION OF OUTCOME MANAGEMENT

Outcome management can be described as 'a partnership between managers and individuals and teams who, through the use of dialogue, develop a common agreement about expectations and goals' (Armstrong, 2001). It is a process of development that leads to an agreement about path of development and improvement. It also enables employees to control and develop their own performance, guided and supported by their leaders and peers and the organisation. In that sense, outcome management is a holistic process which relates to all aspects of the organisation's business, including personnel and financial policy and the strategic direction of the organisation. Outcome management can help ensure that the focus is not just on the administrative system, but on the behaviour of clinical and managerial leaders, teams and individual employees. Outcome management not only focuses on results, but also involves processes and competences of people.

Outcome management is therefore based on the premise that staff will contribute fully to the realisation of organisational goals if they know and share these goals and participated in their development. It also recognises that the realisation of the goals depends on the competences of staff and teams and the degree to which they are supported by the organisation and their leaders in terms of resources, processes and systems.

Outcome management succeeds or fails with the interpersonal relationships between individuals, and teams and their leaders between team members and between teams. Outcome management involves the implementation of a management system that is purposefully focused on improving results. The results are obtained by individuals and their contribution depends on the quality of the leadership, their motivation, clarity about what is expected of them, their knowledge, competences and skills, the ways in which they are influenced by the organisation and the ways they influence the organisation. This requires:

- effective leadership development;
- staff motivation through involvement, room for individual development and reward for good performances;
- clear roles and job descriptions;
- continuous training and coaching of employees and teams.

These components of a strategy to create a receptive local context for outcome management are covered in greater detail in Chapter 4.

DOES OUTCOME MANAGEMENT WORK?

In health care we aim to apply those interventions whose effectiveness is scientifically proven and based on evidence. But what do we know about the effectiveness of management systems? How effective is outcome management? Are there indications that outcome management does indeed result in improved performance? Our starting point is performance management in a business context.

Arthur Andersen published the results of a performance management study in 400 large corporations (De Waal 2001). Performance management is a management philosophy strongly focused at obtaining good and sustainable business results. Performance management begins with a strategic process that takes internal and external factors into account and arrives at clearly defined and measurable strategic goals. These goals are subsequently operationalised. The principal strength of the model lies in the systematic application of performance measurement and performance assessment, the periodic assessment of the performance in order to be able to take timely action. This system is usually supported by a reward structure which is based on the contribution made by the employees to the performance of the organisation.

The study dealt with the question: do organisations that have implemented systematic performance management do better than organisations that have not implemented performance management at all, or have implemented it in a less systematic manner? The comparison generated the picture shown in Figure 3.7.

The organisations that had focused on performance measurement achieved considerably better results on all indicators.

The study also compared the performance and particularly the financial results between the businesses that did or did not have a formal performance management system. De Waal (2001) summarised advantages of performance management (see Figure 3.8). Performance management systems enable the

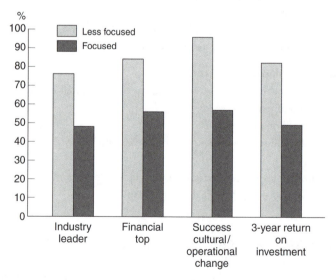

Figure 3.7 *Effects of structured performance measurement (De Waal 2001).*

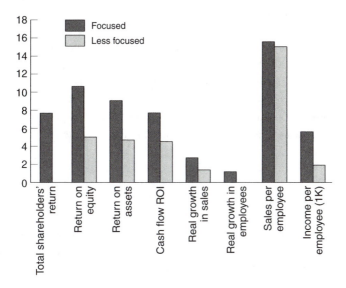

Figure 3.8 *(Non)performance of management-oriented organisations (De Waal 2001).*

corporate strategy to be translated into clear, measurable goals. It provides timely signals that lead to actions before real problems can arise. Performance management supports the principle of the learning organisation through its orientation towards continuous improvement. Finally the culture of the organisation is influenced by the fact that the members of the organisation are aware of what is important.

Outcome management in the health care sector has not yet been widely applied and evaluated on a systematic basis. Research on outcomes can be grouped into a number of categories.

Effects measurements

These are the typical *clinical trials* which examine whether there are differences in outcome between two or more treatment forms. They do not involve systematic feedback to treatment professionals. Results are published only long after treatment has occurred and little is reported about the implementation of the findings.

Diagnostics measurements

These measurements focus on identifying non-treatment related factors that may influence outcomes. As regards feedback and results, the same factors apply to effects studies (Grol 2001).

Quality improvement projects

A care team identifies a problem and corrects it, using the PDSA cycle. Many articles have been published about this, virtually all of them success stories. The improvements reported are mostly process improvements: shorter waiting times, better flow and shorter length of stay in hospital. A project that has 'ended' per definition mostly stops after the realisation of the desired improvement. These results may include an indication of the capacity of the project team to accomplish improvements.

Outcome management

Research is being conducted on the effects of elements of outcome management such as benchmarking. However, no studies have been carried out on the impact that benchmarking has on health care outcomes.

Application of guidelines

A number of studies have been conducted on the effects that feedback has on the degree to which social workers apply guidelines or protocols. The results of these studies mainly show positive effects of such a form of feedback. An example is a study into the effects of feedback on drug workers in a drug rehabilitation clinic, where the application of guidelines increased from 42 per cent to 81 per cent (Andrejewski *et al*. 2001).

Systematic forms of outcome management avant la lettre

A number of studies have been conducted regarding the effects of a more systematic form of feedback to professionals. One study looked into the effect of measuring the degree of coverage of vaccination programmes and giving feedback. The number of vaccinated 2-year-old children between 1988 and 1994 were compared. Annual feedback on vaccination rates was given to the programme leaders in the state of Georgia but not to local leaders in other states. Georgia started out with the same vaccination coverage as the rest of the USA, namely 53 per cent. In 1993, this had increased to 60 per cent across the USA, but to 90 per cent in Georgia. The authors explain the key differentiating factor was the systematic feedback the Georgia programmes had received over an extended period of time (Le Baron *et al*. 1997).

There is another important element here. Not only is it vital that indicators are present and that data are gathered, but also feedback for the teams responsible is equally important. The way and the frequency in which feedback is provided determine whether or not permanent improvement processes are created.

Another study examined diabetes patients between 1994 and 1998, with treatment staff receiving information on a yearly basis about key process and outcome indicators. The results show that in a number of process measurements improvements occured in terms of lab studies and medication, but not in outcome measurements such as acute heart attacks, brain haemorrhages or foot amputations. There was no control group (Petitti *et al.* 2000).

Also at team level the effects of feedback on the outcomes of results have been examined. In one of the few controlled studies at team level into the effects of feedback, 609 psychiatric patients were split up in four groups. In two of the groups, treatment staff received feedback; in the two control groups, no feedback was given. Providing feedback on outcomes prolonged the treatment time and improved the outcomes in patients with a negative prognosis. In the feedback group, twice as many patients showed considerable improvement compared to the patients in the control group, and three times fewer patients suffered a deterioration in their condition. Feedback in patients with a good prognosis led to shorter treatment times with the same clinical outcomes (Lambert *et al.* 2000). Incidentally this study also illustrates the importance of measuring patients' variables (prognosis) as well as process and outcome indicators.

CONCLUSION

These studies do not allow hard conclusions about the extent to which outcome management improves health care results.

We can learn a great deal from attempts to gear professionals to results. Indicators are often of dubious quality and oversimplified indicators are chosen to make measuring possible. The context in which outcomes are applied also is too simple: results are fed back without attention being paid to other aspects such as guidelines, quality systems, process indicators and the need to encourage team involvement.

Some studies suggest that feedback can be useful when provided by a respected professional using evidence-based guidelines and if it fits within a policy of continuous improvement (Grol 2001). This assumption is strongly supported by an analysis of sixteen review articles which measure the effects on the improvement of health care, achieved through a combined approach. This incorporates evidence-based processes *and* attention to training *and* the application of principles of total quality management *and* assurance *and* feedback on results. This analysis shows that only that combination leads to very significant quality improvements, certainly when compared with the isolated application of these strategies.

Grol (2001), in his review study on research into health care quality improvement interventions, concludes:

> They all point in the direction of the need for building bridges between the different approaches to quality improvement. There is a need for integrated methods and comprehensive programs that combine, for instance, evidence-based guidelines, clinical pathways, indicators for continuous assessment, and quality improvement projects embedded within a wider quality system of a hospital or a practice.
>
> (Grol 2001)

Outcome management is a combined approach in the sense that it applies principles of evidence-based, certified or accredited health care processes, professional education and training, feedback on health care results in the context of total quality management. There is sufficient evidence, from healthcare and other sectors that the individual components of outcome management help to deliver better outcomes for patients. Outcome management provides a 'package' of evidence-based approaches. Its potential is very promising.

DISCUSSION QUESTIONS

1   What are the implications of the approach to outcome management described in this chapter for our team?
2   How could outcome management be combined with other approaches to quality improvement that our team or organisation is already using?
3   What level of feedback cycle should we aspire to? (First, second, third or fourth feedback cycle?)
4   How will we measure the results of our outcome management strategy?

REFERENCES

Andrzejewski, M.E., Kimberley, C.K., Morral, A.R. *et al.* (2001) Technology transfer through performance management: the effects of graphic feedback and positive reinforcement on drug treatment counselor's behavior. *Drug and Alcohol Dependence,* 63(2): 179–186.

Armstrong, M. (2001) *The performance management audit.* Cambridge: Cambridge Strategy Publications.

Des Harnais, S. and McLaughlin, C.P. (1994) The outcome model of quality, in C.P. McLaughlin and A.D. Kaluzny (eds) *Continuous quality improvement in health care.* Gaithersburg, MD: Aspen.

De Waal, A. (2001) *Power of performance management: how leading companies create sustained value*. New York: John Wiley.

Grol, R. (2001) Improving the quality of medical care: building bridges among professional pride, payer, profit and patient satisfaction. *Journal of the American Medical Association*, 286(20): 2578–2585.

Grol, R. and Casparie, A.F. (1995) Kwaliteit van zorgonderzoek. *Tijdschrift voor sociale gezondheidszorg*, 73(4): 237–244.

Joint Commission (1998) *Using performance measures to improve outcomes in behavioral health*. Report from *Joint Commission on Accreditation of Healthcare Organisations (JCAHO)*. Oakbrook Terrace, IL: JCAHO.

Lambert, M.J., Whipple, J.L., Smart, D.W. *et al.* (2000) The effects of providing therapists with feedback on patient progress during psychotherapy: are outcomes enhanced? Paper presented at conference on Behavioral Healthcare Tomorrow, Washington, DC. Published (2001) *Psychotherapy Research*, 11(1): 49–68.

Le Baron, C.W., Chaney, M., Baughman, A.L. *et al.* (1997) Impact of measurement and feedback on vaccination coverage in public clinics 1988–1994. *JAMA*, 277(8): 631–635.

Lyons, J.S., Howard, K.I., O'Mahoney, M.T. and Lish, J.D. (1997) *The measurement management of clinical outcomes in mental health*. New York: John Wiley.

Nelson, E.C., Splaine, M.E., Batalden, P.B. *et al.* (1998) Measuring clinical outcomes at the frontline, in C. Caldwel (ed.) *The handbook for managing change in health care*. Milwaukee, WI: Press ASQ QualityPress.

Nelson, E.C., Batalden, P.B., Huber, T.P. *et al.* (2002) Learning from high performing frontline clinical units. *Joint Commission Journal on Quality and Safety*, 28: 472–493.

Petitti, D.B., Contreras, R., Ziel, F.H. *et al.* (2000) Evaluating the effect of performance monitoring and feedback on care process, utilisation, and outcome. *Diabetes Care*, 23(2): 192–196.

Chapter 4

Setting the scene

John Wilderspin and Helen Bevan

KEY POINTS OF THIS CHAPTER

■ Organisational conditions that enable performance improvement to flourish
■ Steps that healthcare leaders can take to set the scene for performance improvement

INTRODUCTION

Chapters 2 and 3 have described the underlying principles of good performance management and the framework within which we are working. This chapter considers the conditions necessary to create tangible, long-lasting performance improvement. Creating an environment and an infrastructure where change can flourish is more important as a predictive factor for success than any specific performance intervention (Ham *et al*. 2002). Many studies of successful change have highlighted the contributing role of a receptive local context for change. Characteristics of a receptive context include effective clinical and managerial leadership, clear strategic goals, collaboration and teamwork and learning from mistakes (Garside 1998; Pettigrew *et al*. 1998; Shortell and Kaluzny 1998; Ham *et al*. 2002; Greenhalgh *et al*. 2004; Maher and Gustafson 2004).

Setting the scene by focusing on context should be the initial priority of any leader embarking on a performance improvement strategy:

> Context (should be treated) neither just as descriptive background nor as a source of opportunity and constraint for change but as something which must be accessible and understood by the innovating group and ultimately mobilised to achieve practical effects.
>
> (Pettigrew *et al*. 1998)

There have been some examples of quick performance turnaround but none have succeeded in sustaining performance without simultaneously investing effort for the future. These foundations are multilayered, and are interdependent; there is no magic bullet or simple solution to this issue (NHS Modernisation Agency 2004). However, learning from healthcare organisations with the most ambitious performance improvement strategies suggests a number of categories for leadership attention (Reinertsen 2004). These are shown in Table 4.1.

BUILD THE WILL FOR CHANGE

First of all, do the organisation's leaders have a clear picture of what 'success' looks like? Is it based purely on the expectations of one head office, whether that be an elected government, or a private or not-for-profit organisation, or is it in the vision of one person such as the chief executive, or a small group of like-minded

Table 4.1 *Steps in setting the scene for performance improvement*

1 *Build the will for change*
  - identify clear aims
  - channel leadership attention
  - define the case for change
  - present the change as further improvement of the present

2 *Generate evidence and ideas*
  - gather, share and evaluate knowledge
  - know the best in your field
  - compare your current performance with the best

3 *Build on the voice of the customer*
  - enable patients to be the decision makers in their own care
  - genuinely involve patients and the public in performance improvement

4 *Execute change*
  - create incentives and 'attractions' for change
  - focus on results
  - build leadership capability

5 *Engage the whole system*
  - work with all stakeholders, inside and outside the organisation
  - promote professional teamwork for performance improvement
  - establish the need to change
  - empower staff

6 *Sustain the changes*
  - make progress on all fronts
  - make performance improvement a line responsibility
  - create the conditions for ongoing success

Source: adapted from Reinertsen 2004

individuals? Much better that it reflects the views and aspirations of all the organisation's stakeholders; patients and users, the local public, staff and partner organisations as well as the hierarchy within which the organisation functions. The more inclusive the process, the greater the likelihood of achieving real and sustainable change in the longer term (Axelrod *et al.* 2004).

The process of developing this 'picture of success' will be instructive in itself. Although different stakeholders may have some different perspectives and aspirations, there will also be many common themes. Equally, stakeholders' views will be based in part on their perceptions of the organisation's current strengths and weaknesses; an invaluable guide as to where improvement efforts will need to focus. Recognising the multiplicity of aspirations is in itself important; healthcare organisations do not have single aims, but rather complex sets of objectives, which need to be reconciled. Successful organisations have readily accepted this paradigm, and developed strategies for dealing with ambiguity, rather than ignoring it (Axelrod *et al.* 2004).

This vision of success needs to be couched in a number of different ways. Clearly, it must include measurable objectives relative to the core business of the organisation, and the major preoccupations of its stakeholders. For example, what is going to be done to improve access to services, or the quality of outcomes, or the level of resources to be used? Just as important however, is to reflect the key values of the organisation; do you see your staff as partners or as resources? What relationship do you want to have with your key suppliers? How do you think senior leaders should conduct their business? In some ways these are more permanent yardsticks of success than more tangible objectives; the aspirations of politicians, shareholders and the public can be changeable, but the expectations of how the organisation and its staff behave are more deep-rooted.

Once the organisation has defined, or at least given some shape to its key success criteria, these need to be communicated back to stakeholders, especially staff. This process needs to be strategic (where do we intend to be in five or ten years' time?) as well as operational (what do we need or want to have achieved by the year end?).

It also needs to be as simple, and all embracing as possible. The cliché is of the cleaner at NASA's Cape Canaveral launch site who, when asked what his job was, replied 'to put a man on the moon'. Not all of us can be so succinct, but it is certainly important that success can be as easily understood by staff and the public as by senior managers. Measurability is important, but so is relevance to the lives of all those who have a stake in the organisation. The currency of leadership is attention. How leaders 'spend' this attention determines the focus and actions of people throughout their organisations (Bibby and Reinertsen 2004).

Senior clinical and managerial leaders in healthcare organisations have a responsibility to bring together the strategic aims of the organisation, its operational imperatives and specific performance improvement projects. The involvement of senior leaders in such projects makes an unequivocal statement about the importance of performance improvement work and sets a powerful example for others to follow. In some cases, it will be enough for senior leaders to set direction and leaver local clinical teams to drive their own improvements. However, the greater the scale of performance gap to be filled, the more crucial the attention and will of senior leaders becomes (Bibby and Reinertsen 2004; Maher and Gustafson 2004; Reinertsen 2004).

Senior leaders need to make the business case for performance improvement visible and explicit (Fry *et al.* 2002; NHS Modernisation Agency 2004; Reinertsen 2004). They need to specify the anticipated benefits from performance improvement initiatives, using a 'balanced scorecard' approach. They should use the same business planning models that work for other organisation-wide goals such as financial performance. Clinical quality, strategy, finance and operations need to be connected. The plan for quality improvement cannot exist independently of the strategic, operational and financial plans (Fry *et al.* 2002).

'Those who ignore history are condemned to repeat it.' It is the job of organisational leaders to plan for the future, and to be positive in their expectations that what is to come will be better than that which went before. This is particularly true of new leaders who have no stake in an organisation's past. However, even in organisations which are by any yardstick performing poorly, this enthusiasm for the future is not shared by everyone. Sometimes this is about fear of change, or even unwillingness to change, but often it is because there are many good things that were done in the past, and those good things represent hard work, and a pride of achievement.

Respecting the achievements of the past, and being seen to build on them, is crucial to gaining commitment to change, and further improvement. Indeed, paradoxically, positioning radical, even transformational, change as a continuity of the present (building on what is already good) rather than a break with the past, may get better results (Fry *et al.* 2002). Equally, it is important that leaders understand where their organisation has come from, before embarking on a new direction; the past is as much part of the journey as the future, and the two parts need to fit together. This does not mean that organisations always have to be as they always have been, but progress always represent evolution as opposed to something completely new.

Cultural analysis is to understand what currently works, and why, and in particular who makes things happen, or stops them happening. These are key pieces of the jigsaw of creating a receptive context (Garside 1998; Shortell and Kaluzny 1998; Ham *et al.* 2002).

Once the organisation, and its leaders, are clear about their future direction, and are able to see it in the context of what has gone before, they have some meaningful yardsticks of current performance. As referred to earlier, the process of setting a future direction (and indeed of understanding the past) will produce a

41

wealth of evidence about current strengths and weaknesses. Some of this evidence may be subjective, but usually a consistent pattern emerges. The process will have helped create a picture of capability (do we always hit our deadlines, or do we always miss them?), capacity for change (are staff keen to develop, or satisfied with the status quo) and values (are services run for the benefit of users, or the staff?). It will also highlight priorities for short-term action ('we never stuck within the budget') and strategic development ('managers and clinicians just don't get on'). Critical to this process is prioritisation; which things have to be done to ensure survival, and which things must be done to improve performance in the longer term? This is the hardest aspect of scene setting; many organisations go through the process described above, but come up with a huge shopping list of things that ought to be done, and try to do these all at once, ending up achieving little or nothing. Successful organisations think hard about which actions will bring the most reward (as well as those which really are critical to survival) and focus their efforts on ensuring those things are actually delivered (Reinertsen 2004).

GENERATE EVIDENCE AND IDEAS

'Knowledge management' is a term in fashion; books on the topic populate countless airport bookstores. Although more sophisticated techniques are undoubtedly being developed, often supported by advances in information technology, the basic principles are as old as history. Knowing that there is a better way of doing things, sharing evidence of success (or failure), teaching new skills; all of these rely on the use and transfer of knowledge. Yet again, part of the success of knowledge sharing relates to attitude, as well as technique. One of the 'cultural artefacts' of many healthcare organisations is that they are strongly averse to importing ideas from elsewhere; this is sometimes referred to as the 'not invented here' syndrome (Greenhalgh *et al.* 2004). One can speculate as to why this culture exists; it is, however, a major obstacle to rapid performance improvement. Attention must be paid to this issue if successful knowledge management is to be embedded.

Assuming this can be done, attention should be paid to setting up robust systems to gather, share and evaluate knowledge. This applies to all aspects for which the organisation is responsible, including the organisational development process it is applying to itself. Therefore, if the organisation is to be successful in developing, delivering, and constantly adapting good healthcare services, it must have systems to gather knowledge internally and externally, share that knowledge with appropriate staff, and constantly evaluate the delivery of these services. Equally, if the organisation is to develop itself to be successful, leaders and staff must have access to knowledge about their own performance, and the performance of others, to help them to improve.

Assessing where you are, relative to where you want to get to, is very important. However, it should not be done in isolation. The organisation should also benchmark its performance; where possible against an agreed standard, or at the very least against the performance of others (Joss 1994; Ernst & Young 2004). Ambitious healthcare organisations take steps to identify 'best in the world' performers to set a standard to aspire to (Reinertsen 2004).

Many healthcare systems have developed relatively sophisticated frameworks to measure the performance of individual organisations. These are usually based on the key concerns of stakeholders (e.g. access to services, quality of care, cost etc.), technical measures of performance (usually clinical or professional best practice) and international comparisons. Examples of this are the British National Health Service (NHS), where each healthcare organisation is externally audited against national targets and standards, and allocated a performance rating (on a scale of 0 to 3 'stars') (Ferlie et al. 2002). Critics of such systems are concerned that even relatively sophisticated systems do not reflect the overall complexity of health care provision. However there is no doubt they act as a spur to improvement in respect of specific targets. (The arguments for and against are explored in more detail in Chapter 12.)

Comparison against these 'gold standards' can be done at different levels of the organisation. Many successful change programmes make use of 'measurement for improvement', asking participants to devise, a challenging target, relative to their own local priorities then measuring their improvement in performance against that target, as they adopt new working practices. Where such absolute measures do not exist or cannot be agreed upon, it is also possible to compare performance with others. If the parties to change are all agreed on the need for change and improvement, this can be very beneficial, as it acts as a spur to self-assessment and analysis. However, where a change process is being resisted, this type of benchmarking often simply leads to futile argument; whether the comparison is valid, whether the resources available to both parties are comparable, whether the constraints are as great in the organisation which it is being compared against.

This process of comparison is a foundation for improvement; increasing understanding of priorities; giving a picture of the relative size of the task, setting a baseline against which to measure change. It also starts to engage the organisation's stakeholders in the *need* for change, a prerequisite which is explored later in this chapter.

BUILD IN THE VOICE OF THE CUSTOMER

The most radical shift in the culture of public services recently has been the realisation that we exist to serve our patients and the wider public, and that everything we do should be geared towards that aim. It seems extraordinary that we should have ever lost sight of that, but so much of what we do is driven by the needs of other, often more vocal and powerful stakeholders, that it is easy to forget this simple truth.

It is an axiom in the business world that successful organisations focus obsessively on the needs of their customers. In the private sector, the central point of any quality focused organisation is the customer and is said to be the 'ultimate arbiter of quality' (Ferlie *et al.* 2002). This has not always been the case in health care, particularly in the public sector in the past. Success has been construed in different ways; financial performance, growth in physical size, research output have often been seen as more important than providing a service which is safe, high quality, and shaped around individual patients' needs. This is no longer acceptable. Even where patients do not pay directly for their health care, they are increasingly vocal about their needs and expectations, and express their views indirectly through the ballot box. This means that politicians are concerned to ensure that public health services are more responsive, even if the managers of local services have not recognised this change in public expectations. There are significant gains to be made by shaping services around the needs of patients rather than around the needs of the organisation. It is recognised that in comparison to the private sector the concept of the customer in health care is more complex. In health care there are multiple stakeholders involved – patient, carer, staff, management and government – and each may have different definitions of quality which can potentially result in conflicting interests (Mazur and Zuther 1996; Penny 2002; Sweeny and Griffiths 2002; Clarke *et al.* 2004). However to provide optimal care for patients we must consider them the most important customer. In trying to understand how to provide the best care possible organisations must examine their services with patients rather than in consideration of patients (De Feo and Barnard 2004).

In many systems, there are now direct links between the views of patients and the public, and the measured performance of healthcare organisations. At its most basic, this may mean the existence of a real, or managed 'market', where the preferences of patients impact directly on the bottom line, and often the survival of health care organisations. Even where this is not the case, organisations are inspected, and publicly rated, partly on the basis of their 'customers' views'. At worst, poor patient and public perceptions are now far more likely to be shared in the media, leading to an image of poor performance, whatever the protestations of the organisation about its success in terms of other indications.

Systematic research into customers needs and expectations is a continuous activity in commercial organisations where it is claimed that only by understanding your customer can you effectively deliver and improve services (Department of Health and Social Security (DHSS) 1983).

In health care, this is a huge task and is at times less evident:

businessmen have a keen sense of how well they are looking after their customers. Whether the NHS is meeting the needs of the patient, and the community, and can prove that it is doing so, is open to question.

(Berwick *et al.* 2005: 35)

Nevertheless, there has been an increase in the role of the customer in the development of government publications and policy which is one indicator that there is progress in moving away from the role of passive recipient. The concept of the customer as advocated in general quality management terms has proven quite difficult for health care to grasp. Nonetheless any insights into the 'voice of the customer' can only be of benefit as many would argue 'the better the organisation can understand and meet the needs of its diverse customers, the more successful it will be in the long run' (Berwick *et al.* 2002: 35).

It is often perceived that recognition of patient and public views needs to be undertaken as some sort of 'defensive measure'. This is far from the case. Those organisations that have positively addressed the need to involve patients more in their own care, and the public more in the running of their health service, have gained on many fronts. Crucially, when patients and the public feel genuinely involved, they quickly become allies, not enemies. Most people want their health services to succeed; they have a vested interest in it doing so, and an instinctive desire to be proud of local institutions and their staff.

Where patients and the public are involved in shaping their own care, or developing services, it has been recognised that they bring a wealth of experience and insight which on a day to day basis has often escaped the attention of busy staff. There are significant efficiency gains to be made by focussing service development around the needs of patients rather than around the needs of the organisation, these have included improvements such as reduction in waiting times and improvements to flow and general efficiency of the process (Kerr *et al.* 2002).

This should not be a surprise; patients want their service to be as efficient and effective as possible. They rightly want the best, but that does not necessarily mean greater expense, but instead greater imagination and flexibility. If organisations want to perform well, and be successful, patients need to be involved in all aspects of the improvement process; from the development of the vision, to the delivery of detailed aspects of their own care.

EXECUTE CHANGE

Real change, sustainable improvement in performance happens only if the majority of stakeholders want things to change for the better (Axelrod *et al.* 2004). Even in situations where the stakeholders themselves are dissatisfied with the status quo, the aversion to making change can be strong. There are many reasons for this: fear of change itself, concern that proposed changes may be for the worse, or a vested interest in the status quo for reasons of income or personal standing (Maher and Gustafson 2004). In today's fast moving world, holding together the status quo is a big enough job; the effort required to change can feel a step too far.

Breaking with the magnetic attraction of the present is a major step in itself. However, if the performance of the organisation is to change fundamentally, there must also be a process which sustains the changes; to make the break with the past irrevocable (Maher and Gustafson 2004). So how do we get people to embrace change, if the impulse to carry on as now is so strong?

There is considerable research into the reasons why people become prepared to change. Everett Rogers has set out how individuals going through a change process will fall into differing categories of preparedness to change; at one end of the spectrum are the innovators, who will be at the vanguard of the change process, at the other will be the 'laggards', who find the change deeply uncomfortable and have to be dragged kicking and screaming. Rogers also writes of the way in which those in the middle of the spectrum (the 'silent majority') can be swayed for or against change through the reaction of 'opinion leaders' (Rogers 1995). (This is also explored in Chapter 10.)

Importantly for a managed process of performance improvement, these opinion leaders are not necessarily those individuals who hold positions of formal authority. Nevertheless their reaction to change will be critical, and considerable attention must be paid to them if a receptive context for change is to be established.

Importantly, Rogers also identifies that one's position on the 'diffusion curve' of adoption is not fixed in stone; in respect of some issues individuals may be seen as 'laggards' whereas in other spheres of activity they may be seen as innovators, and vice versa. Recognising that a particular change is attractive for some, and anathema to others is important; recognising that a reframing of the reasons for change can result in a shift in attitude is crucial.

The importance of creating 'attractors' is explored more fully by Paul Plsek (2001) in his work on managing complexity. Plsek argues that the 'machine metaphor' which dominated management practice during the twentieth century is inappropriate; setting out a detailed prescription for change, and expecting everything to go to plan is untenable in a field as complex as that of human behaviour. Plsek goes on to describe how the application of simple rules, rather than detailed plans, is more likely to get organisations; or systems, to move in broadly the same direction. He also describes the importance of 'attractors', in getting individuals to embrace change. Arguing that to force individuals down a particular path is both hard work and often futile, Plsek urges leaders instead to describe the attractions of their vision of change, in terms which appeal to individuals and to the group.

How would this work in the context we are describing in this book? Instead of managers berating their staff for 'poor performance', and expecting them to improve, it requires leaders to explore with staff why the present is no longer tenable, and how things could be better; for them, their colleagues and for those they serve.

Of course, identifying attractors is not a simple business; there is unlikely to be one size which fits all. For some, the reason for change must be described in rational terms, followed up by evidence. For others, it is a question of appealing to their values; how can change allow them better to achieve the things they hold most important. Of course, in seeking to identify the key attractions, the process of analysis described in the previous section will prove invaluable.

The aspirations of stakeholders in respect of their service (whether as providers or users), are key pieces of evidence if leaders want to create an 'attractive' vision of change. However, as we have explored above, it is also important to pay respect to the past before encouraging people to move forward.

Of course, it would be naive to assume that all attractions can be seen in positive terms. Even if the leaders of an organisation are clear that performance must improve, and can persuade the majority of the necessity to change, there will be some whose stake in the status quo is too great for them to embrace change willingly.

Here, the incentives for change may need to reflect the 'unattractiveness' of staying as we are. At its most extreme (and this should be in a minority of cases) there may be need to use sanctions for refusing to accept change, and certainly, there needs to be clarity as to why the status quo is unacceptable.

Even in this group, however, there will be some benefits of any proposed change which can be accentuated, There will also be 'opinion leaders' who can help persuade the 'laggards' to accept the need for or inevitability of change.

Whatever, it is crucially important to keep this group in perspective. Rogers' research suggests that this group are usually in the minority, they may be vocal, and important, but most of the work of creating a receptive context needs to be focussed on the majority, including the innovators and 'early adoptees' of change.

Second, a disproportionate use of sanctions may turn this group into perceived 'victims' or 'martyrs', heightening the fear of change amongst the 'silent majority', and turning the laggards into the 'opinion leaders' with an ability to sway the majority to reject change, not embrace it.

It would be wrong to talk about creating a 'receptive context' and not acknowledge the impact that competition can have on people's attitude to change. In classical management theory, particularly as applied to private sector organisations, competition is seen as the engine with which to drive change. The market, with its opportunity for success, and fear of failure, is seen as the best way to ensure that organisations always strive to improve, and to align themselves with the needs of their customers (Boak and Jones 2002).

Although we believe there are other motivators for change, It would be foolish to discount the possible benefits of competition in the healthcare setting.

On the positive side, many healthcare workers are competitive individuals, striving for excellence, or at least to be better than their peers. When linked with some form of tangible reward, either financial or in terms of status, this can produce dramatic improvements in performance. Equally, the negative aspects of competition (failure, loss of status, or income) can be used to challenge complacency, and make the status quo seem very unattractive.

However, there are downsides to competition, which means that it should not be used as the only club in the bag. First, in many health care sectors, there is no true market, and the consumer does not have real choice. So, effective proxies have to be introduced to ensure that competitive behaviour is focussed on satisfying the needs of service users, and not some other lesser objective.

Second, the incentives of competition (and the sanctions for failure) are often focussed on the consequences for individuals. This runs counter to the known benefits of multidisciplinary, and multi-organisational teams. Creating incentives for whole teams, which do not reward part of the team at the expense of the whole, is a sophisticated exercise which needs to be thought through.

Not withstanding the possible negative consequences of competition, the possible benefits in creating a receptive context should not be dismissed. As with all the other methodologies described in this section, it should be considered, against the local context, and taking account of the people involved.

High calibre leadership

If good senior leadership is essential to initiate organisation wide change and improvement, it is evident that these leadership skills need to be replicated throughout the organisation if the essential changes are to spread, be sustained, and for the organisation to be able to adapt to changing circumstances. Crucially important for health care organisations is the promotion of clinical leadership; to make a real difference in clinical performance and outcomes for pateients, clinicians have to be involved in leading the process.

Good clinical leadership however, is not sufficient; in the best organisations there is a partnership and mutual respect amongst clinical and professional managers. This is not simply because the non-clinical aspects of the organisation need to be well managed to allow the clinicians to perform. It is also due to the blend of skills of clinicians and managers, and the personal chemistry which adds real value, and creates a mutual support network which sustains individuals efforts when the going gets tough.

There are two key components to a development strategy to establish 'leadership for improvement':

- ■ *Invest in leadership development.* Faced with the range of challenges described earlier in this chapter, it is not surprising that many organisations pay lip service to 'real' leadership development. It requires investment; funding and remitting people with the right calibre, high calibre development resources, and of course, time. Many organisations either ignore this investment, or try to side step it by simply replacing one set of leaders with another. Leadership development *may* require moving some people on from their current roles. However, wholesale changes are usually hugely disruptive, often leading to deterioration in performance, and if the new leaders are not invested in, they too will fail.

- *Develop 'improvement skills' in your leadership.* Even organisations which are staffed by leaders of experience and management expertise will struggle to hold their position in the dynamic environment of healthcare. It is becoming increasingly clear that a new set of skills, connected to the ability to continuously improve services is required by both leaders and front line staff. Some of these skills, particularly those related to the management of people, build on 'traditional' good management practice. Others, such as statistical process control, measuring for improvement and an understanding of how to work effectively in a complex environment, are much more sophisticated. These are not replacements for 'traditional' skills, such as budgetary management, which remain essential to good governance, and high performance. Instead, they are an add-on, which will allow leaders more easily to move their organisations forward, and to enable them to remain flexible in our fast moving environment.

Change management expertise

Many traditional management skills are about maintaining the organisation in equilibrium, rather than bringing about a transformation in performance. These skills are not to be decried; a lack of them is usually symptomatic of poorly performing organisations. However, to move organisations onto a higher plane of performance, and to keep them there over a long period of time, requires additional skills. As set out above, this skill set is now being properly enunciated in terms of a discipline of improvement based on the experience of quality and service improvement in many health systems since the 1980s. (This is explored in more detail in Chapter 6.) In essence it focuses on four main areas:

- how to involve users, carers, staff and the public in improving health services;
- using a 'whole systems' approach to the provision of services, rather than focussing on individual departments, or even individual organisations;
- developing individuals, and organisations in a systematic way;
- initiating and sustaining improvement in the way all of us carry out our work.

The discipline encompasses the latest thinking which apply to all of these themes, whether in terms of technical approaches to providing services in the most efficient way, or in the way key stakeholders can be empowered to contribute effectively to making services even better.

As with any aspect of performance management, this approach will be really effective only if it is understood, and utilised, by those who are responsible for the organisation. Sharing these skills with middle managers, or the leaders of a discrete part of the organisation will bring some benefit, but there will be an exponentially greater benefit if *all* leaders and managers are in possession of these skills. At the very least, line managers, whether at senior, middle or junior level, need to understand this new way of managing, and be sympathetic to its application. If they do not, there will be conflict, and the organisation will revert to the tried and tested, 'tried and tested', of course, only in terms of giving you what you've always had in the past, not what you will need in the future.

As well as giving line managers these new skills, however, many of the organisations that perform best actually retain staff who are experts in 'change management'. There are a number of good reasons for this. First, the discipline of improvement, like other aspects of management, is constantly being updated, and keeping up to date with best practice is a difficult task for busy line managers. Second, there is a need to share the skills of improvement, to teach them, and coach others. This is very difficult to do on top of a busy day job. Third, facilitating change and supporting others who are undergoing change is virtually a job in itself. Simply managing the status quo is enormously time consuming and challenging; even where line managers understand the need for change, and have the skills to implement it, finding time to make it happen is a big ask. Supporting line managers with skilled and respected facilitators allows those changes to happen more quickly, with a better chance of sustainability.

Skills and capability development

In describing the building blocks for change, we have already talked about three different sorts of skill or capability: leadership, change management and maintenance management. We have already referred to the need to invest in the people who have these skills, and constantly help them to develop those skills further. This applies equally to the multiplicity of other skills and capabilities that are required of complex health care organisations. This isn't simply a question of management skills; high performance in health care is ultimately down to the quality of clinical care that is delivered to patients.

It follows, therefore that a key building block of success is a comprehensive human resources (HR) strategy, aligned with the vision for the organisation, and reflecting all the issues which were highlighted in the analysis of current strengths and weaknesses. We always talk about 'our staff being our biggest asset'; developing an effective HR strategy is the opportunity to give meaning to these words. Recruiting and maintaining the best people, training and developing them, managing their performance and maximising their potential; without these foundation stones, high performance cannot happen.

One factor that is sometimes overlooked is the development of a workforce which remains flexible enough to cope with the constant, fast moving changes in healthcare, and in society. In part, this is a question of attitude; as referred to above on creating 'receptive context', different people have different abilities to cope with particular sorts of change. Recruitment, selection and development processes need to take account of this, and help staff to respond positively to changes in their jobs and their environment. Giving staff opportunities to try out different roles; to see things through others' eyes can be a useful part of such a policy. One small example of this is in the organisations we referred to above whom employ skilled facilitators to work alongside line managers. Sometimes these people are career facilitators who do this job permanently. Often however, the organisations will move line managers into these roles (and vice versa) as a means of developing skills, and avoiding staleness in their current roles. This also helps staff to feel part of the whole organisation, rather than simply identifying with 'their' department or function.

ENGAGE THE WHOLE SYSTEM

Proper recognition of the prime importance of patients does not mean that staff should now be seen as unimportant. While it is true that staff interests have sometimes held a disproportionate sway in the provision of health services, there have also been many instances where staff have been disenfranchised in change processes, and their legitimate concerns ignored.

As we referred to earlier in this chapter, staff are our greatest asset. Even in this technological age, the quality, effectiveness and cost of most of our activities will be based on the judgement, behaviour and competence of our staff. Where those staff feel valued, understand their contribution to patient care, and are well trained, the performance of the organisation is likely to be good. Where they feel disenfranchised, undervalued and ill equipped, it is not possible to perform at anything better than a mediocre level.

Proper appraisal systems and good performance management of individual staff is critical to the effective performance of the organisation. They are also important as a measure of ensuring that staff feel valued, and fairly treated. However, if staff are going to go the extra mile, to strive to achieve excellence, they need more than good performance management. They also need to be involved, to contribute positively to the way their service, their department and their organisation is run. This does not necessarily mean that they will be formally involved in the management of the organisation (though in some places this philosophy is actively espoused). It does mean, however, that staff are properly 'empowered' able to improve the things that affect their lives, and the services they provide to others. This doesn't imply anarchy; all of us work within constraints and most staff respect that. However, it does mean that staff are able to deploy their knowledge, skills and close observation of how things work at the front line, without constant reference to others, and the need to seek permission.

As with the shift to increased user involvement, the empowerment of staff may require a fundamental shift in the way organisations have historically been run. In particular, it may require some senior staff to reappraise the way they view others at different levels in the healthcare hierarchy. These are difficult challenges when those senior staff are also required to keep the show on the road, and simultaneously lead major change. However, if the organisation is to transform its performance, and harness the capability of all its key assets, this is a shift that must be undertaken.

SUSTAIN THE CHANGES

It is worth considering at this point whether successful change management is sufficient by itself to lead to sustainable improvements in performance. Many of the preconditions for successful change management are undoubtedly essential to high performance. Good leadership, support for improvement, performance measurement; these are prerequisites to making real change happen, and also to keep it happening. However, the key to real high performance lies in the ability to make change happen over the long term, to react to new circumstances, and to maintain momentum. This is the difference between the organisations which hit the headlines for one or two years, and those which remain at the top for ten, fifteen or twenty-five years.

The ability to sustain improvement is critical to good performance management. It needs to be built in to every facet of the organisation, the way new projects are initated, the way performance is measured, the way investment decisions are made, the way managers interact with their staff. The case study which accompanies this chapter, and studies of other high performing organisations demonstrate this. Real success did not happen overnight; the foundation stones were meticulously laid, the essential conditions have been carefully nurtured, and the leaders have always had an eye to the future as well as a sharp focus on the present.

Before embarking on a process of performance improvement, all leaders must have a strategy for sustainability; without it, impressive early gains may fade away, and the organisation will slip back into mediocrity.

We have made reference to complexity before in this chapter, in respect of the way human organisations work as complex adaptive systems rather than as machines. This makes performance management an inherently complex process in any organisation which achieves its objectives principally through the contribution of people rather than machines. However, healthcare organisations are faced with added layers of complexity, which are not shared by all other human enterprises. This begins at the basic level of defining who our clients are; whom we exist to serve. Clearly that starts with our patients, but for many health systems it also includes a responsibility for the health of the wider population. However these 'clients' are not always the paying customer; they are often represented by public commissioners or authorities, or private/voluntary insurance companies. These bodies in turn represent the financial interests of the taxpayer, shareholder, national or local government. Even meeting the needs of this complex array of clients and customers only tells half the story; healthcare organisations also have to work with the aspirations and requirements of other stakeholders. In common with all organisations they must be legal, safe and act as good corporate citizens, but as part of the fabric of public services, they also need to work with, and support the activities of other public service providers. The importance of healthcare to the public also means that it is the continual object of political and media interest, or at worst, interference.

Another prerequisite for sustainable improvement is a well-developed information infrastructure. This includes good information technology, but equally important are the skills to utilise information effectively, at every level of the organisation. Information is the engine that helps drive change, and improvement. Health services are lucky in that many of their staff have had sound training on the use of information; for diagnosis, monitoring of treatment regimes and clinical audit. We are also lucky that many of our users are hungry for information about the services we provide. But we don't necessarily exploit our good fortune; information systems have often been neglected, information skills allowed to wither, and informed practice whether clinical or managerial has not been championed.

Information management is important for many reasons. For health care to be of a technically high quality, good information about individual patients, and the wider public, needs to be robust, timely and easily accessible. In order to make the best use of our resources, we need to be able to measure our performance, in comparative terms, and against defined objectives. Crucially, if we are to move from a 'paternalistic' service to one which engages patients as 'partners in care', we need to be able to keep patients informed in a way we have never aspired to before. As with knowledge, our processes for gathering, sharing and evaluating information need to be carefully thought through and well maintained. This topic is important so it needs to be properly considered at the onset, rather than as an afterthought.

CASE STUDY

Sustained performance improvement at an organisational level: King's College Hospital, London

King's College Hospital is a good example of an organisation which has used many of the principles set out in this chapter to transform, then sustain its performance at a high level.

King's is a teaching hospital in south London. Like a number of London's teaching hospitals, it was deliberately sited in an area with considerable social deprivation, and its catchment population remains relatively deprived today. Interestingly, there remains a strong social ethos amongst senior doctors and other staff: eschewing the greater opportunities for financial reward in other parts of London, they see it as a key part of the hospital's mission to contribute to the development of the local community.

By the 1980s, King's had lost its position as a pre-eminent teaching hospital. The hospital's Emergency Department had a reputation for long waiting times and poor service, culminating in open criticism from local politicians and the public. A new chief executive was brought in to improve performance, and he began a process of transformational change which restored King's reputation, and has continued ever since.

The initial process of transformation divided into two parts:

- using external consultants to work with staff in the hospital;
- a second (arguably more successful) phase which was led by the hospital's own staff and focussed to a greater extent on improving the experience of patients.

Key features of this process of transformation were the following:

- A clear commitment to improve radically the performance and level of service of the much-maligned Emergency Department. This included recruitment of new high-calibre senior staff and capital investment, but also a fierce determination to prioritise key resources (such as beds) for emergency patients, rather than established priorities such as research and tertiary services.
- Using the vision of transformed emergency care to focus effort on radical redesign of the hospital's internal processes. This was underpinned by a formal 'transformation programme'.
- Use of a 'balanced scorecard' methodology for internal performance management purposes.
- Investment in dedicated 'improvement facilitators' working alongside line managers and clinical staff to support changes in practice.
- A clear human resources strategy focussed on recruiting high calibre staff and continuous development of new skills.
- A widely communicated set of 'values and behaviours' for all staff.
- Close working and mutual respect between clinicians and managers.

Since the original process began, King's has now had three different chief executives. They have each brought new perspectives and approaches to the leadership task, but have also continued to build on the past and maintain the core principles outlined above.

The most recent episode in this ongoing process of change has been participation in the 'Pursuing Perfection' programme. Working with local partners, and other programme participants in the UK, Europe and the USA, the objective is to transform further the delivery of health care, leading to improved clinical outcomes, greater satisfaction for patients, and the optimum use of scarce resources.

The hospital is now intending to move on to a further process of change, the 'Operational Transformation Programme'. In essence, this will ensure that clinical professionals are more engaged in production management, enhancing the efficiency of systems and processes but also focussed very strongly on improving the experience, outcomes and safety of care for patients.

CONCLUSION

This chapter has described the spade work which needs to take place if the organisation wants to be successful over a long period. Some of the processes and building blocks will not show dividends for some time, and in these days of instant gratification it will be necessary to deliver some short-term gains alongside this painstaking laying of solid foundations. However, we are clear that if the scene is not set in this way, and on a comprehensive basis, then the roots of success will be shallow, and the appearance of improvement will be short lived. The chapter also focuses principally at the level of the whole organisation, rather than the clinical micro-system as is the case in the remainder of this book. This is deliberate; although good outcomes for individual patients can be achieved by high-performing teams working in isolation, consistently good outcomes require the whole system to be working effectively.

REFERENCES

Axelrod, R., Axelrod, E., Beedon, J. and Jacobs, R. (2004) *You don't have to do it alone: how to involve others to get things done.* San Francisco, CA: Bernell-Koeheler.

Berwick, D., Godfrey, A. and Roessner, J. (2002) *Curing health care: new strategies for quality improvement.* San Francisco, CA: Jossey-Bass.

Bibby, J. and Reinertsen, J. (2004) *Leading for improvement: whose job is it anyway?* www.modern.nhs.uk/pursuingperfection

Boak, G. and Jones, H. (2002) *Leading innovation and change in the Health Service.* Chichester: Kingsham Press.

Clarke, C., Reed, J., Wainwright, D., McClelland, S., Swallow, V., Harden, J., Walton, G. and Walsh, S. (2004) The discipline of improvement: something old, something new? *Journal of Nursing Management*, 12: 85–96.

Coers, M., Gardner, C., Higgins, L. and Raybourn, C. (2001) *Benchmarking: a guide for your journey to best practice process*. London: Amer Productivity Centre.

De Feo, J. and Barnard, W. (2004) *Juran Institute's six sigma: breakthrough and beyond*. New York: McGraw-Hill.

Department of Health and Social Security (DHSS) (1983) *The NHS management inquiry report*. London: DHSS.

Ernst & Young (2004) *Straight talk about clinical quality from health care CEOs*. Ernst & Young White Paper. James L. Reinertsen and Mark Finucane for Ernst & Young, April 2004.

Ferlie, E., Aggarwall, K. and McGivern, G. (2002) *Assessing the impact of large-scale quality-led change programmes*. Report for the Department of Health Strategy Unit. London: Centre for Public Services Organisations, Imperial College Management School.

Fry, R., Barrett, F., Seiling, J. and Whitney, D. (eds) (2002) *Appreciative inquiry and organizational transformation: reports from the field*. Westport, CT and London: Quorum.

Garside, P. (1998) Organisational context for quality: lessons from the fields of organisational development and change management. *British Medical Journal, Quality in Healthcare*, 7(suppl.): S8–S15.

Greenhalgh, T., Robert, G., Macfarlane, F., Bate, P. and Kyriakidou, O. (2004) Diffusion of innovations in service organisations: systematic review and recommendations. *Milbank Quarterly*, 82(4): 581–629.

Ham, C., Kipping, R., McLeod, H. and Meredith, P. (2002) *Capacity, culture and leadership: lessons form experience of improving access to hospital services*. Birmingham: Health Services Management Centre.

Joss, R. (1994) What makes for successful TQM in the NHS? *International Journal of Health Care Quality Assurance*, 7(7): 4–9.

Kerr, D., Bevan, H., Gowland, B., Penny, J. and Berwick, D. (2002) Redesigning cancer care. *British Medical Journal*, 324: 164–166.

Maher, L. and Gustafson, D. (2004) *Sustainability toolkit*. www.modern.nhs.uk/sustainability

Mazur, G. and Zuther, R. (1996) *Voice of the customer: tutorials of the eighth symposium on quality function deployment*. Ann Arbor, MI: QED Institute.

NHS Modernisation Agency (2004) *Ten high impact changes for service improvement and delivery*. www.modern.nhs.uk/highimpactchanges

Penny, J. (2002) Building the discipline of improvement for health and social care: next steps for NHS improvement: the early vision and way forward. MA Management Board, November, unpublished paper.

Pettigrew, A., Thomas, H. and Whittington, R. (1998) *Handbook of strategy and management*. London: Sage.

Plsek, P. (2001) Redesigning healthcare with insights from the science of complex adaptive systems (Appendix B), in Institute of Medicine, *Crossing the quality chasm: a new health system for the 21st century*. Washington, DC: National Academy Press.

Reinertsen, J. (2004) *Theory of leadership for the transformation of health care organizations*. www.modern.nhs.uk/pursuingperfection

Rogers, E.M. (1995) *Diffusion of innovations*. New York: Free Press.

Senge, P. (1999) *The dance of change: the challenges of sustaining momentum in learning organisations*. London: Nicholas Brearly.

Shortell, S. and Kaluzny, A. (1998) *Health care management: organization, design and behaviour*. Albany, NY: Delmar.

Sweeny, K. and Griffiths. F. (2002) *Complexity and healthcare: an introduction*. Abingdon, Oxon: Radcliffe Medical Press.

57

Part II

Building blocks of performance management in health care

Chapter 5

Teamwork and performance

Phil Glanfield

KEY POINTS OF THIS CHAPTER

- Teamwork and high performance
- Individual, professional autonomy and teamwork
- Implications of different tasks and different teams
- Understanding the quality of teamwork

INTRODUCTION

CASE STUDY

An everyday story of teamwork

Sharon is an orthopaedic consultant at an English hospital. There she has three operating sessions each week and sees ambulatory patients in an outpatient clinic. Clinically she is particularly interested in non-invasive techniques and pain control. Some of her colleagues come to her for advice on these issues, others don't. It seems to her that a number of practices in the orthopaedic department are out of date. Most of the time Sharon enjoys her work; some days are better than others. Tuesday and Friday are usually good days when the theatre sessions always seem to go well.

Sharon is concerned about the number of referrals she is receiving from general practitioners – are they all necessary? Sometimes it is difficult to make a decision based on the limited information in the referral letter. There isn't enough time to see everybody and it is difficult to get hold of the GP. She wonders what happens at the other nearby hospitals.

The hospital has recently been downgraded within the government's annual performance rating system. Last year it was classified as a high performing hospital. This year it has been downgraded to a rating of 'poor performing' because of its financial performance and waiting times in the Accident and Emergency Department (A&E). Sharon hasn't noticed any significant difference in the hospital before or since the rating was announced. She knows there are problems in A&E because they are always looking for beds. Her clinical colleagues at a neighbouring hospital joke with her about being a 'poor performing doctor'. She doesn't think that is funny!

Sharon's story will help us to explore contemporary teamwork in this chapter. She and we know when we are working in a good team because even the most challenging of tasks is enjoyable, we have a sense of purpose and of being in this together. We are learning on the job and we all take pride in the results that we see. And, uncomfortable as it is, we must also acknowledge that close-knit teams are capable of getting things badly wrong while being convinced that they are doing a good job. This happens in the boardroom (Enron) and on the frontline of care (Argyris 1990).

So what is the relationship between teamwork and performance improvement? What does teamwork mean in today's complex and ever-changing world? How can we create the kind of teams that we would aspire to work in and that gets great results?

SERVICE DELIVERY, TEAMS AND WORKING LIFE

Teamwork in contemporary working life calls into question some of the traditional ways of thinking about teams and organising. The very word 'team' conjures up a picture of a small group of people who work alongside each other and are engaged in a common task with a common purpose. And yet, as Sharon illustrates, we often belong to a number of teams simultaneously: Sharon moves in and out of different teams in the same day, from the theatre to the ward to a multidisciplinary case conference. Team or workgroup, membership is often temporary;[1] rotas change, people come and go, new people join because of a new task or a reorganisation. Changes may be due to training requirements for clinical staff and career development for managers but not everybody moves. Sharon has been a consultant for five years and is beginning to find the turnover of managerial staff frustrating. She seems to keep going over the same ground with different people.

Paradoxically interest in effective teamwork has increased in parallel with our interest in individual, professional accountability (O'Neill 2002). This can be a significant stumbling block in the development of multidisciplinary teams (Savage and Moore 2004). It is important to hold onto this as a paradox, not something to be resolved in favour of the individual or the team; both are vital. Effective multidisciplinary teams provide better patient care (Zwarenstein and Bryant 2000) and individual professional accountability for patient care is inescapable.

Sometimes the team is invisible to the patient who sees only individual care providers in a sequence of encounters. Poor communication may become obvious to the patient if relevant information does not move as fast as they do. But the results of good, effective teamwork are likely to be the product of many interacting factors and may be unacknowledged and taken for granted. The team may be virtual in high or low-tech ways. For example, telemedicine can be an effective way of making scarce resources and skills go further and email and phone conferences may be the most efficient way of swapping and creating information and intelligence. Even in circumstances where the team does not meet, as patients, we would want the group of people involved in our care to work together 'as if' they were a high performing team.[2]

Of course this begs the question of what constitutes high performance. The hospital that Sharon works in has been rated as poor performing on its past year's performance on some very specific indicators. What does that say about the whole organisation? More importantly what does past performance tell us about the capacity of the organisation and the teams within it to improve?

WE HAVE A PROBLEM!

The multifaceted nature of today's teamwork presents us with a problem with our traditional notion of teambuilding. Typically we think of team development as a linear process that happens over time: 'storming, forming, norming, performing' (Tuckman 1965). In addition we pay attention to the psychological profiles and preferred behavioural style of individual team members and the team as a whole (for instance Belbin 2003). There is an underlying assumption of a balanced team with the *right* amount of the various ingredients or styles. Many organisations invest in teambuilding activities which are intended to accelerate the process of team development and bond the team together. Often these activities are 'off the job' and even outdoors with a tenuous connection to the task at work. We draw parallels with sporting teams which may not be appropriate and exclude from the conversation those who are not interested in sport. Sharon prefers the arts and is bored by endless talk of golf!

In a health care setting, there are unlikely to be any circumstances in which team performance is as easy to measure as a sporting team and there are other awkward questions. What happens if workgroups are not static in their membership, if one person is not able to pick a team from scratch with the 'right' profile? What happens if we can't get the team together or we can't afford to spend regular teambuilding time with each of our several teams? What if we don't have time to wait for the team to go through its stages of development?

TEAMWORK AND BEST PRACTICE

There is an interesting tension inherent in writing a chapter about teamwork in a book which draws heavily on quality improvement methodology which is rooted in a rational, scientific paradigm. In the scientific paradigm cause and effect can be established by breaking things down into their component parts and quantifying their impact. Once the causal connection has been isolated then we can predict and measure the impact of changes and plan and control to achieve the desired outcome. This engineering perspective on the world has served us well through the industrial revolution, the growth of technology and the development of medical science. Through fundamental research, application development, trial and error medical science has created powerful and effective diagnostic and therapeutic interventions so that in many circumstances we know what constitutes best practice. We call this an evidence base. This way of thinking about how we understand the world in which we live has become so dominant that it goes unquestioned and has become universally applicable; it informs orthodox ideas about teams and teambuilding. This leads us to understand teams by breaking them into their component psychological parts and to accelerate development through linear, diagnostic and therapeutic processes. We expect to be able to plan and manage teams based on some evidence about best practice.

The problems with the application of scientific thinking to a social context are well illustrated through the example of implementing evidence-based medicine. Typically evidence based medicine is understood as 'a body of evidence, separated from its social context, that can be unilaterally transmitted from the research setting – where it is known – to the world of practice – where it is not' (Wood *et al.* 1998: 1730). Usually the focus is on the production of high quality knowledge that 'speaks for itself'; theory (evidence) is isolated, proved and must therefore be used. Where there is attention paid to implementation

> the discussion is normative, linear or 'top down' in tone, using the language of 'planned change'. The use of incentive structures is also proposed to promote compliance. There is a search for effective interventions and change levers such as the development of educational programmes. Local change champions should be informed and motivated to implement desired change.
>
> (Ferlie *et al.* 2000: 97)

Sometimes there is recognition that the evidence does not speak for itself, something else is needed to achieve a change in practice. Change needs to be *engineered* through a variety of *mechanisms*. So the paradigm that developed the evidence also informs the approach to implementation. However, numerous studies have shown a modest relationship between scientific evidence base and clinical behaviour change. 'This confirms the long-established proposition that "science-push" is by itself a weak influence on behaviour' (Ferlie *et al.* 2000: 97). Ferlie also concludes that 'the micro politics and capacity of the local clinical group as a whole also determine rates of local learning and change' (Ferlie *et al.* 2000: 101). This underlines the importance of the team and workgroup to effective practice. Arguably the most importance characteristic of a team is that the individuals learn from and with each other as they go about their task.

LEARNING AND INTERDEPENDENCE

Stacey (2003) takes up this theme in his description of learning as an activity of interdependent people and begins to shape a different understanding of team. Earlier we touched on the question of individual professional autonomy and teamwork. Often this is posited as a dilemma that must be resolved in favour of the team or the individual; which is the superior authority? Stacey (2003) frames such situations differently, as a paradox 'a state in which two diametrically opposing forces/ideas are simultaneously present, neither of which can ever be resolved or eliminated'. For the clinician, accountability to her or his profession and, at the same time, accountability to the local team or organisation is an everyday reality. Providing health services is complex and complicated; different professions have different perspectives and make different contributions. Physicians and surgeons will often see the world differently and teams operating at the interface of health care and social care are likely to take a different perspective again.

From the patient's perspective, each and every contribution is important and it is equally important for each contribution to be provided in a timely way. In other words, healthcare is a highly interdependent activity in which all the actors are co-dependent. Any change or improvement in one area has implications for the whole. Innovative practice emerges from day to day conversations as staff grapple with the exigencies of a particular patient's condition and circumstances. And this is not planned in the sense of working to a blueprint or master plan. No one individual can be said to be 'in control' in the sense that others follow their orders, rather 'widespread coherent, evolving patterns emerge from local interaction' (Stacey 2003). Often difference in a workgroup or team is seen as a problem but here difference, paradox, conflict is valued because the interaction of those differences gives rise to new patterns, new and better ways of providing a service.

> This view of organisation focuses attention on the way in which ordinary everyday conversations between people are perpetually creating the future, in the present, in the form of shifting patterns of communication and power relations. What is being perpetually created is nothing other than inseparable individual and collective identities.
>
> (Stacey 2003: 8)

65

CASE STUDY

Sharon looks at her email and marvels at the latest management speak from the Human Resources Director. What can he mean? She is glad to be distracted by Sam, another orthopaedic specialist who she likes but sees as a bit of a stick in the mud as he has worked in the same way for years. He jokes: 'At your email again, shouldn't you be seeing patients? We've got performance targets to hit!' It dawns on Sharon that this is the chance she has been waiting for. 'Actually I am,' she says. 'I'm answering queries from general practitioners and physiotherapists about possible patient referrals'. Sharon goes on to describe a project she has been involved in with primary care clinicians and the two hospitals.

> I offered to use my practice to test out potential improvements. To start with we collated the available data about each step of the patient journey, from end to end, and developed a way of reporting this information routinely so everyone could see what was happening. We called it our 'dashboard'. The information revealed that some issues I thought were problematic, quality of referral and referral letters, were working well but improvements could be made in other areas by redirecting referrals to a physiotherapist and better selection of diagnostic tests. We have set up an electronic discussion forum so that primary care clinicians can discuss potential referrals with me. They email and I respond each day at a time that suits me. The results have been encouraging: patients in most pain are seen more quickly, other patients are treated earlier avoiding the need for surgery, I need fewer outpatient sessions because fewer patients are directly referred to me so I am able to spend more time in theatre. I think we should do this across the orthopaedic team.

SO WHAT?

If we take the interdependent, co-created clinical activity that we see in Sharon's work as our starting point (rather than an abstract notion of teamwork) then we can begin to explore what it might mean for our understanding of, and approach to, teams. In the case study we have looked at only a small part of Sharon's working day and yet it is apparent that she works in a number of different teams that have different tasks and characteristics. We might think of these different examples as:

■ *Physical teamwork:* when Sharon turns up for a theatre session her team does not have to discuss what they are going to do and who is going to do it; everyone knows their job and they get on with it. On Tuesdays and Fridays it is usually the same anaesthetist and most of the team have been together for some time so they have got to know each other well. Things 'just happen', often there is no need to talk, but there is always time for a chat.

- *Virtual teamwork:* the project team that Sharon was part of met a few times as a small group but the project itself covers lots of people in different locations. It would be hard, if not impossible, to identify everyone who was affected by it. Sharon has met some of the people she 'meets' in the electronic referral forum but by no means all – and it doesn't seem to matter.

- *Distributed teamwork:* some teams seldom get together, if at all, and yet they develop a strong sense of shared values, belonging and working practice. Sharon discovers that her hospital has been working with a national team set up to work with 'poor performing' healthcare organisations to help them to raise their performance:

CASE STUDY

Sharon gets talking to Alex for the first time. Alex explains that she works with a national team which provides support to local health care organisations that have been assessed as having performance challenges through the national performance rating system. Alex explains that it is a relatively new team doing a job that hadn't been done before. The team members live all over the country and travel a lot as the geographical distribution of the health care organisations they work with changes every year. They also spend a lot of time on the phone. Alex explains:

> It's a great team to work for. There are about fifty of us working with forty or so organisations each year – all types of organisation, primary care, secondary care, mental health and ambulance services. Most of us have clinical backgrounds, some managerial. We all have a mixture of general and specialist skills. I don't know everybody that well but it is a very supportive team. It needs to be because you never know what you are walking into and often the situation is very difficult – you find people who are angry and hurt, situations that have been problematic for a long time. In the early stages we work with people, inside and outside the organisation, to agree priorities and find the people with energy to tackle some of the problems. We will then pull together the people from our team with the most appropriate skills and availability. The groups that we work in change all the time but the team is very democratic and we talk things through. We do some different things, like we all get to choose our own line manager. This means that we have to make the choice ourselves and find someone we want to work with. Sometimes you wonder what difference we can make in a relatively short time but we must be doing something right: 80 per cent of organisations that we work with gain a higher national performance rating within a year.

IMPLICATIONS FOR TEAMWORKING

So if we can identify some very different types of team addressing different tasks what are the implications for team development? Critchley and Casey (1984) have described a way of thinking about this (Figure 5.1).

We can see from Sharon's experience that in the operating theatre she is working with 'unshared certainty' most of the time. The need to share is low because the procedure is routine, roles are well defined, each person knows what to expect of the other. Of course if something unexpected happens or something goes wrong, uncertainty increases dramatically as does the need to share in order to resolve the problem. When working in the virtual team on the referral project, Sharon is primarily working in the zone of cooperation. Every patient is different, what suits one may not suit another and there are a range of choices about the referral pathway – things can get complicated. There is some need to share in order to develop common understanding between the various parties involved

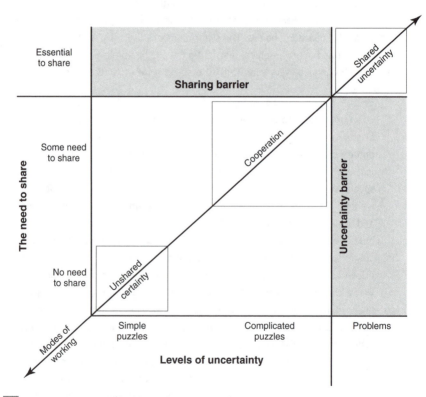

Figure 5.1 *Criteria for team development.*

Source: Critchley and Casey 1984.

about what should happen. Some of this might be formal sharing, such as a special meeting to review the expected pathway for patients with a particular condition, or it might be day-to-day sharing in the sense that those involved learn from their experience of making, discussing and treating referrals and they adjust their practice accordingly. In any event what is required is a sufficient level of compromise, give and take and goodwill from all parties in order for cooperative ways of working to develop. In her distributed team Alex is dealing with anxiety-provoking, shared uncertainty most of the time. The team often tackles a problem with no known answer and multiple, highly contested possibilities.[3] The demands on the team change week by week so that resources must be used flexibly. So there is a need for high levels of sharing and for team members to work closely together to integrate their different types of specialist knowledge and their particular experience.

It is important to note that these are only illustrations and the links between physical team and unshared certainty, virtual teamwork and cooperation, distributed teams and shared uncertainty, are not fixed relationships. From time to time, as circumstances change or a crisis occurs, all team types will need to operate all modes and that can be hard. For example, Alex's team may be flexible and responsive to local circumstances but try telling them to do the routine things in the same way at the same time (timesheets and expenses for example) and watch their response!

Critchley and Casey (1984) explore this issue further by developing their model to consider different approaches to team development (Figure 5.2).

It is common sense (which can be remarkably uncommon!) that polite and pleasant social skills are needed to carry out a straightforward and well understood, routine tasks. As Sharon found on Tuesdays and Fridays, things seem to go better when she has easy relationships with her colleagues. In the project work, Sharon is lucky to be working in a health community with a long history of cooperation between different agencies. The relationships are well established and there was sufficient trust to focus on and improve a task by cooperating. This is described in the literature as social and intellectual capital (Mayo 2001). Where high levels of capital exist it is likely to be implicit and taken for granted. As Sharon found 'it is just the way things are around here' – there is no need for soul searching. However, where such capital does not exist, change and improvement becomes a risky business. In low trust relationships, we are likely to think the worst of someone's actions and intentions. If social capital is not sufficient to sustain cooperation, it will be woefully inadequate for tackling conditions of shared uncertainty where task and feelings require equal attention. In Sharon's case it may be that there are some very difficult unresolved issues that are shaping the hospital's performance, for instance, tension between physicians and surgeons over the use of beds and the perceived disruptive effect of emergency admissions.

69

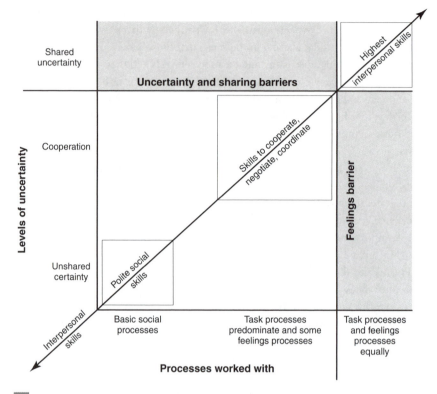

Figure 5.2 *Approaches to team development.*

Source: Critchley and Casey 1984.

'WE ARE WHAT WE TALK ABOUT': EXPLORING THE QUALITIES OF TEAMS

In discussing social and intellectual capacity we are beginning to explore the earlier question about the capacity of a team or workgroup to improve its performance. The performance of the team is likely to be assessed through quantifiable outcome and output measures. Considering the capacity of a team to improve itself directs our attention to the *quality* of the team. So how do we make judgements about this?

At the start of the chapter, it was suggested that we 'just know' when we are part of a good or bad team. This is because we draw our satisfaction and frustration from the quality of conversation we have (or do not have) with our colleagues. Indeed the quality of conversation has been found to heavily influence the judgements we make about the performance and quality of our health services, much more so than any hard data that is available (Goddard *et al.* 1999). The following framework (see Glanfield *et al.* 2004) is based on an analysis of findings from public inquiries within the English National Health Service, experience and organisational theory that emphasises the importance of the everyday experience of people involved (see Gergen 1999; Stacey *et al.* 2000; Shaw 2002). It is useful in exploring what is going well as much as what is not going so well. It is not suggested that the framework covers everything that is important about every team, just some of the most important things that are common to most situations. Nor is it suggested that this qualitative approach is an alternative to quantitative analysis – each informs the other and both are equally valid. The intention is to focus on the day-to-day experience of people (who are part of or connected to a team), how they relate to each other, and what happens as a result. Let's use it to explore Sharon's teams. You will notice that each of the five dimensions has a title and a conversational expression in everyday language.

Leadership and direction – 'I'm confident and trusted in leadership'

Leadership operates, formally and informally, at all levels. The extent to which people have confidence and trust in *their own* leadership and the leadership of others is crucial. It is noticeable that Sharon had enough confidence in herself to take up a leadership role in the project. She is concerned about some of her colleagues' practice which she might explore with the formal leaders of the orthopaedic service. How do they interpret their leadership responsibilities? How supportive will they be? How well does Sharon know them?

Quantity and quality of connections – 'I am well connected'

Healthcare is a complex and complicated affair with many people, most importantly the patients themselves, contributing to effective treatment. In Sharon's story the virtual team were working together in order to manage these complications. They were helped by working in a well-connected health community with a history of cooperation. Often the health communities with the most problems are the most fragmented; underperformance and fragmentation feed off each other. In other words the local 'relationship landscape' varies from place to place (Kauffman 1993). Sharon may get on with her orthopaedic specialist colleagues but how likely are they to want to protect their professional power?

Power and authority – 'I can use power with others to make things happen'

The exercise of power is necessary to bring about change and, for an improvement to last, there must be an appropriate redistribution of power within any given context. Sharon felt she had authority to act, with others, not in a unilateral way.

Equally, Sharon had to be prepared to relinquish some of her power to others for them to make referral decisions rather than everything coming through her. By allowing others to take more control over their own work the overall results were improved. In the case of Alex's team the members are encouraged to make their own choices, according to local circumstances, and power moves around between team members as different people take responsibility and call others to account depending on the circumstances. Alex describes her team as democratic; there is a sense of belonging.

Inclusion and contribution – 'I find out what's going on'

This has two meanings. First, I find out what is going on because people tell me (formally and informally), and second, if I don't know, I know where to go to find out and I am taken seriously. Clearly Sharon was well informed about her own area of work and was taken seriously. She was less well informed about the position of the hospital overall. Did this matter? It might do if Sharon had tried to find out more, if she had some improvement ideas or simply wanted someone in authority to listen to her frustrations about the day to day allocation of beds. A common feature in situations of failure are stories where some people knew what was going wrong but they could not make their voices heard and so they give up (Argyris 1990). And all of this matters when it comes to the 'bottom line' performance of the team.

Control of core business – 'I know what we do works'

We saw in the story the importance of the 'dashboard' – allowing all those involved to see what is happening as patients move through a process of treatment. Of course it is not enough to measure and report. In Sharon's case they were able to bring together existing data about patient pathways in new ways so that useful information was created and acted upon. As we have seen, information or evidence rarely speaks for itself. Its application is highly dependent on the social context.

CONCLUSION

This chapter has sought to demonstrate that there is an important relationship between teamwork and high performance and that the pattern of teamwork often changes frequently as we move through the working day. In seeking to improve team performance, therefore, we need to pay attention to the task and the demands that the task places on the interrelationship of team members. In shaping our approach, we need to take into account the pre-existing quality of the local relationships (social capital) and we should pay at least as much attention to the quality of a team as we do to its quantifiable performance.

DISCUSSION QUESTIONS

1   How does the multifaceted nature of today's teamwork influence working on performance improvement?
2   How could we determine the quality requirements of a team according to the nature of a team?
3   How could we 'just know' when we are part of a good team?
4   What role could leadership play in developing a team?
5   What factors do we need to take into account when giving feedback on outcomes to a team?

NOTES

1   For the purposes of this chapter we regard the terms team and workgroup as synonymous.
2   Some research suggests that physical proximity does not automatically generate teamworking and may be detrimental.
3   Reg Revans (1998) draws an important distinction between answerable puzzles, where the task is to find the answer, and problems with no known or agreed solution.

ACKNOWLEDGEMENTS

Where to start – with every team I have ever worked in or with? Perhaps not, so thanks to Jay Bevington, Murray Anderson-Wallace and Lucy Appleton for the joint venture that is the qualitative framework. Bill Critchley for his insight and excellent article. Nick Naftalin and Alex Tobin for helping to 'keep it real' and most of all to the best team ever, the Performance Development Team.

REFERENCES

Argyris, C. (1990) *Overcoming organisational defenses.* Boston, MA: Allyn & Bacon.

Belbin, M. (2003) *Management teams: why they succeed or fail.* Oxford and Boston, MA: Butterworth Heinemann.

Critchley, B. and Casey, D. (1984) Second thoughts on team building. *Management Education and Development,* 15(2): 163–175.

Ferlie, E., Fitzgerald, L. and Wood, M. (2000) Getting evidence into clinical practice: an organisational behaviour perspective. *Journal of Health Services Research and Policy,* 5(2): 92–102.

Gergen, K. (1999) *An invitation to social construction.* London: Sage.

Glanfield, P., Bevington, J., Anderson-Wallace, M. and Appleton, L. (2004) Getting to the heart of the matter. *In View,* 4 (December).

Goddard, M., Mannion, R. and Smith, P. (1999) Assessing the performance of NHS hospital trusts: the role of 'hard' and 'soft' information. *Health Policy,* 48: 119–134.

Kauffmann, S. (1993) *The origins of order: self organisation and selection in evolution.* New York: Oxford University Press.

Mayo, A. (2001) *The human value of the enterprise.* London: Nicholas Brearley.

O'Neill, O. (2002) *A question of trust: the BBC Reith Lectures 2002.* Cambridge: Cambridge University Press.

Revans, R. (1998) *The ABC of action learning.* London: Lemos and Crane.

Savage, J. and Moore, L. (2004) *Interpreting accountability: an ethnographic study of practice nurses, accountability and multidisciplinary team decision making in the context of clinical governance.* London: Royal College of Nursing.

Shaw, P. (2002) *Changing conversations in organisations.* London: Routledge.

Stacey, R. (2003) Learning as an activity of interdependent people. *The Learning Organization,* 10(6): 325–331.

Stacey. R., Griffen, D., and Shaw, P. (2000) *Complexity and management: fad or radical challenge to systems thinking.* London: Routledge.

Tuckman, B. (1965) Development sequence in small groups. *Psychological Bulletin,* 63: 349–399.

Walshe, K. and Higgins, J. (2002) The use and impact of inquiries in the NHS. *British Medical Journal,* 325: 895–900.

Walshe, K., Harvey, G., Hyde, P. and Pandit, N.R. (2004) Organisational failure and turnaround: lessons for public services from the for-profit sector. *Public Money and Management,* special issue on public sector turnaround, 24(4): 201–208.

Wood, M., Ferlie, E. and Fitzgerald, L. (1998) Achieving clinical behaviour change: a case of being indeterminate. *Social Sciences and Medicine,* 47(11): 1720–1738.

Zwarenstein, M. and Bryant, W. (2000) Interventions to promote collaboration between nurses and doctors. *The Cochrane Database of Systematic Reviews,* Chichester: John Wiley.

Chapter 6

Improving performance by improving processes and systems

Helen Bevan and Richard Lendon

KEY POINTS OF THIS CHAPTER

- Potential of process and system improvement as a key strategy for performance improvement in healthcare
- How many existing approaches to performance fail to maximise the potential of process improvement
- Characteristics of an optimal process improvement strategy
- Steps in a strategy for process improvement

INTRODUCTION

A key strategy for performance improvement is a focus on *process*. A process is a set of linked activities that convert a series of inputs to an outcome (Slack *et al.* 1998). A process has the following characteristics:

- a starting point and an end point;
- a purpose or aim for the outcome;
- rules governing the standard or quality of inputs throughout the process
- links and relationships to other processes.

(NHS Modernisation Agency 2002)

Every patient who encounters the healthcare system goes through a process. Patient processes may be short and simple:

- a patient consultant with a primary care physician which results in the patient being reassured about potential symptoms;
- a check-up with a dentist which leads to the patient receiving a clean bill of oral health.

Other processes are highly complex, involving multiple professions and healthcare organisations:

■ the process of assessment, diagnosis and treatment for a patient with cancer which leads to improvement outcomes and life expectancy;
■ the support process for an older person with multiple long-term conditions, the outcome of which is reduced risk of future hospital admission in a crisis situation.

Healthcare processes are more likely to be complex than simple. Even a relatively straightforward process such as a diagnostic testing process will involve many different inputs. These might include the doctor who requests the test, the clerk who arranges the paperwork, the nurse who carries out the test and the scientist who interprets the results.

The point at which responsibility for the patient is passed is called a 'handoff' (NHS Modernisation Agency 2002). Healthcare processes may involve literally hundreds of handoffs. They do this without considering how it contributes to the wider process of care or how changes in one part of the patient process will have knock-on, often unintended consequences downstream (Institute of Healthcare Improvement 2003; Mango and Shapiro 2001).

An example is the challenge that many hospitals face across the world in managing patient demand for emergency care (Haraden and Resar 2004). Typical symptoms of the problem include patients having to wait for many hours to see a doctor in the Emergency Department and, once assessed, lack of availability of a hospital bed. Patient safety may be compromised. In some countries, such as the USA, ambulances are turned away, depriving the organisation of important income. However, this problem is not just about the Emergency Department. Care processes in the Emergency Department do not exist in isolation. They are part of a wider system of care. Many hospitals have chosen to expand capacity in their Emergency Departments in response to the demand problem. Rather than relieving the situation, it may make it worse or create even more complexity in the system (Silvester et al. 2004). It is like broadening the large end of a funnel without increasing the capacity in the neck (Haraden and Resar 2004). Typically, the real causes of the emergency problem are downstream in the system where processes for different groups of patients (emergency and elective) cross and use common resources such as specialist doctors and diagnostic testing services.

Many of the performance problems in healthcare organisations are the result of problems in the way that healthcare processes are organised and delivered across the healthcare system. Problems such as variation in clinical outcome, excessive patient waiting times, high costs of care, even needless deaths in hospital can be tracked back to issues around healthcare processes and the flow of patients through the healthcare system (Mango and Shapiro 2001; Murray 2000; Silvester *et al.* 2004; Wolstenholme 2002). A focus on healthcare process is a key priority in improving healthcare performance.

APPLYING INDUSTRIAL PROCESS IMPROVEMENT METHODS

Over the past period, a variety of methodologies for process improvement from manufacturing and service operations have been switched to healthcare. These methods include lean thinking, which seeks to eliminate activities or process steps which do not add value to customers (Womack and Jones 1996; Bicheno 2000); queuing theory, which is utilised to reduce delays in systems (Hall 1991); the theory of constraints, which seeks to eliminate bottlenecks in processes (Goldratt and Cox 2000); six sigma, which aims to reduce variation and create defect free services (De Feo and Barnard 2004) and system dynamics which identifies process flows at the macro level of the whole organisation (Wolstenholme 2002).

In this book, we position outcome management as an integrating approach which builds on and complements existing quality improvement strategies. We apply a similar philosophy in our approach to process improvement. We do not recommend a single superior methodology. Rather, our approach seeks to take aspects from many of these toolkits and create our own methodological package for healthcare.

We find that these industrial approaches, based on many years of improvements knowledge in other sectors, can make a significant contribution to performance improvement in healthcare. However, they need to be translated for a clinical environment. This includes reframing the methods into a language that clinical and managerial leaders can relate to, providing specific clinical examples and case studies and creating clinical champions for the application of these techniques (Ferlie and McNulty 2002).

As these process improvement methods become more commonplace in healthcare and their benefits are demonstrated, they are contributing to a new mindset amongst healthcare leaders about how to systematically improve care (Mango and Shapiro 2001; NHS Modernisation Agency 2004; Silvester *et al.* 2004).

CHANGING THE PERFORMANCE MANAGEMENT MINDSET

We can demonstrate the change in mindset by contrasting the prevalent leadership approach to performance improvement with the emerging approach. Table 6.1 shows the components of a typical current healthcare performance improvement strategy adopted by healthcare leaders:

For many healthcare organisations, the performance management system is typically designed to prevent performance failure, to avoid failure in meeting

77

Table 6.1 *Typical current health care performance improvement strategy*

- Design the system to prevent performance failure
- Create awareness of standards, targets and performance requirements and raise leadership intent to deliver them
- Seek to improve the performance of specific departments, specialties, practices or parts of the system
- Work harder
- Implement measurement systems to monitor compliance with the required performance

Source: NHS Modernisation Agency 2004

minimum performance standards (i.e. wait times in the Emergency Department, or time to thrombolysis for patients with heart attacks) and achieve key targets and goals such as maximum wait times for elective, emergency and cancer care. The underpinning aim is to 'pass' the required performance or quality standard. Executive leadership teams seek to ensure that everyone who contributes to a particular goal is aware of what is required of them and is personally committed to achieving the goal. In the current system, we also tend to focus on improving a particular department, specialty, practice or part of the system, rather than seeking to raise the performance of the system as a whole. Targets are frequently achieved by staff working harder; more hours or at a higher level of intensity (NHS Confederation 2004; Silvester *et al.* 2004). In this approach we are raising performance by treating the symptoms rather than the disease itself.

By contrast, the process improvement philosophy which has grown from the use of industrial process improvement methods, starts from a different mindset. The system should be designed not just to avoid performance failure but to enable ongoing improvement across the whole organisation. The components are shown in Table 6.2.

Table 6.2 *Optimal health care performance improvement strategy*

- Design the system to continuously improve
- Take a process view of patients across the boundaries of specialities, functions and departments
- Work smarter by
  - focusing on the bottlenecks that prevent smooth patient flow
  - managing and reducing causes of variation in patient flow
  - segmenting patients and designing processes for them according to their specific needs
- Implement measurement systems for improvement that reveal the true performance of the system and the impact of any changes made in real time

Source: NHS Modernisation Agency 2004

This approach takes the process view, following the patient journey through the system. In this approach, we are now seeking to treat the disease that is causing the symptoms which may be unnecessary delay, poor clinical quality or high cost. Performance can be improved by removing activities that do not add value for patients and by simplifying and speeding up processes. Evidence tells us that clinical process improvement can achieve apparently contradictory objectives – improving the quality of care, patient and staff experience as well as reducing waste and enhancing value for money (Mango and Shapiro 2001; Silvester et al. 2004).

Healthcare organisations with this optimal performance mindset work smarter, rather than harder. There are three high impact ways of doing this.

The first aspect of working smarter is to address the bottlenecks that are a constant characteristic of traditional healthcare processes. We should actively seek out bottlenecks and address the factors that cause them. A bottleneck is the stage in a patient process under the most pressure. It creates queues, and slows down the whole process. It might be the most time-consuming step (rate limiting step) in a specific patient process. It might be a 'functional' bottleneck, where two or more patient flows converge on a single function such as diagnostic tests or an assessment unit.

The quest to improve healthcare performance requires us to systematically identify and then eradicate bottlenecks in patient processes across the whole healthcare system. Evidence suggests that by doing so, we can reduce organisational complexity, speed up care and eliminate 'hassle' factors for patients and staff (Goldratt 2002; Silvester et al. 2004).

The second aspect of working smarter is to understand patient flow and recognise the importance of addressing variation in patient flow. Flow means moving patients through the system in a timely and efficient manner so that every patient gets the right care from the right staff, with the right information at the right point in time (Institute for Healthcare Improvement 2002).

Variation is the enemy of smooth patient flow through the system. Variation creates peaks and troughs in patient demand and in the capacity of the healthcare system to meet that demand. Variation is endemic and intrinsic to healthcare processes (Mango and Shapiro 2001; Silvester et al. 2004).

Natural variation is an inevitable characteristic of any healthcare system. Steps need to be taken to manage it (Haraden and Resar 2004). Sources of natural variation include differences in the symptoms and diseases that patients present with, the times of day that emergency patients arrive and socio-economic or demographic differences between patients. The patient variables that are the topic of Chapter 10 are classic examples of natural variation in the healthcare system.

By contrast, artificial variation is created by the way the system is managed. Sources of artificial variation include the way we schedule elective admissions, the working hours of staff, how staff study leave and staff vacations are planned and

the availability of clinical equipment. Artificial variation has a much more significant impact on patient flow than natural variation. Indeed it is the major cause of
waits and delays in the system (NHS Confederation and NHS Modernisation
Agency 2004; Silvester *et al.* 2004). It is usually driven by the personal preferences
and priorities of staff, rather than actual demand for a service; for instance a surgeon wanting to operate on a Monday morning rather than a Friday afternoon. As
it cannot be managed like natural variation, steps should be taken to eliminate artificial variation.

The third aspect of working smarter is to segment patients according to their
specific needs and preferences. Segmentation identifies patients with similar needs
and/or preferences, and groups them together so that a specific pathway can be
designed for them and specific resources can be allocated to them. An example is
a strategy for people with long-term conditions such as diabetes and asthma.
Rather than having a 'one size fits all' support strategy for people with long-term
conditions, we can group or segment patients by their level of risk. So a person
with mild disease could be offered a disease specific education programme or
expert patient programme to help with self-care. A patient with more severe disease or multiple diseases might be offered one to one support in the community
to avoid crisis and prevent hospital admission.

Segmentation also means designing the system to meet the needs of each
group, so that variation is reduced and capacity matches demand at every stage in
their journey. An example is segmentation of patients who attend the emergency
department. They can be grouped or streamed according to whether they have
'major' or 'minor' needs. A separate process flow is established for each stream of
patients with dedicated clinical staff for each stream. In this way, artificial variation is avoided because staff are not being constantly moved between minor and
major patient streams. This way, the needs of all patients are met. By working out
the detailed resources required by each patient group, the flow of patients through
the whole system is improved and variation, queues and subsequent delays are
avoided. Patients are safer, satisfaction rates are higher and the potential for effective outcomes is enhanced.

A major problem with many prevalent methods of performance measurement
in healthcare is that apparent improvements in performance (waiting times,
patient and staff experience, clinical outcomes, activity and/or cost) may be due
to the natural variation in the performance of processes. Even if there is a statistically significant change in average performance, the improvement is often not sustainable because the underlying causes of variability in the process have not been
addressed.

As a result, a growing number of healthcare organisations are adopting measurement systems for improvement. This involves using *statistical process control*
techniques to plot key measures over time (Carey and Lloyd 1995; Hart and Hart
2002). This enables us to understand the natural variation and the true perform-

ance of the system and the impact of any changes made. Some forward thinking healthcare leadership teams will now only accept performance data that is presented in this way.

A STRATEGY FOR PROCESS IMPROVEMENT

The steps in a strategy for process improvement are shown in Table 6.3. Table 6.3 is a summary of the process improvement steps championed by a variety of industrial approaches as applied to healthcare (Silvester *et al.* 2004). The first step is to *understand the system* at a *macro* level, for instance at the level of a whole hospital or at the level of all surgical patients. This might involve analysing the pattern of emergency and elective admissions to the hospital. Hospital leaders often assume that it is the natural variability of emergency admissions that threatens the ability of the hospital to manage its elective workload and avoid last minute cancellations of elective patients. Yet, macro-level process mapping shows that it is more likely to be the artificial variation of the pattern of elective scheduling that prohibits the organisation from meeting the needs of both emergency and elective patients (Haraden and Resar 2004; Institute for Healthcare Management 2003; Silvester *et al.* 2004).

Table 6.3 *A step-by-step strategy for process improvement*

1 *Understand the system*
   - understand the demand and capacity of the system at a macro level and the impact that different flows have on each other, for example, emergency and elective admissions processes
   - map patients' journeys through the clinical process

2 *Simplify the process*
   - reduce the number of steps involved
   - reduce the number of, or eliminate, bottlenecks in the process

3 *Control the variation*
   - identify patients with similar flow characteristics and separate these flows where appropriate

4 *Reduce the variation*
   - measure the demand and capacity continuously over time
   - understand the causes of variation that affect the demand and capacity of the system
   - take steps to manage natural variation
   - eliminate artificial variation

5 *Make the system safe for patients and staff*
   - set the capacity appropriately to minimise the delay for all patients
   - monitor the variation using statistical process control methods

Source: adapted from Silvester *et al.* 2004

Understanding the system at a *micro* level involves mapping the journeys of specific groups of patients through the healthcare process (NHS Modernisation Agency 2002). Process mapping is one of the most powerful ways for multidisciplinary clinical teams to understand the real problems from the patient perspective and to identify opportunities for improvement. Typically, this takes the form of a facilitated four hour workshop attended by representatives of all the staff groups who contribute to the patient process in addition to service users. Even a relatively straightforward patient process can result in a process mapping workshop of forty to fifty people! The benefits of patient process mapping are shown in Table 6.4.

Having mapped the patient journey, the team should analyse the map for issues and opportunities. Analysis might include:

- The number of steps in the patient process – this is often a revelation to staff;
- The time each step takes;
- The number of handoffs in the process;
- The constraints and bottlenecks in the process;
- Which steps actually add value for patients;
- Which steps generate the most problems for patients.

Table 6.4 *Process mapping benefits*

A map of the patients' journey will give you

- a powerful starting point for any improvement project, large or small
- the opportunity to bring together multidisciplinary teams from primary, secondary and social care and from all levels in the organisations
- the ability to create a culture of ownership, responsibility and accountability for the improvement effort
- an overview of the complete patient process, helping staff to understand, often for the first time, how complex the system can be for patients, for instance, how many times the patient has to wait (often unnecessarily), how many visits they make to the hospital or clinic and how many different people they meet
- a mindset-changing dialogue between staff and service users about the actual experience of the process
- an aid to help plan effectively where to test ideas for improvement that are most likely to contribute to outcomes and aims
- brilliant ideas from staff who do not normally get the opportunity to contribute to service organisation but who really know how things work
- a way to get people who work across the same patient process talking to each other and understanding each others' perspective
- an end product – the patient process map – which is easy to understand and highly visual

Source: NHS Modernisation Agency 2002

Key questions can then be asked (NHS Modernisation Agency 2002):

- Is the patient getting the most appropriate care that will lead to the best outcomes?
- Is the most appropriate person giving the care?
- Is the care being given at the most appropriate time?
- Is the care being given in the ideal place?

Steps should be taken to *simplify the process* to reduce the number of handoffs, to eradicate delays in the system and to maximise the parts of the process that add most value to patients.

One of the most effective strategies for *controlling the variation* in the system is to identify patients with similar needs, who can flow through the system at a similar rate, and separate these where appropriate. An example is segmenting surgical patients by whether they are undergoing relatively minor, low-risk procedures (short stay) rather than more complex, high-risk procedures (longer stay). This is an alternative to the traditional model of segmenting patients by speciality. A specific process can be developed which minimises the potential for delay, clinical error and variation in the flow (NHS Modernisation Agency 2004).

In order to *reduce the variation*, steps should be taken to measure demand and capacity and match them continuously on a daily basis (Silvester *et al.* 2004). Demand can be defined as the number of patients with the requirement for the service being referred to (or presenting themselves for) the service on an hourly, daily, monthly or annual basis. In order to understand demand, to minimise variation in the system and ensure smooth process flow, we need to know who these patients are and what their needs are. We need to match our capacity (people, buildings and equipment) to this demand. Yet many healthcare organisations do not actually measure demand. They measure activity (the work that their clinical teams actually carry out). Activity is a very poor basis for planning capacity. Planning on the basis of activity rather than patient demand increases the potential for variability in the system (NHS Confederation and NHS Modernisation Agency 2004; Silvester *et al.* 2004).

Analysing patient demand helps us to understand the natural variation in the system, which is caused by differences between patients and the symptoms they present with. Demand and capacity need to be measured in the same currency (such as minutes required) so that discrepancies between demand and capacity can be identified. Typically, the problem this analysis identifies is not lack of capacity to meet patient demand. Rather the problem is typically a mismatch between variation in patient demand and variation in the patterns of capacity to meet the demand (Silvester *et al.* 2004). This analysis identifies the artificial variation caused by the way we typically plan capacity. It enables us to plan to eliminate this variation and enable patients to flow smoothly through the system in line with their needs.

Having analysed the variation in the system and taken steps to eliminate artificial variation we need to *make the system safe for patients and staff* by monitoring and controlling the variation on a continuous basis. This means analysing changing patterns of demand and ensuring that the capacity in terms of staff and equipment are continuously available to meet them. It means planning staff schedules, holiday and study leave so that the appropriate capacity to enable patient flow is always available.

CONCLUSION

Process and system redesign is one of the most effective strategies for improving healthcare performance. The biggest barriers are mindset barriers – the way that organisational leaders and clinical teams think about how care is delivered. Giving patients timely access to safe, appropriate care is a critical aspect of high quality care and effective outcome management.

DISCUSSION QUESTIONS

1 What is the potential for process improvement in your organisation or your area of clinical specialism?
2 What are the sources of natural and artificial variation in your system? How might you manage and eliminate them?
3 What steps could you take to improve your processes?
4 How will you measure the outcomes?
5 How can you get access to the specialist technical expertise you might need to help you analyse demand and capacity and reduce variation?

REFERENCES

Bicheno, J. (2000), *The Lean Toolbox*. Buckingham: Picsie Books.

Carey, R.C. and Lloyd, R.C. (1995), *Measuring quality improvement in healthcare: a guide to statistical process control applications*. Milwaukee, WI: American Society for Quality Control.

De Feo, J. and Barnard, W. (2004) *Juran Institute's six sigma: breakthrough and beyond*. New York: McGraw-Hill.

Dettmer, W.H. (1998) *Breaking the constraints to world class performance*, Milwaukee, WI: American Association for Quality Control.

Ferlie, E. and McNulty, T. (2002) *Re-engineering healthcare*. Oxford: Oxford University Press.

Goldratt, E. (2002) *Theory of constraints*. Great Barrington, MA: North River Press.

Goldratt, E. and Cox, J. (2000) *The Goal*. Aldershot: Gower.

Hall, R.W. (1991) *Queueing methods for services and manufacturing*. New York: Prentice Hall.

Haraden, C. and Resar, R. (2004) Patient flow in hospitals: understanding it and controlling it better. *Frontiers of Health Services Management,* 20(4): 3–15.

Hart, M.K. and Hart, R.K. (2002) *Statistical process control for healthcare*. London: Duxbury Thomson Learning.

Institute for Healthcare Improvement (2003) *Optimising patient flow*. www.ihi.org

Mango, P.D. and Shapiro, L.A. (2001) Hospitals get serious about operations. *McKinsey Quarterly,* 2: 74–85.

Murray, M. (2000) Modernising the NHS: patient care: access. *British Medical Journal,* 320: 1594–1596.

NHS Confederation and NHS Modernisaiton Agency (2004) *Leading edge: breaking the rules: is capacity the problem?* www.nhsconfed.org/publications

NHS Modernisation Agency (2002) *An improvement leaders' guide to process mapping, analysis and redesign.* www.modern.nhs.uk/improvementguides

NHS Modernisation Agency (2004) *Ten high impact changes for service improvement and delivery.* www.modern.nhs.uk/highimpactchanges

Silvester, K., Bevan, H., Steyn, R., Lendon, R. and Whalley, P. (2004) Reducing waiting times in the NHS: is lack of capacity the problem? *Clinician in Management,* 12(3): 105–111.

Slack, N., Chambers, S., Harrison, A., Harland, C., Harrison, M. and Johnston, R. (1998) *Operations Management*. London: FT Pitman.

Wolstenholme, E. (2002) *Patient flow, waiting and managerial learning: a systems thinking mapping approach*. Leeds: Leeds Business School.

Womack, J. and Jones, D. (1996) *Lean thinking: banish waste and create wealth in your organisation*. New York: Simon and Schuster.

Chapter 7

The outcome quadrant

Jan Walburg

KEY POINTS OF THIS CHAPTER

- Clinical outcomes
- Functional outcomes: quality of life
- Patient opinions
- Cost of treatment

INTRODUCTION

To undertake outcome management preparations have been made with the composition of a team and specification of a care process for the team to manage. The task is now to combine the team and its process with the selection of outcome measures. In order to introduce and clarify the situation, it may be helpful to first take a look at a patient.

CASE VIGNETTE

John is 59 years old and in treatment for heart problems. The complaints first presented themselves when John was 50. Examination showed the flow of blood to his heart to be obstructed by contracted vessels in a few places. John underwent angioplasty. Since then, he has been on medication and followed a special diet. When John was 54, the complaints reappeared. Examination revealed narrowed vessels in a place which does not lend itself to angioplasty. John was given blood thinners and has managed in such a manner.

John's medical story is not a particularly spectacular story and typical of many. Nevertheless, from the perspective of outcome management, a few principles stand out. The care process already spans a period of nine years and may continue for some time. John has been seen by various health care professionals: his family doctor, the outpatient department at the hospital and the department of heart and lung diseases. In each instance, John comes in with a specific medical problem and a number of expectations with regard to treatment, the costs of treatment and the quality of the remainder of this life. John similarly leaves each particular care episode with certain treatment effects, an opinion with regard to the treatment and an idea of how he will proceed with the rest of his life.

A number of principles that also hold for other treatments are illustrated by this treatment example.

- The care took place over a period of time in which treatment is sometimes provided separately and sometimes in combination with other care providers.
- The outcomes were not definitive outcomes but changes in the health situation of the patient, which then give rise to new or other health issues.
- The majority of the care is provided for patients with chronic illnesses, which means that no real end to the treatment can be identified.
- That which changes under health influence of treatment is more than just the medical-technical aspect. The patient has expectations which get adjusted with regard not only to the treatment but also his or her quality of life. Outcomes thus have multiple components.
- The health care process is often a combination of parallel processes:
  - the diagnostic process involving the laboratory and radiology departments among others;
  - the medical-technical procedure performed by the doctors responsible for the angioplasty;
  - the nursing process;
  - the process of lifestyle adjustment under the guidance of a dietician.
- Some of the process outcomes are specific, such as widened blood vessels and changed patterns of consumption.
- Some of the outcomes are general and generic, such as opinions regarding the care process or changed quality of life.

All of the preceding is presented as background information for further consideration of the different outcomes which can be seen to occur as a consequence of a care process. Multiple outcomes which encompass the majority of the consequences of a care process will thus be considered:

- clinical outcomes or the disease-specific outcomes associated with the diagnosis;

- functional outcomes associated with the manner in which the person can function during daily life;
- patient opinions regarding the quality of care;
- the costs of the care process.

The four categories listed above largely correspond to the outcome categories which are sometimes referred to with the term 'clinical value compass' (Nelson *et al.* 1998). We have opted to use the term 'outcome quadrant'. Limiting ourselves to the aforementioned four categories is by no means meant to exclude the importance of other variables. There is a lot to be said, for example, for the opinions of the staff with regard to the care process. The focus within the outcome quadrant, however, is on the results of treatment.

CLINICAL OUTCOMES

The care process leads to changes in the health of the patient. From the perspective of not only the patient but also the care provider, health can be broadly conceived as not only the absence of illness but also – as defined by the World Health Organisation – everything which has to do with a state of 'complete physical, mental and social well-being'. Health in its broadest sense is represented within the outcome quadrant by the quality of life indicator. Within the framework of the measurement of care outcomes, a more limited conception of illness and health will be utilised with specific attention to perceptible changes in the symptoms or medical status of the patient.

Why clinical outcomes?

It has already been observed that the literature on improvement of the quality of care is very process oriented. Most of the specific indicators are process oriented and intended to indicate whether the medical staff do what they are supposed to do (or not). Such process indicators are obviously of great importance and therefore merit a position in any system of health care management. However, improvement of such indicators basically leads to greater conformity to the current rules and regulations – at best.

In addition to process outcomes, it is also interesting to determine which concrete clinical outcomes are realised and which procedures lead to improved clinical outcomes. Even for teams which dutifully adhere to the same treatment protocols, not only outcome differences as a result of (patients') different case-mix but also differences of emphasis during the course of treatment can be detected. The differences in clinical outcome can stem from attempts to intervene earlier in the development of the illness, better consultation with the referring doctor, greater involvement of the family in treatment, greater involvement of the patient, clearer instructions for aftercare, the particular backgrounds of the medical professionals involved and so forth.

The monitoring of clinical outcomes can give both professionals and patients insight into treatment progress but also (progress with respect) insight into what can be expected. The non-occurrence of an expected effect can prompt adjustment of the treatment and/or diagnosis. And in this respect, there are four important reasons to measure clinical outcomes:

- to monitor treatment and make timely adjustments;
- to inform the patient of treatment progress in relation to own or professional expectations;
- to improve the treatment process on the basis of aggregated outcomes;
- to improve professional knowledge of possible treatment for a particular diagnosis on the basis of outcomes aggregated across multiple teams.

Clinical outcomes: more detailed consideration

Clinical outcomes are the result of a care process in which the clinical state of the patient is initially assessed to determine a diagnosis. Thereafter, a treatment plan is formulated, treatment is undertaken and the clinical state of the patient is again assessed (see Figure 7.1).

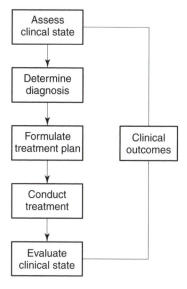

Figure 7.1 *Health care process.*

The difference between initial assessment of the clinical condition of the patient and assessment following treatment is the clinical outcome of the care process. Clinical outcomes have a number of shared features.

- Clinical outcomes represent the changes which occur in the body of the patient, the changes which occur in the patient's biochemistry, physiology or microbiology, and the changes in patient symptoms. Physiological changes include such measurable values as blood sugar levels, blood pressure levels, cholesterol levels and various other laboratory values. The clinical outcome, then, is the normalisation of the biochemical state, physiological function and microbiological flora (Benson 1992). Changed symptoms can be the visible or tangible consequence of physiological changes. The clinical outcome in this case is disappearance, decreased severity or stabilisation of the symptoms.
- Another shared feature of clinical outcomes is that they typically pertain to extended treatment episodes which can sometimes overlap. Measurement is only a static momentary indicator, and the objective of such measurement can differ from time to time. The objective of measurement in cases of chronic illness can certainly vary over time. As depicted in Figure 7.2, for example, interventions X, Y and Z can have very different objectives and thus lead to outcomes B, C and D for one and the same patient.
- Particularly with regard to clinical outcomes, confusion can occur between outcome and process indicators. In Figure 7.3, the differences between structure, process and outcome indicators are therefore depicted regarding the process of diagnosis and treatment.

Figure 7.3 demonstrates the importance of using different indicators and clearly distinguishing the indicators.

Clinical indicators need not reflect the adequate conduct of treatment. In fact, clinical indicators typically reflect the quality of the care process with the meaning of determined in relation to various patient and process characteristics.

Having explored these issues, we are now in a position to define clinical outcomes: Clinical outcomes are those characteristics of the care consumer (or patient) in relation to a specific illness or disorder which can change over time as a result of a care intervention. This definition emphasises, first and foremost, the characteristics of the patient or care consumer. The patient thus constitutes the

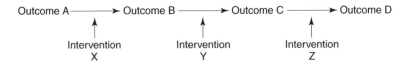

Figure 7.2 *Course of care over time.*

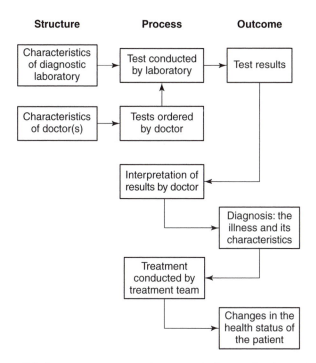

Figure 7.3 *Structure, process and outcome indicators for diagnosis and treatment.*

Source: Donabedian 1992.

unit of analysis independent of who makes the diagnosis or how things are measured. Second and third points of importance are as follows: the definition concerns characteristics which can change over time and the change must be a reasonable result of treatment. Changes caused by matters external to treatment fall outside the definition of clinical outcomes. And the demonstration of a causal relation between the care process and clinical outcomes requires the use of solid measurement instrumentation.

Existing systems of clinical indicators

The clinical outcome indicators differ for almost every care intervention. Over the years, different models have been developed to register indicators and thereby detect any problems with the quality of care or the organisation of such.

Joint Commission

In 1994, the Joint Commission initiated the measurement of clinical results within the Indicator Measurement System (IMSystem) Project in the USA. The IMSystem is a comparative national measurement system composed of indicators developed by professionals. The relevance, reliability and validity of the indicators have been thoroughly tested. The IMSystem was developed to help health care organisations measure and improve their performance and to support the Joint Commission in its evaluation of health care organisations.

A stepwise approach is followed. Expert validity is of initial importance for the selection of an indicator. Thereafter, the extent to which an indicator reflects the possibilities for improvement or the so-called predictive validity of an indicator is examined. Finally, the extent to which the indicators influence processes within the organisation and thereby improve patient outcomes is examined as part of the validation process (Nadzam *et al.* 1993). The participating organisations supply facts and information, which are then returned to the organisation on a quarterly basis in the form of a control card, management review card and comparison card (Walburg 1997).

ORYX is an initiative on the part of the Joint Commission to incorporate outcomes and performance management into the accreditation process (Lee *et al.* 2000). The initiative is also intended to present a flexible and affordable approach to the support of quality-improvement activities within organisations accredited by the Joint Commission and thereby improve the value of accreditation (Joint Commission 2002). Accredited organisations are given the opportunity to measure their performance, use this information for internal quality-improvement purposes and thereby demonstrate the organisation's responsibility for quality care to external auditors (Lee *et al.* 2000). ORYX thus provides a link between the outcomes of care and accreditation (Joint Commission 2002). Trends and patterns are made visible and, with this information, efforts to improve the quality of care can be undertaken.

Quality Indicator Project

The Quality Indicator Project (QIP) was developed by the Association of Maryland Hospitals and Health Systems (MHA). At the initiative of seven hospitals in the city of Baltimore, Maryland, and in cooperation with the MHA, a system to work on internal quality control was sought (CVZ 2001). The measurement of clinical care performance was the primary objective, and various indicators were identified and developed for this purpose.

A coherent system of clinical indicators tailored to general and psychiatric hospitals, on the one hand, and outpatient and admitted patients, on the other hand, was developed, validated and tested for its reliability (Paepe and Quaethoven 2000). The QIP is a system which can be used to evaluate professional care on the basis of a set of clinical indicators and thereby promote continued quality improvement on the part of the relevant organisation (Huppes 2001). In the mean time, the QIP has grown into a worldwide organisation. In order to meet the need for explicit guidance of the group of participating hospitals and coordinate the participation of all non-US countries, which have their own national coordinators, the Centre for Performance Sciences (CPS) has been established.

The QIP is, in principle, an information system used to map a primary care process by situating it in time (i.e. determining trends) and positioning it with respect to other care processes (i.e. comparing care processes). This two-sided approach entails the collection of clearly care-oriented information. And on the basis of such information, the quality of the care can then be evaluated, monitored and – where possible and necessary – improved (Paepe and Quaethoven 2000).

The QIP has developed 20 indicators and 194 ratios for acute care to date. A variant of the QIP specifically developed for the field of psychiatry also exists. That is, 11 indicators and 87 ratios have been identified for psychiatric care. Organisations which join the QIP select those indicators and ratios which are most informative for their purposes. They then collect the necessary information and are informed with regard to trends and positioning.

The measurement of clinical outcomes

The simplest manner to measure the outcome of care is to have a health care professional decide whether a change in the condition of the patient is related to treatment or not. This is easy and inexpensive, but the reliability and validity of such judgements are not particularly clear. In marked contrast is the use of the 140 outcome indicators developed for the treatment of diabetes: the use of such indicators has been shown to be reliable and valid but also quite complicated and expensive.

When it comes to the measurement of clinical indicators, just *what* we measure, *how* we measure and *when* we measure all play a role. With regard to *what* to measure, it is critical that the choice of an indicator be determined by precise specification of the care process. Only on the basis of such information can the relevance of an indicator be determined and the different objectives of different disciplines be considered. With regard to *how* to measure, not only such methodological factors as reliability, validity, specificity and sensitivity obviously play a role but also such practical factors as the amount of effort required to measure an indicator in terms of time and money.

With regard to *when* to measure, initial measurement at the start of treatment is the natural starting point. Just when to measure thereafter depends on the type of indicator, which may call for daily measurement or only measurement after an extended period of time. There is also a relation between when to measure and the nature of the illness. In the case of chronic illness, the measurement process may never come to an end although the nature of what is measured may change over time.

End measurement is often difficult. Many patients simply fail to appear towards the end of treatment, which makes final measurement rather difficult.

Measurement at fixed intervals or according to a particular schedule is therefore recommended, also because regular measurement prevents dependence on only pre-test and post-test data.

Clinical outcomes and outcome management

In the stepwise approach to the measurement of clinical outcomes, as depicted in Figure 7.4, the following steps can be distinguished.

Step 1 Identification of treatment objectives

The objectives of the treatment process are often not determined by the treatment team alone. There are others involved in the determination of treatment objectives such as the patients themselves and insurers. There are also different disciplines with their own objectives often involved in a team. Nurses, for example, have very different clinical objectives than medical specialists. Finally, one must keep the possibility of shifting objectives in mind.

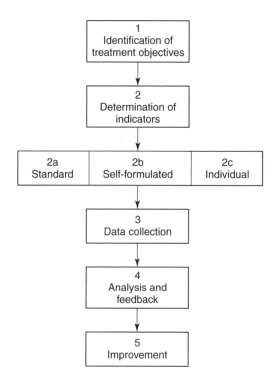

Figure 7.4 *Stepwise measurement of clinical outcomes.*

A distinction should be made between long-term versus short-term objectives, or objectives should be formulated per phase of treatment. Objectives can be specified with the aid of a flow chart or clinical path calling for the following:

- illness-specific and generic treatment objectives;
- professional objectives stemming from different disciplines;
- individual objectives based on the desires of the patient or the specificity of the pathology for a particular patient.

Step 2 Determination of indicators

In the determination of the indicators, a selection can be made of:

- indicators which indicate the presence of a complication in connection with the illness or the treatment thereof (such as infection or decubitus);
- indicators which reflect progress in the direction of the desired treatment objectives. In both cases, three scenarios may apply:
  (a) standard indicators;
  (b) self-formulated indicators;
  (c) individual patient indicators.

Standard indicators

It is very possible that for the relevant care process, a reliable, valid and feasible set of indicators has already been determined on the basis of a review of the research literature and/or the development of the relevant treatment guidelines. The use of such standard indicators is attractive for a number of reasons: prior experience with them, previously determined statistical properties (reliability, validity), availability of a standardised measurement method, instructions for the use of the indicator and comparability of results across teams. In other words, one must have very strong arguments to depart from the use of an available standard.

Self-formulated indicators

It is conceivable that the specificity of the treatment and/or treatment objectives require the formulation of special indicators. This must certainly be done when there are no standard indicators available as yet.

One can formulate indicators oneself by following the steps presented in Table 7.1 and expanded below.

1 Identification of the exact clinical area proceeding from general to specific. In such a manner, various objectives for the formulation of an indicator can be stipulated.

95

Table 7.1 *Self-formulation of indicators*

1   Specify objectives

2   Review literature

3   Formulate rough indicators

4   Agree on indicators

5   Experiment with indicators

6   Determine statistical and methodological characteristics of indicators

7   Set indicators

2   A review of the literature can provide insight into existing indicators together with their statistical and user characteristics. The guidelines associated with treatment can also be taken into consideration as these frequently point to indicators.

3   On the basis of steps 1 and 2, a group of experts can make an initial selection of indicators. The expert group is composed of clinical experts from the area of illness; others involved in the chain of care associated with treatment; patients who have already undergone treatment for the illness; and methodological experts. In a number of sessions, different domains are delimited together with the experts and rough indicators formulated on the basis of these choices. The authority of the experts is of considerable importance as they must convince other specialists of the value of the selected indicators. The experts can next rate the importance of the rough indicators along a five-point scale to provide a measure of their construct validity.

4   On the basis of the preceding, a set of rough indicators is agreed upon.

5   The indicators are then experimented with in actual practice to determine their statistical properties, whether or not an indicator is measurable and manageable in actual practice and whether the different indicators do not require too much effort on the parts of the team and patients.

6   The observations from actual practice are considered by the group of experts.

7   The final set of indicators is now set.

Individual patient indicators

It may also be necessary and useful to formulate – in addition to or instead of standardised generic indicators – a few patient-specific indicators at times. This is done on the basis of the individual diagnosis and treatment plan. The indicators should be made as simple and unambiguous as possible and thereby fit into a simple measurement scheme. These indicators are only used to monitor individual patient progress and cannot be aggregated at a higher level for purposes of analysis or benchmarking.

Step 3 Data collection

Once the indicators have been established, the compilation of data follows. However, the relevant data are often recorded in the medical file using the different registration systems from the laboratory and radiology departments, for example, which makes it difficult to merge the information into a single set of indicators. One solution is the electronic case file, which contains all of the data on a patient in a very accessible and easy to process format.

Step 4 Analysis and feedback

Evaluation and feedback are undertaken by the team of experts and the various professional groups involved in the treatment. Mutual trust and respect play an important role here as defensive reactions or accusations can undermine the purpose of outcome measurement. Particularly with regard to clinical indicators, professional pride can play a role, which means that the relevant outcomes must be analyzed in an objective and specific manner with concrete questions in mind. Only then can the professionals enter into an open discussion of outcomes and areas for improvement.

Step 5 Improvement

Efforts to improve the outcomes of treatment can proceed according to the principles elaborated in Chapter 10. A nice example of improvement for complications accompanying cerebrovascular accident (CVA) is the overview of possible preventive measures presented in Table 7.2 (Treurniet 1999).

Summary: the measurement of clinical outcomes

In order to monitor treatment, to inform the patient and to improve treatment, the measurement of clinical outcome is important. This measurement follows the formulation of a mission and the treatment objectives. A distinction is often made between long-term and short-term objectives. The specification of objectives and indicators is based on illness-specific and generic treatment objectives and on individual objectives based on the patient's specific needs. Many standardised outcome indicators are available.

FUNCTIONAL OUTCOMES: QUALITY OF LIFE

Medical treatment is aimed at the cure of illness or prevention of more severe illness. The most important outcomes of the care process are thus the clinical outcomes. Nonetheless, treatment can also have clear consequences for the physical, psychological and social functioning of the patient. And for patients, the functional

Table 7.2 *Measures to prevent possible complications as a result of immobility in CVA patients*

	Complication	Possible preventive measures
Skin	Decubitus	Early mobilisation Regular repositioning of body Daily skin examination Use of pressure alleviating mattress Intestinal and bladder treatment Good diet
Intestines	Constipation Faecal impact Faecal incontinence	Early mobilisation Enema High-fibre diet Sufficient liquids
Bladder	Urinary tract infection Urine retention Urine incontinence	Hydration Early mobilisation Examine secondary causes of retention Bladder training Catheterisation, if necessary
Heart and blood vessels	Orthostatic hypotension	Early mobilisation Wear support hose Slow shift from lying to standing position (via sitting position) Sufficient liquids
	Deep venous thrombosis and lung embolism	Early mobilisation Wear support hose Administration of subcutaneous heparin

outcomes of treatment may be just as important as the clinical outcomes because functional outcomes relate to the quality of life or the second set of outcomes to be considered here.

Why quality of life?

Within the field of health care, outcomes at a number of levels are – in principle – pursued (Benson 1992). As depicted in Figure 7.5, the first and most fundamental level involves the biochemistry, physiology and microbiology of the patient.

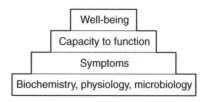

Figure 7.5 *Levels of outcome.*
Source: Benson 1992.

The second level concerns the symptoms or visible characteristics of an illness. In outcome terms, this level falls under the rubric 'clinical outcomes'. The third level involves the functional capacities of the patient or, in other words, the capacity of the patient to act, react and interact during daily life. Three dimensions of such functioning can be distinguished: the physical, psychological and social. The fourth and final outcome level is often referred to as well-being or happiness and is thus the most sweeping outcome of medical intervention.

The care provider or clinician is generally oriented towards the first level because this level typically reflects the basis of an illness and improvement at this level can influence other levels. The symptoms of an illness are considered next, and then the rest.

The patient, however, often has a very different perspective. The well-being of the patient is at issue and thus constitutes his or her major concern, as depicted in Figure 7.6.

The preceding is formulated in rather general terms as the perspectives of the care provider and patient tend to correspond more strongly in cases of acute or serious illness than in cases of chronic illness. The most important point here is that the capacity to function should be one of the desired outcomes of treatment for both the care provider and the patient; the general outcome indicator used for this purpose is 'quality of life'.

A good example of this is the chemotherapy that is given patients with meta-stasised breast cancer, which is not curative but related to considerations of the quality of life, for instance (Essink-Bot and de Haes 1996). A second reason to include quality of life in the outcome quadrant is that quality of life may actually

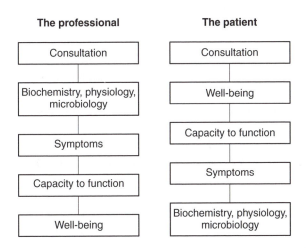

Figure 7.6 *Different perspectives on objectives of health care.*
Source: Benson 1992.

constitute the treatment objective at times. In the case of support for chronic psychiatric patients, for example, one does not so much 'treat' as attempt to maintain some quality of life.

A third reason to include quality of life in the outcome quadrant stems from the fact that consideration of the effects of treatment on the quality of life may determine the choice between two different treatments with comparable effects on symptoms at times.

Fourth, a weighing of clinical outcomes, quality of life, patient opinions of care and costs is needed to discuss the results of the outcome quadrant. For example, improved quality of life may justify higher costs at times.

Existing systems of measurement for quality of life

The existing systems of measurement for quality of life can be traced back to three basic types:

- Measurement instruments which are health related and thus measure a particular aspect of the individual's health condition. Such instruments will be considered in further detail below.
- Measurement instruments stemming from cost-effectiveness studies such as QALY (Quality-Adjusted Life Years) which combines estimates of the number of life years with estimates of the quality of life or – stated more technically – $QALY = V(Q) \times Y$, where Y is the number of estimated survival years and $V(Q)$ is a correction factor with V representing the quality of life associated with health status Q. V dead has a value of 0 and V healthy has a value of 1. The cost-effectiveness of health programmes is then measured by calculating the cost price per QALY.
- Quality of life questionnaires based on a particular model or theory such as quality of life conceptualised as 'the degree of correspondence between expectations and reality' or 'the capacity of the individual to meet his or her own needs'. Such questionnaires are situated too far away from clinical use and will therefore not be considered further with the present context.

When those instruments which measure quality of life most closely to health status are considered in greater detail, generic instruments versus illness- or domain-specific instruments can be distinguished.

Generic questionnaires

Generic instruments measure the quality of life in terms which are relevant for each and every person and thus irrespective of the presence or absence of a specific diagnosis. Generic instruments encompass the physical, psychological and social domains. Given that the health status of the individual is expressed in such generic and generalisable terms, however, generic instruments are less sensitive than illness-specific measurement instruments.

Illness-specific questionnaires

Illness-specific measurement instruments address those dimensions of health most influenced by the illness in question. Very few illness-specific instruments have been developed. In Table 7.3, a few of the questionnaires are listed (Essink-Bot and de Haes 1996).

In mapping the state of health for a particular patient group, estimates for specific domains, functioning or health may also be of interest. An example is pain. Using standardised domain-specific questionnaires specifically developed for this purpose, it is possible to make comparisons to other patient groups and groups of healthy people. In Table 7.4, a few domain-specific questionnaires are listed.

Multidimensional measurement instruments

The search for comprehensive and meaningful indicators of health status reveals very few instruments with an adequate degree of reliability and validity together with easy applicability (Jenkinson and McGee 1998) and while various

Table 7.3 Illness-specific questionnaires

Cancer	Cancer Rehabilitation Evaluation System – Short Form
	EORTC QLQ-C30+ specific modules
	FACT-G+ specific modules
	Rotterdam Symptom Checklist
CARA	Chronic respiratory questionnaire
	Quality of life questionnaire for CARA patients
	Medical psychological questionnaire for CARA patients
	Living with asthma questionnaire
Heart disease	Medical psychological questionnaire for heart patients
Diabetes	Diabetes symptom checklist

Table 7.4 Domain-specific questionnaires

Pain	McGill Pain Questionnaire (MPQ-DLV)
Depression	CES-D
	Hospital Anxiety and Depression Scale
Anxiety	State-trait Anxiety Inventory
Fatigue	Multidimensional Fatigue Inventory
ADL	Barthel Index

instruments have been developed to measure the effects of a treatment intervention, they all have the disadvantage of being either very global in nature or aimed at specific clinical pictures.

Attention to the use of multidimensional measurement instruments to establish general health state and quality of life has therefore increased (van der Zee and Sanderman 1993). And for purposes of outcome management, a generic measurement instrument constitutes the best option. Frequently used generic measurement instruments are the Short Form 36 (SF 36), the Nottingham Health Profile (NHP) and the Sickness Impact Profile (SIP). The major advantage of these scales is their broad applicability and their demonstrated reliability and validity (Drummond *et al.* 1997).

Sensitivity to change is an indispensable feature of any health status instrument when used as an outcome measure. In addition, it is critical that the significance of any change in the outcome scores have an unambiguous interpretation.

Medical outcome study (MOS SF 36, SF 20)

One multidimensional measure of health status is the Short Form 36. This measurement method is a product of the Rand Corporation's Health Insurance Experiment (HIE) and the subsequent Medical Outcome Study (MOS). The HIE and MOS are long questionnaires which map the general state of health and thus constitute the precursors to the SF 36. The purpose of both questionnaires was to assemble patient-related outcome measures in addition to traditional clinical and laboratory measures of health and illness (Jenkinson and McGee 1998). The SF 36 health status questionnaire has been used worldwide since 1990.

Nottingham Health Profile

The NHP was developed in the United Kingdom and is based on the health status perceptions of laypeople. The conceptual basis for the NHP is that the definition of health status should reflect the layperson's perceptions as opposed to the professional's (Bowling 1997: 43). The developers of the NHP argued that despite various attempts to develop self-report measures of health status, a short, easy to complete and generic instrument had yet to be developed (Jenkinson and McGee, 1998 32). The NHP was then developed on the basis of a large number of interviews among non-professionals regarding the consequences of illness for behaviour.

One criticism of the NHP is that it provides only a very superficial overview of the effects of illness. In the United Kingdom, the NHP has been used to evaluate the outcomes of different treatments from the perspective of the patients and to measure the perceived health status of patients before and after undergoing a particular procedure (Bowling 1997).

Sickness Impact Profile

The SIP was developed as a measure of perceived health status and as an outcome measure for use in the evaluation of health care across a wide range of health problems and illnesses and different demographic and cultural groups (Bowling 1997: 40). Illness is measured in relation to its impact on behaviour, and the SIP emphasises illness-related dysfunction rather than the illness itself. The SIP has been made sufficiently sensitive to detect differences in health status in terms of less morbidity (Bergner *et al.* 1981). The SIP was also developed using standard psychometric methods.

EuroQol

The EuroQol is the most frequently used questionnaire for quality of life research in Europe. The EuroQol group was founded in the mid-1980s with the development of an international measurement instrument for use in economic evaluations of health care as its objective (Jenkinson and McGee, 1998). The instrument had to be short because it was expected that it would be used in addition to other questionnaires.

The EuroQol instrument measures health status using five items:

- mood
- mobility
- pain
- self-care
- daily activities.

The response possibilities are:

- 'no problems'
- 'some problems'
- 'many problems'.

Given that the questionnaire consists of only a small number of questions, it is easily included in patient-based research. The limited number of health states also makes the appraisal task relatively easy for the general public. The immense amount of work involved in the development of the EuroQol has made the instrument one of the most widely accepted outcome measures in Europe. The instrument is seen to provide not only a practical and easy measure of health but also present health differences in a meaningful manner (Jenkinson and McGee, 1998). There are also some objections to EuroQol as a measure of health, however. Given the small

103

number of questions and response categories, for example, the sensitivity of the EuroQol is assumed to be limited (van Busschbach 2001).

In Table 7.5, various multidimensional measurement instruments are compared with respect to a number of structural properties.

Quality of life and outcome management

The recording of an index for the quality of life can proceed according to a number of steps with the team first asking itself whether quality of life is a meaningful indicator in connection with the medical activities of the team. If the treatment is not very drastic, consideration of clinical outcomes alone may be sufficient. In keeping with the flow chart presented in Figure 7.7, the steps to determine the quality of life for purposes of outcome management will be considered further below.

Summary: the measurement of functional outcomes and quality of life

For the patient, quality of life is a very important outcome of the treatment as it reflects the capacity of the patient to act, react and interact during daily life. Many questionnaires have been developed to measure this conceptually vague concept. These questionnaires can be generic or specific to an illness. It depends on the treatment team and the patients to decide whether comparability is more important than specifity. And sometimes, the treatment is aimed at a specific aspect of quality of life, at anxiety or pain for example.

PATIENT OPINIONS

The treatment offered by a health care organisation is aimed at patients. And information on the opinions of patients with regard to their treatment is therefore needed to improve treatment and bring treatment more into line with what patients expect. For this reason, most health care organisations have one or the other form of patient satisfaction measurement available to them. Such measures are often very generic and typically provide very little information on specific components of the care process. Just how the organisation should use the results of such measurement to realise actual improvement is also not always clear.

If we really want to improve the health care process and consider the opinions of the patient to be important in this light, then another manner of handling patient opinions is called for. That is, a decentralised, close to the patient and continuous check of whether or not the health care process is meeting the expectations of the patient is necessary.

Table 7.5 Multidimensional measurement instruments

	SIP 36	SIP 68	NHP	COOP/WONCA	SF-20/MOS 24	SF/RAND-36	EuroQol
Number of items	36	68	38 + 7	6	20/24	36	6
Administration duration (min)	20	10	5	5	5	10	2
Response categories	yes/no	yes/no	yes/no	5 categories with pictures	more than one type (3–6 categories)	more than one type (2–6 categories)	3 categories plus thermometer
Reference period	today	present	at the moment	2 weeks	3 months/1 week	4 weeks/1 week	past week
Developed for age group	adults	adults	adults	14 years	adults	16 years	12 years
Designed for diagnostic purposes	varied	varied	general population	patients consulting family doctor	varied	varied	varied

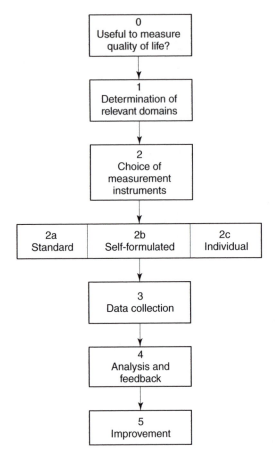

Figure 7.7 *Determination of quality of life for purposes of outcome management.*

Why patient opinions?

Seeing that patients have positive opinions with regard to their health care is important for a number of reasons.

- *Humanistic reasons.* When patients come into contact with health care, they are often very vulnerable and fearful. They are sick, in pain and worried. The warm human provision of services is therefore a duty of care professionals.
- *Medical reasons.* A patient who is well informed, handled with respect and involved in treatment to the greatest extent possible is more inclined to adhere to treatment guidelines than other patients. It has been repeatedly demonstrated that satisfied patients adhere to treatment recommendations or instructions better than other patients (Benson 1992).

- *Outcome reasons*. Sometimes the evaluation provided by the patient constitutes a direct outcome measure. In a number of circumstances, such as those associated with pain or psychiatric problems, the success of the treatment can be indicated only by the patient.
- *Quality-improvement reasons*. Patient opinions provide insight into the quality of care processes, and this information can thus be used for improvement purposes.
- *Efficiency reasons*. A dissatisfied patient requires more attention than a satisfied patient.
- *Market reasons*. Competition is playing an increasingly important role in the provision of health care. For patients, the quality of the service appears to be a decisive factor.

When health care is under pressure, as in much of the world, providers tend to fall back upon purely medical qualities: 'As long as the medical treatment is okay.' They underestimate the interwoven nature of the quality of the medical care provided and the other services provided. And, in such a manner, the health care sector makes itself extremely vulnerable to commercial initiatives which provide equally good or perhaps less good medical care but clearly shine with respect to the quality of the other services provided.

In other words, there are plenty of reasons for health care organisations concerned with the improvement of outcomes to include patient opinions as part of what they consider.

Patient opinions: more detailed consideration

Many organisations acknowledge the importance of patient opinions and thus try to gain an impression of such. However, the manner in which patient opinions are dealt with has a number of shortcomings. Every author uses his or her own definition of patient satisfaction. Across studies, thus, patient satisfaction is conceptualised in very different manners. An analysis of the literature reveals the following dimensions:

- general satisfaction
- accessibility
- costs
- general quality
- humanity
- competence
- provision of information
- administrative procedures
- physical environment

- handling of psychosocial problems
- continuity of care
- outcomes of care.

There are countless such lists stemming from factor analyses of surveys or some other methods of analyses. And there are large differences in the nature of the outcome measures.

Sometimes the opinions of the patient actually constitute the outcome measure. In cases of pain or anxiety, for example, only the patient can evaluate the extent to which such feelings play a role before, during and after treatment. The situation is very different when a consumer-oriented study specifically requests an evaluation of the service component of the care. And there are also questions more or less solely aimed at the evaluation of specific care outcomes. 'Did the treatment help you?' constitutes the outcome measure, thus.

In other words, patient satisfaction may be examined using three completely different questions. The real issue, then, is whether it makes sense or is even possible to conceptualise patient satisfaction within a single definition.

Patient involvement

Patients are rarely asked to evaluate treatment from their own perspective. Sometimes a questionnaire will be constructed in consultation with a particular patient organisation, but this is often then the end of any patient involvement. Patients are rarely asked what they consider important for themselves and rarely involved in the discussion of treatment results.

Existing systems of measurement for patient opinions

Most theories assume that patient opinions are the result of the weighing of the expectations which someone has against the actual provision of services. I expect to be helped immediately but have to wait 15 minutes, so my opinion is negative. I expect a wait of at least 30 minutes but am helped after 15 minutes, so my opinion is positive. In other words, the opinion is viewed as the result of a comparison of the experienced service to some standard. Comparison leads to an opinion or feeling which is either positive or negative, and this is known as the 'value-expectation model' with Linder-Pelz as an important proponent (Harteloh *et al*. 1992). Stated most simply, to the extent to which experience exceeds expectation, the chances of a satisfied patient increase (Harteloh *et al*. 1992). The preceding model is depicted in Figure 7.8.

Other models of patient satisfaction (Williams 1994) are discrepancy theory in which satisfaction is assumed to be the result of what someone desires and the extent to which that desire is met; satisfaction theory in which satisfaction is assumed to be the difference between that which is desired and that which is received in the form of positive experiences and reward; and balance theory in which the perceived balance between input and output relative to the gains of others under similar circumstances is assumed to determine satisfaction.

Research on the value of the different models has not produced convincing evidence in favour of one or the other. Even in the most carefully conducted research, for example, no unequivocal support for the role of expectations and opinions can be found. Other factors are consistently found to play a major role in the explanation of patient opinions and satisfaction. And it is certainly possible that expectations are not stable and thus change during the course of a medical process.

One model in which it is attempted to integrate the many different aspects of patient satisfaction is the client satisfaction model as proposed by Zeithaml *et al.* (1990) and outlined in Figure 7.9.

The client satisfaction model was developed on the basis of focus groups of clients from different service-providing sectors. The information provided by the focus groups showed clients – irrespective of the type of service – to use basically very similar criteria to evaluate the quality of service (Parasuraman *et al.* 1985). A total of ten determinants of the perceived quality of service initially emerged. These were later collapsed to create five dimensions for evaluation of the model: tangibility, reliability, service, trustworthiness and empathy (Harteloh and Casparie 1998).

Measurement

The measurement of patient opinions is typically done with the aid of a questionnaire. Such a questionnaire usually requires a value judgement with regard to the care provided. Given that patients do not want to appear ungrateful, really critical judgement is often not provided. The result is that most patients (80 per cent to 90 per cent) report being satisfied (Harteloh *et al.* 1992) and the responses to such questionnaires do not lead to the identification of problems in the health care process.

It is also the case that questionnaires administered after treatment are often not returned, which causes the response rate to drop under the desired 50 per cent.

Figure 7.8 *Value-expectation model.*

Source: Harteloh et al. 1992.

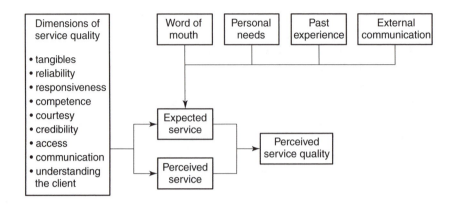

Figure 7.9 *Client evaluation of quality of service provided.*
Source: Zeithaml et al. *1990.*

Furthermore, the majority of the questionnaires assess just how 'satisfied' patients are with specific aspects of the care while points of dissatisfaction are much more important for the identification of those aspects in need of change or improvement.

The reliability and validity of the majority of the questionnaires used to measure patient satisfaction are unknown. Questionnaires also force patients to make judgements with regard to matters which may be trivial to them, and the utility of such questionnaires can therefore be very limited depending on the objective motivating their use and the context of their use.

There are many methods other than the questionnaire to attain information from patients. Among the possibilities are:

- observation: the judgements of patients and their reactions to the care;
- participant observation: going through the care process oneself;
- telephone inquiry;
- focus groups;
- semi-structured or fully structured interviews;
- complaint analyses;
- critical-incident analyses;
- exit interviews;
- process analyses in which patients are followed during the care process and asked about their experiences.

Each of the aforementioned methods has its own advantages and disadvantages. Different methods can perhaps be applied in combination and depending on the situation. For example, a focus group can provide information on what patients expect or desire, and this information can, in turn, supply questions for a questionnaire or exit interview.

A number of conclusions with regard to the measurement of patient opinions can be drawn on the basis of the preceding overview.

- It is of critical importance that the evaluator of care outcomes and the evaluator of the quality of the service provided be aware of the opinions of patients; only then can the direction for the improvement of activities be properly determined.
- The measurement of patient opinions must be specific and suited to those patients receiving a particular form of care.
- The measurement of patient opinions should be reliable, valid and based on explicit conceptualisation of the quality of care and the evaluation of such.
- The patient should be proactive and fully involved in the measurement and improvement of the quality of care.
- Patient opinions should be analysed and reported back to those teams with direct responsibility for the care process and also with the authority and capacity to transform this knowledge into concrete improvement activities.

Patient opinions and outcome management

In this section, just how the opinions of patients can be incorporated into outcome management will be considered. As depicted in Table 7.6, a proactive perspective on the measurement of patient opinions and their complete involvement in the measurement process will be adopted.

Step 1 Operationalisation of vision

An organisation or a team which is just starting with outcome management does not do this without its own vision of what constitutes good care. A few of these

Table 7.6 *The measurement of patient opinion*

1 Operationalization of vision
2 Inventory of patient desires and expectations
3 Development of standards
4 Selection of measurement instrument
5 Data collection
6 Analysis and feedback
7 Improvement

expectations and desires can also be derived from the contributions of patient groups and current developments within the field.

A team thus has to make its vision of good care tangible to patients and team members. It also needs to be aligned with the vision of the whole organisation.

Step 2 Inventory of patient desires and expectations

Different methods can be used to reveal the aspirations of patients involved in a specific care process. In each case, it is critical that direct communication occur between those requesting help and those providing help and that patients in the different phases of the treatment process be involved in such communication. Active interaction is critical as only in such a manner patients and staff can help each other formulate their expectations.

Once expectations with regard to the care process have been stipulated in the form of – for example – a clinical path, a more specific inventory of the desires of patients with regard to the different phases of care can be made. With the use of a clinical path, one can even record the specific wishes of the individual patient. As depicted in Figure 7.10, patient desires generally appear at three levels: the organisation, the team and patient group and the individual patient.

When all the desires of the patients have been recorded, these are again considered in a joint session involving the team and patients.

Step 3 Development of standards

Once the different desires and expectations of patients have been considered, the formulation of concrete objectives and accompanying standards for care can be undertaken.

Figure 7.10 Patient opinions in layers.

Step 4 Selection of measurement instrument

As already indicated, different methods can be used to collect information from patients. The simplest method is the questionnaire supplemented with at least a detailed complaint procedure and, for example, exit interviews with a sample of patients asked to reflect upon the care provided in a structured manner.

There is a lot to be said for active involvement of patients in the selection of the instrument to be used to measure their opinions and for giving them a role in the collection of such data. However, responsibility for the collection of information on patient opinions lies with the team leader.

Step 5 Data collection

The team determines the frequency with which information on the opinions of patients should be collected. The team should also formulate some measures to minimise the chances of non-response or incomplete response on the part of patients when given, for example, a questionnaire.

Step 6 Analysis and feedback

It is again possible (and recommended) that patients be involved in the analyses of the information collected on patient opinions and the formulation of feedback with regard to the results of such for the care team. Patients can be involved in the analyses and provision of feedback in different manners. They can help interpret the results or discuss the results with the care team.

Step 7 Improvement

The improvement step will be considered in much greater detail elsewhere. Suffice it to say that numerous opportunities present themselves for patients to participate in the improvement process and that these opportunities for patient participation should not be missed.

Summary: the measurement of patient opinions and satisfaction

The patient's opinion on the treatment is of importance for various humanistic, medical and market reasons. And it is of course a base for improvement. Measurement is typically done with questionnaires but there are many other options like observation, focus groups and exit interviews. Each with its own advantages and disadvantages. The contents of a questionnaire or of other methods depends on the vision and mission of the team and reflects the needs of the patients. What is being considered as good care and how to make this sufficiently specific in order to make it measurable.

COSTS OF TREATMENT

Treatment costs money. And for purposes of outcome evaluation, the cost of treatment must be calculated. It is certainly possible, for example, that the outcome of a treatment can be enhanced but only at a much greater cost. In other words, a care team must be able to make such trade-offs as part of their efforts to improve the course of treatment.

Why costs?

In light of the rapid developments occurring in the fields of medical technology and other forms of medical treatment together with the increased financial pressures being placed on health care, growing attention is being paid to the actual costs of care. To determine the value of a particular form of treatment, for example, the outcomes and costs of care are now compared with the 'value' represented by the outcomes divided by the costs. And with the incorporation of the costs of care into the process of outcome management, it is possible to achieve realistic comparisons – comparisons across not only organisations and teams but also across time or before and after improvement efforts.

Existing systems of cost calculation

One can speak of four types of costs associated with treatment:

- costs incurred during the course of treatment;
- costs incurred outside treatment;
- direct costs;
- indirect costs.

Direct costs are costs which can be directly related to treatment; indirect costs arise as a secondary consequence of treatment (Rutten *et al*. 2000).

In the following, we will concentrate on the direct costs incurred within the field of health care because determination of the indirect costs and costs outside the field of health care is far too complicated for inclusion within the regular clinical context.

We will, however, include all direct costs and thus those costs also incurred outside the team and even outside the organisation provided they pertain to treatment and care. For example, a reduction in the number of hospital days can be counted as a cost reduction, but the cost of an increased stay in a rehabilitation centre or convalescent home must not, then, be ignored.

The calculation of costs

Once again, our primary interest is in the calculation of the direct costs of health care. In doing this, the time frame selected for consideration is of initial importance. And this, of course, depends on the diagnosis and treatment. In the case of a broken bone, determination of the costs incurred during the treatment itself is sufficient because the remaining costs are marginal or zero. In the case of a chronic illness, however, the situation is much more complicated and the time frame is usually such that all intervention-related costs are included (Rutten *et al.* 2000).

The calculation of costs can be undertaken in a more or less detailed manner. A key factor in the calculation of costs is the extent to which overhead costs are included or not.

Summary: the calculation of costs

Costs of treatment are weighed against the other indicators within the outcome quadrant. If current treatment costs more but also leads to better outcomes than alternative treatment, more in-depth analysis of current treatment in the form of a cost-effectiveness analysis – for example – may be called for. This also holds when current treatment costs less but also leads to poorer outcomes than alternative treatment. In this case, lower costs must be weighed against lower outcomes. If current treatment is less expensive but leads to better outcomes than alternative treatment, then the current manner of working should be continued and built upon. If, in contrast, current treatment is more expensive and leads to less good outcomes than alternative treatment (e.g. treatment elsewhere or in the past), then the current treatment should be modified or redesigned on the basis of a careful study of the alternative.

CONCLUSION

'Outcome of treatment' is a multidimensional concept. In this chapter we selected four outcomes: clinical outcomes, functional outcomes or quality of life, patient opinions or patient satisfaction and costs. With this selection we do not want to exclude other variables. The selection of outcome criteria depends on the mission of the team, possibilities for measurement and statistical aspects of the measuring instruments.

We think that it is less important to select the very best ultimate criteria than to start the process of feedback of outcomes to a healthcare team. Outcome measurement and performance improvement is a long process that will develop over time. It is best to start with a simple set of criteria in order to prevent long administrative and bureaucratic measurement procedures. The fun and challenge is in the discussions on the outcomes, comparing it with the performance of other teams. The administrative perfection of the system can be developed in due time.

DISCUSSION QUESTIONS

1 In the past, many outcome indicator systems have been developed. Why have these systems so seldom been of clinical use?
2 In what cases is the measurement of quality of life of less importance and in what cases is it of very high importance?
3 What other costs of treatment than financial costs can you identify?
4 How can you integrate the needs or the voice of the patient in the measurement of patient satisfaction?

REFERENCES

Benson, D.L. (1992) *Measuring outcomes in ambulatory care*. Chicago, IL: American Hospital Publishing.

Bergner, M., Bobbitt, R.A., Carter, W.B. *et al*. (1981) Development, testing and use of Sickness Impact Profile, in S.R. Walker and R.M. Rosser (eds) *Quality of life: assessment and application*. Lancaster: MTP Press.

Bowling, A. (1997) *Measuring health: a review of quality of life measurement scales*. Buckingham: Open University Press.

Donabedian, A. (1992) The role of outcomes in quality assessment and assurance. *Quality Review Bulletin*, 18(11): 356–360.

Drummond, M.F., O'Brien, B., Stoddart , G.L. *et al*. (1997*) Methods for the economic evaluation of health care programmes*. New York: Oxford University Press.

Essink-Bot, M.L. and de Haes, J.C.J.M. (1996) *Kwaliteit van leven in medisch onderzoe*. Amsterdam: Amsterdam University Press.

Harteloh, P.P.M. and Casparie, A.F. (1998*) Kwaliteit van Zorg: van zorginhoudelijke benadering naar een bedrijfskundige aanpak*. Utrecht: De Tijdstroom.

Harteloh, P.P.M., Sprij, B. and Casprie, A.F. (1992) Patiëntsatisfactie en kwaliteit: een problematische relatie. *Maandblad voor Geestelijke volksgezondheid*, 47(2): 157–165.

Huppes, W. (2001) *Kwaliteit resultaat analyse system: Achtergrondstudie*. Zoetermeer: Raad voor de Volksgezondheid en Zorg (RVZ).

Jenkinson, C. and McGee, H. (1998) *Health status measurement: a brief but critical introduction*. Abingdon, Oxon: Radcliffe Medical.

Joint Commission (2002) *Facts about oryx: the evolution in accreditation. Joint Commission on Accreditation of Healthcare Organisations* www.jcaho.com

Lee, K.Y., Loeb, L.M., Nadzam, D.M. *et al.* (2000) Special report: an overview of the Joint Commission's ORYX Initiative and Proposed Statistical Methods. *Health Services and Outcomes Research Methodology*, 1(1): 63–73.

Nadzam, D.M., Turpin, R., Hanold, L.S. *et al.* (1993) Data-driven performance improvement in health care: the joint commission's indicator measurement system (M system). *Joint Commission Journal on Quality Improvement*, 19(11): 492–500.

Nelson, E.C., Splaine, M.E., Batalden, P.B. *et al.* (1998) Measuring clinical outcomes at the frontline, in C. Caldwel (ed.) *The handbook for managing change in health care*. Milwaukee, WI: ASQ Quality Press.

Paepe, L. de and Quaethoven, P. (2000) Klinische indicatoren als instrument voor kwaliteitsverbetering in Vlaanderen. *Kwaliteit in beeld*, 10(4): 11.

Parasuraman, A., Zeithaml, V.A. and Berry, L.L. (1985) A conceptual model of service quality and its implications for future research. *Journal of Marketing* 49: 41–50.

Rutten van Mölken, M.P.M.H., van Busschbach, J.J. and Rutten, F.F.H. (eds) (2000) *Van Kusten tot effecten: een handleiding voor evaluatie studies in de gezondheidszorg*. Maarssen: Elsevier Gezondheidszorg.

Treurniet, H.F. (1999) *Kwaliteitsbewaking in de gezondheidszorg: Ontwikkeling van uitkomstenindicatoren*. Amersfoort: Drukkerij Wilco.

Van Busschbach, J.J. (1997) Metingen van kwaliteit van leven in farmaco-economische onderzoeken. *Ziekenhuisfarmacie*, 13(1): 52–54.

van der Zee, K.I. and Sanderman, R. (1993) Het meten van de algemene gezondheidstoestand met de RAND-36: Een Handleiding. Reeks: *NCG meetinstrumenten* vol. 3. Groningen: Noordelijk centrum voor gezondheidsvraagstukken rijksuniversiteit.

Walburg, J.A. (1997) *Integrale kwaliteit in de gezondheidszorg: Van inspecteren naar leren*. Deventer: Kluwer BedrijfsInformatie BV.

Williams, B. (1994) Patient satisfaction: a valid concept? *Social Science and Medicine*, 38(4): 509–516.

Zeithaml, V.A., Parasuraman, A. and Berry, L.L. (1990) *Delivering quality service: balancing customer perceptions and expectations*. New York: The Free Press.

Chapter 8

Patient variables and risk adjustment for the assessment of health outcomes

Karin Lemmens

KEY POINTS OF THIS CHAPTER

- The importance of patient characteristics as variables in the outcome of care
- Patient variables with the biggest impact on outcomes of care
- Risk adjustment tools for outcome management
- Methodological issues related to risk adjustment strategies

---

INTRODUCTION

Any team or organisation that implements an outcome management strategy needs to take account of variation between patients and the risk this poses to the achievement of outcomes. Up until this point, a direct and unambiguous relation has been assumed between a specific intervention and the subsequent outcomes. In reality, however, a number of factors other than the intervention itself can influence the outcome of care. Factors related to patient characteristics appear to play a particularly important role. Differences in age, sex, severity of the disorder, comorbidity and the consequences of therapeutic interventions are all reasons for why outcomes can vary between patients (Shin and Johnson 2000a). Outcomes must thus be adjusted for these factors. Risk adjustment is the process by which the factors that influence care outcomes are taken into consideration in assessing potential outcomes. The goal of risk adjustment is to consider the relevant patient variables before relations are drawn between the effectiveness or quality of care and patient outcomes (Iezonni 1997). Other terms for risk adjustment are severity adjustment, case-mix adjustment, comparison of apples and oranges and levelling of the playing field (Shin and Johnson 2000a).

In this chapter, we will first discuss the importance of patient variables. We will then consider the global selection of patient variables for purposes of risk adjustment and assessment of the severity of illness. A number of steps for the final selection of patient variables for purposes of risk adjustment will be outlined. Finally, we will identify a number of methodological problems associated with risk adjustment.

IMPORTANCE OF PATIENT VARIABLES

In this book, we take outcomes to be a measure of the quality and effectiveness of intervention within the field of health care. We further attempt to identify measurement instruments and indicators which constitute good measure of outcomes, on the one hand, and the intervention process, on the other. Patient characteristics must be considered as an important part of the equation because they help to:

- determine treatment;
- interpret outcomes;
- steer the care and determine care capacity.

In this chapter, we focus on reasons for including patient characteristics in the evaluation of health care outcomes in greater detail.

Determination of treatment

The exact nature and content of clinical treatment is based on the needs and wishes of the patient and professional evaluation of the patient's condition. Decisions regarding treatment strongly depend on the clinical picture. Are we considering early-stage problems, severe problems or long-standing chronic problems? Is the problem acute or is there less urgency about time to treatment?

Depending of the type of clinical problem, the identification of various patient variables and patient characteristics may be critical to determine the type of treatment needed. That is, patient variables may constitute an indication for a differentiated form of treatment.

Interpretation of outcomes

Care outcomes cannot be analysed without consideration of patient characteristics. A few examples illustrate the point. The outcomes of treatment for lung cancer are strongly determined by the smoking behaviour of the patient, occupational hazard and family history (Petty 2001). The effectiveness of treatment for depression strongly depends upon, among other things, psychosocial factors in the patient's youth, sex and social structure (Riise and Lund 2001). The success of a kidney transplant depends upon, among other things, the presence of diabetes, similarity of donor characteristics and the presence of certain antibodies (Van Saasse et al. 1996). And as described in Chapter 7, not only clinical outcomes but also such matters as patient opinions and satisfaction depend, at least in part, on such patient characteristics as age and subjective health condition (Rahmqvist 2001).

Consideration of patient characteristics is also of critical importance when benchmarking is part of the system of outcome management. Organisations A and B can, for instance, attain very different outcomes which stem largely from differences in their patient populations. Outcome measures which include patient characteristics generally produce results which are more valuable and less susceptible to critique than in cases of straightforward benchmarking or external comparison of outcomes.

Steering care

Analyses of care outcomes, such as in diabetes care the percentage of patients with glycohemoglobin (HbA1c) greater than 9 per cent with a 1 per cent HbA1c reduction, can also lead to an adjustment of the care being offered and/or provided. We might, for example, notice that too few people from a particular cultural background are seeking treatment for a particular medical problem despite research showing an equal distribution of the problem across the population. An example is undiagnosed diabetes amongst the South Asian population. In such cases, the provision of targeted and culturally appropriate services or information for that particular group may be called for.

Another example illustrating the need for careful consideration of patient characteristics is when a particular treatment is found to be successful for one group but not another. An example is a smoking cessation programme, which is effective for an adult population but does not meet the needs of young people. The establishment of a treatment programme, which specifically takes the particular characteristics of the other group into consideration, may then be recommended.

GLOBAL SELECTION OF PATIENT VARIABLES FOR RISK ADJUSTMENT

Those variables which appear to influence health care outcomes are summarised in Figure 8.1. Among the multitude of variables, two main categories can be distinguished: *illness-related* variables and *non-illness-related* variables.

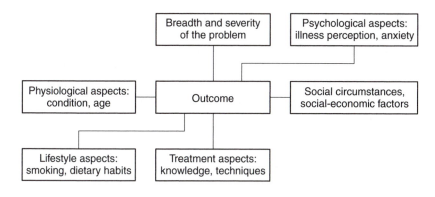

Figure 8.1 *Factors of importance for determination of outcome indicators.*

Illness-related variables

Included in the category of illness-related variables are the acuteness, complexity and severity of the illness. The acuteness of the illness concerns whether or not immediate intervention is required. A threat to a person's own life or a threat to the lives of others may be involved at times. The degree of urgency for each illness is determined on the basis of different criteria. And for purposes of registration in medical records, it is important that the clinical characteristics, which determine the urgency, be explicitly stated.

The complexity of an illness depends on the breadth of the illness while the severity depends on the depth. The complexity of an illness can be determined in terms of the number of diagnosable conditions which may relate to other medical or psychiatric disorders and the general condition of the patient. We will return to the determination of the severity of an illness at a later point in this chapter.

Non-illness-related variables

Ethical considerations place limits on what may be registered. The criterion is usually no more registry than that which is of importance for the interpretation of health care outcomes. The following selection of variables therefore may or may not thus be considered for inclusion in the evaluation of outcomes:

- biographical variables (age, sex, ethnic background);
- lifestyle variables (smoking, diet, alcohol consumption, exercise);
- social-economic variables (social background, profession);
- psychological variables (anxiety, motivation, illness perceptions).

There are several ways to determine the importance of the inclusion of variables not directly related to an illness by means of evaluation of treatment outcomes. This can be done on the basis of the existing literature (i.e. evidence based), on the basis of what the relevant guidelines recommend and/or on the basis of clinical experience and substantiated presuppositions. For example, risk elements for the prevalence of problem behaviour towards others of nursing home residents are cognitive impairment, Alzheimer's disease, other dementia, psychotic conditions and comorbidity (Arling *et al.* 1997).

THE SEVERITY OF ILLNESS

In the evaluation of the treatment of a particular patient, we must always keep the complexity and severity of the illness in mind. Similarly, when we want to analyse outcomes across larger numbers of patients and/or compare outcomes across teams and organisations, we need to consider the severity of the illness before treatment of the patient. There are many other reasons for professionals to consider the severity of patient illness. With adequate differentiation of the severity of the illness, the workload and logistics associated with the required care can be adequately planned. However, prior attempts to apply care weight as a measure of workload have not provided much insight simply because the systems were implemented for only a brief period of time and not evaluated sufficiently. On a different front, institutional and regional budgets should take differences of severity into consideration. It is assumed, for example, that not only the extent but also the severity of psychiatric problems is greater in large cities than in other geographical locations. It is also known that the age differences between certain geographic regions can explain the greater extent and severity of particular illnesses in one region relative to another.

The brief overview presented above suggests that not only clinical professionals but also managers, insurers and policy-makers should be interested in the severity of illness. However, this situation brings certain risks with it as well. The patient or potential patient may be offered unsolicited activities in the form of prevention or screening measures on the basis of the aforementioned figures. Furthermore, the most important reason for the widespread and ongoing discussion of the measurement of illness severity is not so much one of quality improvement as comparison of the effectiveness of hospitals. And in some countries, such as the USA, large commercial interests are involved in the comparison of hospitals. Unfortunately, the most important conclusions from the discussion to date are that different measures of illness severity produce very different impressions of severity and that the morbidity figures adjusted for severity of illness do not provide an adequate indication of the quality of a hospital. Severity measurements thus have a limited value and cannot be used alone to determine whether a health care organisation is performing well or not (Iezzoni 1997). Considerable caution is thus called for in the comparison of outcomes across hospitals and other health care organisations. And beyond this, we should note that the real issue should be improvement of the quality of care and not comparison of organisations. In other words, we should examine health care outcomes and relate these to (among other things) the severity of illness to evaluate the treatment process. Within the context of quality improvement and careful analyses sometimes via individual case files, determination of the severity of illness is not only useful but also crucial. There are two reasons why risk-adjustment should be used when profiling providers on their outcomes. First, providers differ in their patient-mix. Providers caring for sicker patients may be unfairly penalised if unadjusted outcomes are used. Second, judgements of how a provider performed differed depending on whether unadjusted or risk-adjusted measures are used (Berlowitz *et al.* 1998). Risk-adjusted data may provide a more accurate description of true performance and should be encouraged when describing outcomes of care.

Definition

'Severity of illness' is operationalised very differently by authors adopting different perspectives on the issue. Some definitions emphasise the purely clinical aspects and thus speak of only symptoms and the stage of illness. The illness and severity of the illness are thus described in terms of:

- the organs involved;
- pathophysiological changes in the organs;
- etiological variables;
- the severity of the pathophysiological changes.

(Des Harnais and McLaughlin 1994)

Other definitions pay greater attention to the more subjective aspects of illness severity involving patient feelings and the functioning of the patient.

The manner in which severity is measured also depends on the assessment perspective adopted. On the one hand, assessment may be undertaken with the aid of physiological measurement instruments and laboratory tests. On the other hand, assessment may be undertaken via an interview with the patient. Given that both physical and subjective factors play a role in sickness and in health, much can be said for a broad operationalisation of illness severity. We should consider the following dimensions (Almeida and Carlsson 1996):

- The most important determinant of the risk of death is pathology or, in other words, the objective physical characteristics of the health problem such as the severity of the diagnosis, the severity of comorbid conditions and acute clinical stability.
- Whether the symptoms lead to weakness, tiredness, pain or anxiety. The patient is the most important source of information here.

■ Extent of disability or functional loss in the form (for instance) of difficulties walking or no longer being able to wash, dress or feed oneself. A distinction can be made between loss of behavioural, communication, personal care or movement skills, on the one hand, and other more specific skills, on the other hand. The patient is again the most important source of information here.
■ Risk of suffering.
■ Risk of disability.

The last two dimensions primarily concern the patient's prognosis for the future with physical measurements constituting the primary source of information.

Measurement

In the USA, numerous instruments have been developed to measure the severity of illness. This is sometimes done in a generic manner and sometimes in an illness-specific manner (Iezzoni 1997). Among the most frequently mentioned and utilised scales are:

■ Disease Staging
■ All Patients Defined Diagnosis Related Groups
■ Medis Group
■ Apache II and III (ibid.).

None of these scales cover all five of the dimensions highlighted above as critical for the determination of illness severity. The scales all have their strong and weak points. For example, Disease Staging works best to determine the severity of an acute heart attack while the Medis Group works best to determine the severity of pneumonia.

Most of the scales have been developed and used to undertake comparisons adjusted for severity of illness across hospitals with hospital mortality as the comparison variable. Measures based on mortality are by definition not particularly well-suited for outcome management purposes. It is therefore recommended that a suitably valid measure of the severity of illness be sought per illness or, alternatively, an indicator should be developed based on the five dimensions of severity outlined above.

FINAL SELECTION OF PATIENT VARIABLES FOR RISK ADJUSTMENT

In a previous section, we identified patient variables, which can possibly play a role in outcome management. The question, now, is which specific patient variables should we actually include in the design of outcome management? Inclusion of all possible patient variables in the analysis of outcomes is not only impossible but also undesirable. Therefore, we should consider a number of concrete steps for the identification and selection of the most relevant patient variables for outcome management purposes through:

- review of the relevant literature;
- selection of relevant patient variables;
- determination of relations between patient variables and outcomes.

Review of the relevant literature

As we previously mentioned, many different patient variables appear to influence health care outcomes including age, sex, severity of the disorder and comorbidity. Ideally, all variables which can possibly influence treatment outcome should be taken into consideration. In actual practice, however, such complete inclusion is neither necessary nor useful because certain variables tend to be more influential than others and the inclusion of the most influential variables in statistical models generally accounts for the majority of the variance and thus risks adjustment (Kuhlthau et al. 2004).

On the basis of a comprehensive review of the relevant literature, we can identify the most important patient variables for health care outcomes related to a particular illness. In the majority of cases, those patient variables, which influence the outcomes for a particular clinical picture, are known. The variable smoking, for example, frequently occurs in connection with a number of different illnesses including chronic obstructive pulmonary disease (COPD), cancer and cardiovascular disorder. The review of the relevant literature can be supplemented with information from the medical specialists for the particular illness (i.e. via interviews). Medical specialists constitute a particularly important source of information regarding those patient variables, which influence a particular clinical picture.

Inspection of the literature shows different variables to influence COPD outcomes. The Global initiative for chronic Obstructive Lung Disease (GOLD) divided COPD into four phases: the risk phase, light COPD, mild COPD and severe COPD (GOLD 2003). This division can thus be used to correct for the severity of the disorder for comparison purposes. Other patient variables found to influence COPD outcomes are comorbidity, smoking, age and social-economic status.

On the basis of a review of the literature, we can thus identify the relations between patient variables and general health care outcomes for outcome management purposes. Specific patient variables which appear to influence these outcomes can be determined in this way. Different types of outcomes can be identified depending on the purpose of measurement – namely to determine

125

economic indicators, clinical indicators, quality-of-life indicators or indicators of patient satisfaction. Certain outcomes can be measured on a short-term basis while others require longer-term measurement. The time course for measurement may influence the choice of patient variables, as this information must be collected during approximately the same time course as the outcome information (Shin and Johnson 2000b).

Selection of relevant patient variables

Our next step is to select the most relevant patient variables. In the previous step, we attained an overview of those patient variables, which may possibly influence treatment outcomes by relating the literature to outcomes. Consideration of the following can further help us restrict the set of patient variables to the most relevant variables:

- time course for outcome measurement;
- unit of analysis;
- feasibility of measurement for the patient variables;
- required sample size.

(Shin and Johnson 2000b)

The patient variables used for outcome measurement should fit the time course for outcome measurement and thus be measurable across the same period, as mentioned in the previous section.

We can compare outcomes at different levels such as the patient level, the level of the organisational unit or the organisational level. The level of outcome measurement largely depends on the objective of the measurement. Outcome measurement can be used for different objectives: internal improvement, internal measurement of health outcomes for improvement purposes, or external accountability, public disclosure of health care outcomes. When used for external accountability different standards of validity and reliability are requested. For patient variables, the level of measurement must similarly be determined.

The availability of data is of obvious importance in selecting our final patient variables. The most frequently used sources of data for risk adjustment are medical files, administrative and production registration systems and declaration figures (Shin and Johnson 2000b). Information with regard to age, sex and comorbidity is often present in the medical files. Information on the severity of the illness can also usually be found in the medical file. In many cases, administrative and production registration systems contain information on the physiological condition of the patients, aspects of treatment, breadth of the problems, severity of the problems and lifestyle aspects. In addition to the availability of the information itself, the care with which the information has been recorded, the clinical relevance of the information and the costs of final assembly of the information may also play a role in the selection of patient variables. In other words, we must consider all of the above factors when contemplating whether to include certain patient variables for purposes of outcome adjustment or not.

The final number of patient variables to be included in the analyses of the outcomes is also determined in part by the number of patients to be included in the analyses. Statisticians generally recommend at least five to thirty cases for each independent variable included in the outcome analyses (Shin and Johnson 2000b). This means that an organisation with very few patients is not in a position to adjust analyses involving a large number of patient variables.

Determination of relations between patient variables and outcomes

After the specific patient variables have been selected for purposes of risk adjustment, it is important to gain further insight into the expected relationship between the patient variables and outcome variables. Only in such a manner can the most effective method for data collection and the most efficient strategy for analysis of the data be selected (Shin and Johnson 2000b). In most cases, we can obtain information on these relations from the relevant literature. If patient variables are included on the basis of interviews with medical specialists, it is also important that we corroborate their inclusion by the existing literature.

METHODOLOGICAL ASPECTS OF RISK ADJUSTMENT

A risk adjustment methodology is a classification of patients to predict which patients are capable of the realisation of improvement to a greater or lesser extent. The utility of risk adjustment can be determined by comparison of the average outcomes for patients with their initial risk classification. Patients in a low clinical difficulty group should show better outcomes than patients in a high clinical difficulty group (Mark 1999). The significance of the different averages can be measured using a two-sided t-test.

In order to examine outcomes in relation to patient characteristics, different methods of analysis are available. In the literature, different examples of each can be found. Lyons *et al.* (1997) have distinguished the following categories:

- *Division into groups.* The division of a group into subgroups based on differences in particular characteristics for purposes of comparison can be undertaken: for example, heart patients with and without diabetes or psychiatric patients with or without addition problems.
- *Covariate analyses.* Statistical control for differences in patient characteristics is

also possible. In analyses of covariance, the extent to which a particular patient characteristic varies in connection with various health care outcomes is determined. This statistical technique can only be applied when the reliability of measurement for the patient characteristics is above 0.85 (reliability interval).

- *Decision analyses.* That information which is critical for the making of clinical decisions can be identified. Once this information is known, diagnostic decision-making models can be created – for instance – in the form of an algorithm for the assignment of patients to treatment.

- *Analyses of deviations from expected outcomes.* If the outcomes of a treatment deviate from what the clinical team reasonably expected, these particular outcomes can be adjusted for unique patient characteristics. This helps to determine whether particular groups of patients react differently to treatment.

CASE VIGNETTE

Nursing home quality indicators

Quality of care for nursing home residents has received growing attention; therefore a set of nursing home quality indicators (QI) was developed. The QI cover health and functional conditions, emotional and cognitive status, and the use of specific services or procedures. A central issue in designing the QI system was the need to adjust for variation in risk of harmful outcomes. The purpose of risk-adjustment is to remove effects of resident risk from those associated with quality of care provided by the facility. Using a stratification method, it was possible to stratify the residents into high and low risk groups, according to the presence or absence of specific risk elements. For example, risk elements for the prevalence of bladder incontinence are severe cognitive impairment, totality dependent mobility ADL and comorbidity. The QI improvement rates for the high risk population appeared to be significantly higher than rates for the low risk population. After risk adjustment these rates shifted. The conclusion was that risk adjustment helps to target the facilities that otherwise would have been suspect of quality problems, and also gives consideration to facilities caring for a more at-risk population.

Source: Arling *et al.* 1997

The preceding categories of analysis resemble the categories outlined by Shin and Johnson (2000a). However, Shin and Johnson's division is more pragmatic and boils down to two categories of methods for coupling patient variables with outcomes: The use of freely available published risk adjustment methods or the use of techniques of analysis (e.g. stratification, matching, regression analysis). The latter mentioned category corresponds to the categories of Lyons *et al.* (1997).

■ *Published methods.* Existing methods can be used for risk classification. A frequently used method is the Charlson Comorbidity Index (CCI) (Charlson *et al.* 1987). On the basis of diagnostic data, this method can predict death within a year. The method takes the number and severity of comorbid conditions into consideration. Comorbid conditions are assumed to be supplemental. The severity score is determined by adding up the weights assigned to the comorbid conditions which are present, the severity score is determined. In actual practice, this means that the scores for the comorbid clinical pictures are added.

■ *Stratification.* Stratification involves dividing the group into different subgroups on the basis of the selected patient variables. It corresponds to what is simply called 'division into groups' above. For example patients with COPD could be stratified into groups based on the GOLD classification on severity. Once patients are stratified, subgroup analysis can be conducted to compare outcomes across different strata to determine if there are real differences in patient outcomes (Shin and Johnson 2000a). An important aspect of this approach is that it works well only if there are a sufficient number of patients in each subgroup.

■ *Matched groups.* Another manner available to us to control patient variables is to match patients on the basis of patient variables. The outcomes can then be compared to each other on the basis of such matching. There are simple statistical packages available for such purposes. Matching can be used when a

---

CASE VIGNETTE

A model for case-mix adjustment of pressure ulcer prevalence rates

Acute care hospitals participating in the Dutch national pressure ulcer prevalence survey use the results of a survey to compare their outcomes and assess their quality of care regarding pressure ulcer prevention. The development of a model for case-mix adjustment is essential for the use of these prevalence rates as an outcome measure. A logistic model was developed for case-mix adjustment, using age, malnutrition, incontinence, activity, mobility, sensory perception, friction and shear, and ward specialty. This model was found to have content, construct, and internal validity. Case-mix adjustment influenced the hospitals' performance. Conclusions about the quality of care were influenced by the use of case-mix adjusted outcomes as a measure of this quality.

Source: Bours *et al.* 2003

small set of patient variables is being considered. For large numbers of variables, the establishment of comparable groups becomes very complicated and the result may be extremely small group sizes, which greatly reduces the statistical power.

■ *Regression analysis*. We can determine the weight of each predictive variable via regression analyses. Multiple linear regression or multiple logistic regression can be used to determine those patient variables which bear a statistically significant relation to the outcome after any differences in the other risk factors have been taken into consideration.

CONCLUSION

Within the framework of outcome management, controlling for patient variables is a critical step in the interpretation and comparison of health care outcomes. Health care outcomes are determined not only by treatment or intervention but also to a large extent by variables which have to do with the individual patient such as age, sex and severity of the disorder. If these variables are taken into consideration, outcomes can provide very different pictures of reality.

The use of risk adjustment methods will probably never be perfect. For purposes of risk adjustment, we can never include all possible patient variables. Even when the very best methods are used for control purposes, some important attributes will inevitably be left out. That is, we can never completely control for all patient variables. Nonetheless, considerable progress has been made with regard to control for the most important patient variables. Fortunately, selection of the most influential variables appears to be decisive for controlling outcome.

Patient variables could be included in the interpretation of health care outcomes in different ways. One simple manner is stratification. Statistical techniques can also be used to control for patient variables, which calls for the use of large subject samples and reflects a more scientific approach to outcome management. Statistical techniques also make risk adjustment applicable to different levels of working with outcome management.

DISCUSSION QUESTIONS

1   How can you apply the principles from this chapter to the outcome measurement of the care
    - you provide?
    - your team provides?
    - your organisation provides?

2   Pick a specific patient group. This could be a group with particular long-term condition or group that needs a specific surgical intervention. What are illness-related variables that we typically see within this group? What non-illness-related variables might make a difference to their outcomes?

3   What process might you go through to identify specific patient variables?

4   How might you design a risk adjustment system for a specific group of patients?

REFERENCES

Almeida, R.T. and Carlsson, P. (1996) Severity of a case for outcome assessment in health care – definitions and classifications of instruments. *Health Policy,* 27: 35–52.

Arling, G., Karon, S.L., Sainfort, F., Zimmerman, D.R. and Ross R. (1997) Risk adjustment of nursing home quality indicators. *The Gerontologist,* 37: 757–766.

Berlowitz, D.R., Ash, A.S., Hickey, E.C., Kader, B., Friedman, R., Moskowitz, M.A. (1998) Profiling outcomes of ambulatory care: case mix affects perceived performance. *Medical Care,* 36(6): 928–933.

Bours, G.J.J.W., Halfens, R.J.G., Berger, M.P.F., Huijer Abu-Saad, H. and Grol, R.T.P.M. (2003) The development of a model for case-mix adjustment of pressure ulcer prevalence rates. *Medical Care,* 41: 45–55.

Charlson, M.E., Pompei, P., Alex, K.L. and MacKenzie, C.R. (1987) A new method of classifying prognostic comorbidity in longitudinal studies: development and validation. *Journal of Chronic Diseases,* 40: 373–383.

Des Harnais, S. and McLaughlin, C.P. (1994) The outcome model of quality, in C.P. McLaughlin and A.D. Kaluzny (eds) *Continuous quality improvement in health care.* Gaithersburg, MD: Aspen.

GOLD (2003) *Global initiative for chronic obstructive lung disease: global strategy for the diagnosis, management, and prevention of chronic obstructive pulmonary disease.* Bethesda, MD: National Heart, Lung, and Blood Institute.

Iezonni, L.I. (1997) The risks of risk adjustment. *JAMA,* 278(19): 1600–1607.

Kuhlthau, K., Ferris, T.G.G. and Iezonni, L.I. (2004) Risk adjustment for pediatric quality indicators. *Pediatrics,* 113(1): 210–216.

Lyons, J.S., Howard, K.I., O'Mahoney, M.T. and Lish, J.D. (1997) *The measurement management of clincial outcomes in mental health.* New York: John Wiley.

Mark, H. (1999) A four part outcome measurement system. *Journal of Medical Systems,* 23(4): 291–297.

Petty, T.L. (2001) The early diagnosis of lung cancer. *Disease-a-Month,* 47(6): 204–264.

Rahmqvist, M. (2001) Patient satisfaction in relation to age, health status and other background factors: a model for comparison of care units. *International Journal* for *Quality in Health Care,* 13(5): 385–390.

Riise, T. and Lund, A. (2001) Prognostic factors in major depression: a long-term follow-up study of 323 patients. *Journal of Affection Disorders,* 65(3): 297–306.

Shin, G. and Johnson, N. (2000a) Risk adjustment methods for health outcomes assessments: general approaches. *Formulary,* 35: 426–434.

Shin, G. and Johnson, N. (2000b) Selecting patient factors for risk adjustment in health outcomes assessments. *Formulary,* 35: 595–598.

Van Saasse, J.L.C.M., Mallat, M.K.J., van der Woude, J.J. *et al.* (1996). Results of kidney transplant in Leiden. *Dutch Journal of Medicine (Nederlands Tijdschrift voor geneeskunde),* 140(15): 827–832.

Chapter 9

Standards and benchmarks

Jan Walburg

> ## KEY POINTS OF THIS CHAPTER
> - Benchmarking in health care
> - Possibilities of clinical benchmarking
> - Benchmarking with the outcome quadrant

INTRODUCTION

For a team or individual concerned with the improvement of care on the basis of outcomes, looking at only one's own results is not sufficient. A standard or some other material for comparison is needed. In a number of cases, it is possible to derive such a standard from the literature — for example, the number of post-operative infections. In other cases, no standards are available and one's own results will have to be compared to results from the past or results from others in order to gain some significance. Examples are patient satisfaction or the quality of life. In this chapter, the standardisation and comparison of outcomes will be addressed with so-called benchmarking being given the most attention.

STANDARDISATION

When is what one does not good enough? The very best companies in the world aspire to be a so-called six Sigma company with almost no errors and an accuracy standard of 99.9%. Per million products or services according to this standard, only 3.4 can go wrong. For a four Sigma company, the accuracy is almost 99% and

6210 transactions per million can go wrong. For a two Sigma company, the accuracy drops to 70% and 308,537 transactions per million can go wrong. The cost of errors is estimated to be anywhere from 25% to 30% of the return for three Sigma. For four Sigma, the cost of errors is estimated to be about 10% of the return. And for six Sigma, the cost is 2% to 3%.

In the field of health care, error percentages have consequences not only for the cost of care but also for particularly the safety of patients and their chances of recovery. In the USA with its tradition of outcome indicators, it is estimated that some 1250 people per million hospital admissions die (Kerr 1999). The possibly dramatic consequences of medical errors obviously call for high standards. At the same time, we are aware of the fact that overly high standards are not conducive to the motivation of the individual or the team. Policy aimed at the improvement of outcomes should therefore include standards, which can be shifted and formulated increasingly more ambitiously until maybe even a six Sigma level of health care has been reached. The question then is: which standards should be imposed and when should a team undertake measures to improve the outcomes of care?

An outcome indicator must thus contain a basic standard or achievement objective and an action standard or signal for improvement measures. The differentiation of the two standards stems from an awareness of the fact that a team cannot undertake too many quality improvement actions at the same time. The action standard is thus an agreement that performance below the standard is indeed inferior and that action to improve must therefore be undertaken. Some standards can be expressed as a percentage, others in terms of a single incidence. In other words, there are outcomes which are absolutely undesired and both standards are therefore set at zero.

The standards and action standards within a systematic form of outcome management are set increasingly higher in order to continually improve the performance of the team. The team sets both standards, and the standards can also, of course, coincide. Sometimes the standards are based on measurements from the past. Sometimes the professional literature provides an indication. Sometimes a standard is provided by the professional guidelines (CBO 2001). And sometimes the team itself must judge where the standard lies. A few examples of basic and action standards are presented below.

- In the treatment of patients with angina, the basic standard set by the team is that 100% of patients with chest pain as a result of angina should be seen for follow-up within three months of the completion treatment. The action standard is set at 95%.
- In the treatment of angina, the basic standard set by the team is that 95% of patients should be satisfied or very satisfied with their capacity to function while using the medication nitroglycerine. The team comes into action at 90%.

BENCHMARKING

A benchmark is literally a metal sign used in the USA to mark the highest point in a particular region. Applied to organisations, benchmarking can be defined as the search for the best existing methods which lead to superior performance (Camp 1992). Copying from the best, thus, but then done more systematically.

Benchmarking as a business instrument was developed by Rank Xerox which undertook a study of the costs per product at other businesses in 1979. The results showed competitors to sell machines at the equivalent of the cost price of Rank Xerox machines. Rank Xerox then adopted the manufacturing methods from the competitor and, in 1983, benchmarking was named one of the three pillars for quality management. Benchmarking was defined as the continual process of measuring products, services and procedures relative to the strongest competitor or companies recognised as industrial leaders (Camp 1992).

Some examples of benchmarking are as follows (Camp 1992):

- the opportunity to integrate the best methods of working into one's own methods;
- the motivation of professionals to improve;
- decreased resistance to change because one sees that it works elsewhere;
- the possible discovery of technological breakthroughs;
- the pleasure of professionals in the exchange and analysis of results.

In the somewhat sloppy use of the term 'benchmark', it is also sometimes applied to one-time qualitative comparisons of companies. But this is an incorrect application precisely because benchmarking involves much more than this:

- benchmarking is a systematic and continuous process because the target methods and procedures continually change;
- benchmarking is a quantitative process based on concrete forms of achievement in order to make differences in performance as apparent as possible;
- benchmarking is a qualitative analytic process as determination of the best methods before integration into one's own operations must be done with utmost care;
- benchmarking is a practical implementation process because it occurs for purposes of application of the best methods within one's own organisation.

Benchmarking is thus aimed not only at the competitors within one's own sector but also those who perform certain procedures in a superior manner in other sectors. That is, benchmarking outside one's own sector can help identify any errors or inefficient processes which may have slipped into one's own methods.

In hospitals, for example, it is common for people to be awoken in the middle of the night for routine procedures. In a hotel, such matters are arranged very differently. Having to wait for a scheduled appointment is quite normal in the field of health care but virtually nonexistent elsewhere. And for this reason, two forms of benchmarking are distinguished: 'competitive benchmarking' when the same product or service is under consideration and 'world class benchmarking' when a comparison outside one's sector is involved (Camp 1992).

In principle, every process within organisational benchmarking can be viewed from a number of different perspectives (Brouwer 1996):

- strategic benchmarking aimed primarily at long-term financial management;
- client-oriented benchmarking with figures regarding client satisfaction as the starting point;
- cost-oriented benchmarking in which differences in cost structures are analysed.

Topics which have called for benchmarking within the field of health care are not only such concrete matters as waiting times, costs, hospitalisation days and investments but also personnel policy, allocation of overhead, training policy and facilities management.

The benchmarking process

The typical benchmarking process is characterised by a number of phases which are schematically outlined in Figure 9.1 (Camp 1992).

During the *planning phase*, the following are determined: the product, service or process to which the benchmark will apply; which businesses – either inside or outside the sector – to consider; and just how the relevant data will be collected. The *analysis phase* is aimed at gaining sufficient insight into one's own procedures and the procedures used by the benchmark. In what domains is the benchmark better? How much better is the benchmark? And where in one's own company should the better processes be introduced?

In the *formulation phase*, the results of the benchmark are incorporated into one's own goals and preparations are made for the change process. Clear communication of the findings of the benchmarking process largely determines the success of implementation.

In addition to the determination of goals and what is needed to promote implementation, a concrete action plan is next developed in the *action phase*. The necessary changes are also introduced at this time, and the results of the introduction of new or improved methods are monitored.

Finally, in the *mature phase*, the best methods of working are incorporated into one's own standard methods.

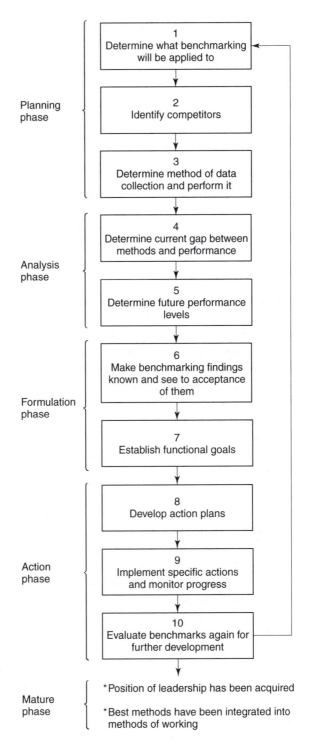

Figure 9.1 *The ten phases constituting the benchmarking process.*

Benchmarking within the field of health care

Within the field of health care, benchmarking is predominantly applied to the administrative aspects of health care organisations. Coopers and Lybrand accounting firms thus compare such variables as technical costs, housing hosts, computer costs and so forth. The organisations then receive an annual report in which one's own institution is compared to the best and the average (Haverhals and van de Vijver 1997).

The efficiency benchmarking which the government encourages goes one step further. That is, the relation between the means which an institution expends and the performance based on such means is evaluated. Increased efficiency can lower costs, which are, of course, of major social concern. The benchmarking undertaken in this connection is thus aimed at comparison of a number of organisations with respect to their efficiency and adoption of the most efficient process as the standard for the sector.

The goal of benchmarking is thus to provide insight for both management and financers. Within the field of health care, various figures and processes are often compared in all kinds of rudimentary manners either within the framework of policy aimed at quality improvement or not. Benchmarking goes one step further in that an organisation systematically compares its outcomes to those of the best organisation within the sector. And this is where the problem for benchmarking within the field of health care becomes most apparent: how do we determine the best institution to serve as a benchmark?

To identify the best institution within the field of treatment and care, one needs data. However, such information is simply not there or only to a very limited extent and mostly anecdotal. Possible points of departure for the relevant benchmarking may then be as follows:

- *The EFQM model.* This model provides scores for the extent to which an organisation has progressed with regard to nine criteria and a total score. This information enables identification of the best institution in general and per criterion for further examination of the manner in which that particular institution achieves such a high score and later adaptation of the methods for introduction into one's own organisation. To the extent that more health care institutions adopt the EFQM model, more possibilities for benchmarking emerge.
- *Patient opinions.* Health care institutions are administering questionnaires to an increased extent to gain an impression of just how patients view the health care services provided. When this is done using a standardised list of items, the possibility of benchmarking according to topic emerges and the best scoring institution can be identified as the benchmark.
- *Process improvement.* Under the influence of the efficiency discussion and the pressure of waiting lists, greater information is becoming available with

respect to waiting and procedures times. These figures constitute a good starting point for benchmarks.

■ *Employee evaluations.* Interest in the evaluation of an organisation by the employees themselves has increased. An important trigger that originates this interest is the scarcity of the labour market.

CLINICAL BENCHMARKS

The term 'clinical benchmarks' is used here to mean benchmarking within the context of clinical results and emphasise that treatment and care are of greater interest here than the management aspects of health care. Defined more strictly, clinical benchmarks are 'the use of clinical data and process analyses to determine the best outcomes, describe the best processes and improve clinical processes to attain the best outcomes' (Barnes *et al.* 1995).

Different forms of benchmarking have been applied within the domain of health care for quite some time already. *Evidence-based guidelines* are strongly based on scientific evidence and the best method of treatment according to the professional group or so-called best practices. For the development of evidence-based guidelines, a systematic procedure is followed to evaluate the available evidence for a medical intervention and formulate an evidence-based guideline. The double-blind clinical trial holds as the strongest form of evidence. The introduction of such guidelines into actual practice, however, has been found to be less than optimal due to the laboratory-like conditions under which the relevant research is conducted, among other things. Clinical benchmarking fits the practice of guideline development quite well because the guideline indicates the best imaginable care process on the basis of the available literature and the benchmarking refines the care via implementation into actual clinical practice and thereby provision of aggregated figures for further development of the guidelines.

Intercollegial evaluation also contains elements of benchmarking. In this case, a group of colleagues evaluates the functioning of a medical practice in order to provide recommendations for quality improvement. The evaluation of outcomes is not so much at issue here as evaluation of the practice in terms of evidence-based guidelines or the state of the art within one's field. When intercollegial evaluation involves the joint evaluation of more than one practice and thus comparison of the care results for one practice to those of other practices, it can strengthen the process of benchmarking.

The benchmarking of clinical outcomes currently occurs only on the basis of national, aggregated databases. The clinically relevant information is then such data as hospital mortality, hospital infection and duration of hospital stay. In the USA, such figures are listed on the Internet with the names of the relevant institutions included. In Western Europe, the databases are often still listed anonymously. The context for such data collection is generally not for purposes of systematic and cyclic quality improvement, however, and is therefore not considered benchmarking.

Benchmarking with the aid of the outcome quadrant

In order to meaningfully benchmark outcomes, the following conditions are needed:

- access to reliable and valid data;
- access to knowledge of administrative routines used to handle data;
- guarantee of strict confidentiality for all participants.

The first two conditions are considered in the other chapters, and the issue of confidentiality is considered in greater detail below.

The professional aim of benchmarking is not only to improve guidelines but also (and primarily) to promote learning and improvement within the teams responsible for treatment and care. Such learning can occur only when team members feel safe and know that information regarding the results will only be externally distributed in an anonymous and aggregated form. Benchmarking can make any differences in within-team results painfully apparent and thus calls for considerable team cohesion, which is also addressed in Chapter 5. A typical benchmarking result is depicted in Figure 9.2.

As can be seen, differences between organisations become abundantly apparent, which means that one organisation is inevitably identified as the best and one organisation is inevitably identified as the worst. The rules for benchmarking must thus guarantee that only one's own organisation knows its position. It can be

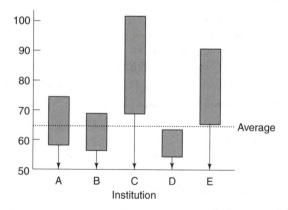

Figure 9.2 *Patient satisfaction.*

further agreed that the best be made known among the participants in order to facilitate the subsequent steps in the benchmarking process. Making the best known to the general public can be counterproductive to the goals of benchmarking. A set of statutes must be established around the benchmarking process. The rules must be made clear, and the following should be agreed upon in any case:

- who owns the data;
- who may use the data and for what purpose;
- who may publish under which conditions;
- which data are to be made known to whom;
- what sanctions apply upon infringement of the statutes.

Integrated into a system of outcome management using a results quadrant, the benchmarking process can proceed as depicted in Figure 9.3 and discussed below.

Analyses by reporting team

To start with, whether or not the data were collected according to the specified administrative routines must be determined. The differences in outcome must be analyzed in conjunction with each other. If a high level of patient satisfaction is found, for example, what were the associated costs and results? Outcomes receive their significance primarily in relation to each other.

Thereafter, the results must be examined in relation to the patient data. Do regional differences exist between patients with respect to lifestyle, ethnic background, sex, social-economic circumstances and so forth? All these matters can influence the outcomes. And an interpretation team must therefore be established to analyse the figures and summarise the findings in the form of a report.

Analyses by care team

The results are next analysed and discussed within one's own team. Questions which may be raised in this context are what are the differences and what may be the cause of the differences? For this purpose, such analytic methods as the cause & effect diagram (fishbone diagram) may be useful.

Identification of best results

Following the analyses, those results that are of relevance to the team and those results that are the best should be identified. In such a manner, those areas displaying such significant differences that improvement is indicated can be identified. And identification of the best organisation for those different areas is also part of this process.

141

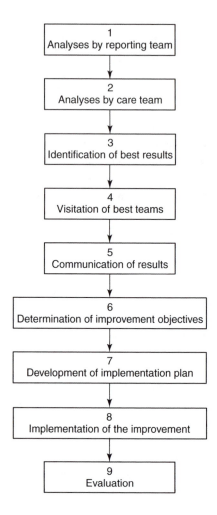

Figure 9.3 *Stepwise benchmarking plan.*

Visitation of best teams

In preparation for a visitation, the relevant documentation should be reviewed. A list of questions can be formulated, and the best team can then be visited for improvement purposes. The relevant processes should be carefully studied at least in part on the basis of the questions which one has.

Communication of results

Within the team, all of the findings – including the visitation – should be discussed in order to be sure that everyone has the same figures available to them and everyone feels equally responsible for the improvement efforts.

Determination of improvement objectives

On the basis of the detected differences, the results of the visitation and the team discussions, realistic improvement objectives can be formulated. Once again, it is important that the team agree on the improvement objectives in order to promote their implementation.

Development of implementation plan

An implementation plan encompasses a general objective, specific sub-objectives, measures to monitor progress, measures to mobilise resources in the form of funds, people, knowledge and sometimes, if absolutely necessary, pilot study.

Implementation of the improvement

During the introduction of the improvement, continuous monitoring of progress should be undertaken. Implementation can best be viewed as a process of trial and error because no change process proceeds exactly as planned.

Evaluation

Whether the desired results are attained or not must obviously be determined. When the desired improvement is indeed achieved, the team should take time to explicitly acknowledge this and celebrate its success. Another component of this step is evaluation of the entire benchmarking and improvement trajectory with an eye to what can be learned for the next cycle.

It should be clear that comparison of one's own results with those of the best is but one component of benchmarking. Actually learning from the best and particularly the implementation of change based on best practice information are of essential importance. One should not be satisfied with a fascinating analysis or interesting visitation. That is, the success of benchmarking depends on effective adoption and implementation.

CASE STUDY

An example of the benchmarking process
The Borges Medical Center is a hospital in Michigan with 426 beds. The hospital initiated cooperation with a number of other hospitals and appointed a multidisciplinary team to benchmark coronary bypass operations. To start with, the team selected a few benchmark hospitals in the area of bypass operations on the basis of particularly low mortality rates. These hospitals were then visited and the procedures followed in the hospitals were carefully studied.

The Borges hospital was next compared to the benchmark hospitals using such simple outcome measures as mortality, duration of stay, heart attack and comorbidity. The patient group was divided into a high risk group and a low risk group. On the basis of the data for a period of one year, the following was found:

- Borges had a lower mortality rate for the low-risk group and a higher mortality rate for the high-risk group;
- Borges had more heart attacks than the benchmark hospitals;
- Borges had a shorter duration of stay for the low-risk group and a longer duration of stay for the high-risk group.

It was next decided to concentrate on the high-risk group for actual improvement purposes. Their own and the benchmark processes were compared, and just where improvement in the treatment process appeared to be possible was determined. This included the degree of adherence to the treatment protocol among other things. The different phases of treatment were then compared per sub-team: pre-operative, patient selection, examination, operation and post-operative care.

The differences between the Borges hospital and the benchmark hospitals were again examined. The benchmarked hospitals were found to do the following relative to the Borges hospital:

- communicate better;
- employ a uniform selection process for patients;
- employ a better scheduling process for both urgent and less urgent procedures;
- employ a better protocol for the use of the 'intra-aortic balloon pump';
- have clearer criteria for the indication of clients for 'precutaneous transluminal coronary angioplasty'.

For each of the improvement possibilities, a working plan was next formulated and a single individual was appointed responsible for the implementation of the plan. Implementation was monitored with the aid of a number of indicators. And the result was that the hospital performed within the borders of the benchmark within a year.

The foregoing example shows how practical and quality facilitating a benchmark activity can be. Before an institution is so far ready for benchmarking, however, extensive preparation must occur. Preparation must be made with regard to the choice of content to be benchmarked and the technical realisation of a measurement infrastructure in terms of skills. Such character traits as curiosity, registration validity and trust with respect to the communication of outcomes must also be attractive to the relevant professionals.

Source: Barnes *et al.* 1995

CONCLUSION

The results of a team can be compared to a standard derived from literature or from historic performance. Even more interesting is to compare the outcomes of care with other teams that are responsible for the same care process in a different setting. This is methodologically complex but at the same time an interesting challenge because it enables teams to compare and discuss outcomes which could start a competition on outcomes.

DISCUSSION QUESTIONS

1 What are traditional standards for comparing clinical outcomes?
2 What is the purpose of clinical benchmarking?
3 What are the criteria for the selection of an organisation for benchmarking?
4 What are chances and risks involved in clinical benchmarking?

REFERENCES

Barnes, D.G., Daston, G.P., Evans, J.S., Jarabek, A.M., Kavlock, R.J., Kimmel, C.A., Park, C. and Spitzer, H.L. (1995) Benchmark Dose Workshop: criteria for use of a benchmark dose to estimate a reference dose. *Regulatory Toxicology and Pharmacology*, 21(2): 296–306.

Brouwer, J.J. (1996) Benchmarken: een gereedschap om te kunnen excelleren. *Checklisten Algemeen Management*, I: A.4.2.-01–12.

Camp, R.C. (1992) Benchmarking, vergelijken met het beste, in *Handboek Integrale kwaliteitszorg*. Deventer: Kluwer.

CBO (2001) *Handleiding ontwikkeling van klinische indicatoren op basis van richtlijnen. Stuurgroep Indicatorontwikkeling*. Utrecht: CBO.

Haverhals, H.J.K. and van de Vijver, F.M.E. (1997) *Benchmarking van de facilitaire kosten*. Alphen aan de Rijn/Diegem: Samson Bedrijfsinformatie.

Kerr, V.E. (1999) Six sigma: can a business quality improvement method be applied to health care. Proceedings of the Outcomes Symposium, Harvard University, Cambridge, MA, 1 May.

Chapter 10

Feedback and presentation of outcomes

Astrid van Dijk

KEY POINTS OF THIS CHAPTER

- The feedback process to the clinical team
- Presenting feedback in a way which motivates the team to make necessary changes in their practice
- Involving patients in the feedback process

INTRODUCTION

The assembled and analysed data have now been returned to the team. Initiation of the feedback cycle is important and should take priority over any desire to perfect the measurement system to any further extent. The quick presentation of feedback regarding the attained outcomes is an important support mechanism for the initiation of a learning loop. The presentation of the results is the point at which a meaningful interaction between the members of a team can emerge. This is also where the active improvement process begins, i.e. what performance management is intended to achieve.

A team reflects on the care outcomes and, on the basis of this, commences with the formulation of improvements in the care processes (Walburg 2004). From the first session in which the results are presented, the importance of regular feedback increases. Professionals also prefer to receive at least part of the results as quickly as possible in order to make use of them to try to improve care processes which are still ongoing.

In this chapter, the different aspects of providing feedback to a team are considered. The basic principles of communication, and the requirements, which these impose on the message (the outcomes), the sender (the transfer) and the receiver (the team), will be discussed.

To start with, the importance of good quality results (the message) should be emphasised. In doing this, extra attention should be paid to the role of the patient as experienced expert in the receipt of treatment/care and in determining the quality of his/her own care. The presentation of the relevant results also requires careful consideration of the person (the sender) to present the results, thorough preparation and the most succinct (often graphic) format for the presentation. In addition, the team (the receiver) must be able to communicate with each other. Basic social skills, team skills and problem-solving skills such as quality techniques are all utilised.

Within this framework, the role of the team leaders (i.e. those responsible for the start and growth of improved outcomes) can be further emphasised. Team development deserves further support in the practical, facilitating and reinforcement senses of the word. That is, the team must give itself time for gradual growth in line with the principles of the learning organisation. Teams are made up of individuals. Not every member has an intrinsic motivation to change their ways of doing things. Usually some members are enthusiastic and some are not. Both types need different sorts of encouragement and different styles of leadership.

The process of transfer is quite complicated in reality and, as depicted in Figure 10.1, it involves a number of intermediate steps.

In this chapter, however, we will concentrate on the main steps.

THE MESSAGE, THE OUTCOMES

Performance management gains in value when the outcomes are presented in conjunction with each other and also analysed and reported in conjunction with a number of patient and process variables. This requires not only thorough analysis of the relationship between the different outcomes but also sufficient insight to keep the interrelationships continually in mind during the interpretation of the results.

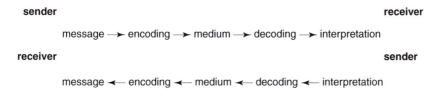

Figure 10.1 *Process of information transfer (Van Beek and Van Dorsten 1997).*

CASE VIGNETTE

Parental satisfaction with information from a psychiatric institution

At a paediatric psychiatric institution, parental satisfaction with the information provided to them and the extent of their involvement in treatment was mapped for all the departments (i.e. outpatient and inpatient). The results showed large differences across the departments for both aspects of parental satisfaction. These outcomes gain meaning only when such factors as the following are considered: the ages of the children (which varied between 4 and 20 years), the length of residence (which varied from six months to longer than five years) and the treatment setting (which could be inpatient or outpatient).

The quality of the outcome: validity and reliability

The presented results must be as a minimum reliable and valid. In fact, guaranteeing the quality of the data is part of the identification of adequate performance indicators. But there are also some rules of thumb for critically inspecting the presented results. For example the checklist for the systematic evaluation of evidence presented in Table 10.1 provides an overview that can be used. Incidentally, not all of the data assembled for performance improvement will fulfil all scientific requirements. To the extent that the data are more quantitative or measured in a more advanced manner the greater the importance of meeting the proper scientific requirements.

Professionals confronted with outcomes without further mention of the variables, which were manipulated or included in the analyses, will not recognise

Table 10.1 *Checklist for systematic evaluation of evidence*

- How reliable are the data?
- How valid are the data?
- Were the relationships between the data and the topic of study well considered?
- How was the subject sample established?
- Are the methods of analysis described?
- Are the new results made known and carefully described?
- What explanations are provided for the results?
- If the results appear to call for change, are they sufficiently convincing?
- Was the data collected and described in an ethical manner?

Source: Øvretveit 1998

themselves or want to recognise themselves in the outcomes. This is because a certain degree of awareness may have emerged during the measurement of the outcomes but the process of adjusting one's thinking, or behaving on the basis of such outcomes is a step further on. Weggeman (1997) distinguishes professionals who improvise (I-profs) and professionals who work routinely (R-profs). The most important difference between the two groups is that the I-profs tend to go beyond the boundaries of collected knowledge while R-profs continually improve themselves and achieve their best performance within the boundaries of already collected knowledge.

The latter group of professionals, however, also runs the risk of becoming overly attached to acquired principles and developing a so-called 'defensive routine' only to defend their already acquired knowledge. Any ambiguity or doubt which may arise on the part of such a professional with regard to the otherwise established value of measured outcomes, may slow the process of thinking about change. The R-prof will grasp at every shortcoming in order to plead for the maintenance of the status quo. In short, the robustness of the message in combination with the status of the sender and the force of the group processes within the team determine the emergence of a meaningful improvement cycle.

Patients' feedback

Outcomes based on questions concerned with patient satisfaction exert their own unique influence on the introduction of improvements and changes. Where the professional does not allow him/herself to be convinced by measurements undertaken from a professional perspective, a message from the perspective of patients often works.

A focus group is, of course, only one of the methods available to us to access outcomes from the patient perspective. We are also familiar, for example, with many forms of patient satisfaction research. A written questionnaire is typically administered to the patient after the conclusion of treatment. The results of one study (Aarsse 2003), however, show information on patient satisfaction alone does not deliver sufficient indicators of quality. Only in combination with other quality indicators can reliable information be attained regarding the actual quality of care, experienced by the patient.

Exit interviews generally provide a wealth of information. The day before discharge, the patient is asked in a one-to-one meeting about his or her experiences and unfulfilled needs. The inventory of needs, in particular, yields information which can be used to introduce improvements in the care process. A variant on this method is the assembly of a panel of former patients to provide feedback with regard to the care received and treatment by the treatment team (with reimbursement of expenses of course). The discussion leader is then responsible for clear communication between the panel of patients and treatment team. For each

149

CASE VIGNETTE

Consulting a focus group

On the basis of a number of considerations (e.g., content of the diagnosis, unambiguity of the diagnosis, dropout during the diagnostic process, degree of direction for follow-up treatment), a standardised method of diagnosis is generally advocated. Rather than stepwise diagnosis on the basis of multiple meetings, a single diagnostic consultation is suggested in which the patient is questioned and examined for about one-and-a-half hours. This suggestion arose from an inspection of the relevant literature and the opinions of leading professional experts. But the relevant professionals consider this unfeasible. The patient is not, in their eyes, able or willing to cooperate for such a long and intensive period of time.

The proposal is next presented to a focus group representing various patients and former patients. The reaction of the patients is very clear: they feel that taking time for such a discussion is absolutely correct and justified. They reason that their problems are sufficiently serious that it is worth the time to consider whether the care process can be improved. And with an eye to travel times and the practical barriers to undertaking such a review, a single consultation is much easier for them.

CASE VIGNETTE

Videotaping an exit interview

A team leader is responsible for the random conduct of exit interviews with patients. He repeatedly notices just how difficult it is to present the interview findings to the team in a way that ensures reflection on current practices actually occurs. The team leader decides to videotape an exit interview with a patient after obtaining permission from the patient to do such. The patient is very critical of the treatment and communication skills of the personnel. One patient actually says:

> and then somebody new comes in and walks along the beds, raises her hand and says "Hi, I'm Eve" to all of us. How am I supposed to know who she is, and isn't the tone a little bit too jolly? We're adult — if not elderly — patients after all.

Instead of reporting the critical remarks back to the team, the team leader plays the videotape for the team. And with the examples clearly formulated from the perspective of a patient, a profitable exchange of opinions takes place on how best staff should introduce themselves to patients.

component of the treatment and care process, for example, experience and suggestions for improvement are explicitly requested.

Finally, two additional forms of patient feedback are worth mentioning. First, patient insights are increasingly being used to instigate new or improved care processes. Rather than ask about experiences after the event, an a priori inventory is taken of the needs and desires of the patient. Proposed changes in an existing care process can also be presented to a patient panel for evaluation prior to actual implementation. A second additional form of patient feedback is measurement of the extent to which a 'therapeutic alliance' has been established. This method is only suited for long-term forms of treatment and care, and it is also clearly based upon the assumption that the extent of effective cooperation between patient and treatment provider is an accurate gauge of the degree of satisfaction on the part of the patient.

THE TRANSFER

In the build-up of a form of outcome-management for a team, the feedback expectations – after intensive preparation for measurement and actual collection of the data – can be quite high. Has the team achieved what they wanted to achieve? And if the objective has not been achieved, why not? In order to find an answer to these questions, it is important that feedback with regard to the attained results be provided to the entire team. That is, every piece of information or summary regarding clinical behaviour, costs or the outcomes of care within a particular period of time should be made known (Grol and Wensing 2001). But how can feedback regarding outcomes best be delivered to the team? One can start by carefully considering the choice of presenter: who is going to deliver the message? Thereafter, the technical preparation of the presentation and the requirements, which the presentation should meet, can be considered.

The presenter

It has already been determined that the point at which feedback is provided with regard to outcomes constitutes an important turning point in the learning process of a team. However, the question of exactly who is going to present the message is not given sufficient consideration in most cases. Is the innovator (member of the quality and research department) responsible for the collection and analysis of the relevant data going to present the message? Is the professional responsible for the relevant care process and/or the quality of the relevant care process going to present the message? Or is the manager responsible for the staff involved going to present the message?

151

Professionals do not always learn in the most obvious manner. In many cases, a clear awareness of the need to improve must first be in place. Boonstra (2000) therefore pleads for the stimulation of 'instability' which he understands to be strong stimulant of the development of an active and permanent learning and improvement cycle in conjunction with work routines. Feedback regarding the outcomes of treatment for professionals constitutes an important prerequisite for the establishment of such a learning and improvement cycle. Interestingly, however, the tidal wave of innovations to date has yet to hit actual practice. Knowing that things need to be done differently apparently does not mean that things actually get done differently. This underlines the need to surround the learning process with the most stimulating and supportive feedback cycles possible, the status of the person presenting the feedback obviously playing a role here. The person must be acceptable to the members of the team receiving the message (Table 10.2). And the presenter must be able to stimulate 'instability'.

In addition to the status and organisational position of the presenter, the extent to which the individual is in a position to design and guarantee a safe learning environment for the team members is of critical importance. Prior to their presentation, whether the results are to be treated as confidential (or not) must be made clear. Does the team have sufficient cohesion to go through the first learning moments together? At what point should the remainder of the organisation be provided with information or a report? And in what form should this be done?

Finally, the role of the presenter of outcome results should be clearly defined prior to the presentation of the results. Is the presenter responsible only for the reporting of findings? Are only facts to be presented and any further analyses undertaken during the meeting itself? Are clarification questions expected and is the presenter expected to answer these? Is the presenter expected to lead the group processes, which emerge either during or after the presentation? Does the

Table 10.2 Advantages and disadvantages of possible presenters

	The innovator (quality and research department)	Professional responsible for care process	Line manager	External expert
Pros	Distant and factual	Involved with substantive knowledge	Involved with both substantive and organisational knowledge	Distant, factual and experienced
Cons	Outsider with no authority to instigate change-management	Unknown authority to management	Possible loyalty conflict (is also part of team)	'Not one of us' and thus little or no identification with the person

---

CASE VIGNETTE

Presenting quality of care outcomes

In the initial presentation of some quality of care outcomes by the person responsible for the operation of a crisis team, the results could be traced back to particular team members despite no use of names. Everybody knew who was the person with the highest caseload and recognised the members of the team who took a long time over their clinical interventions. This created considerable commotion during the presentation and discussion of the results. A number of the team members felt they were being personally attacked and complained to the team leader, because they felt that he was responsible. But the team leader was completely taken by surprise, as he had not been informed of the content of the presentation. Considerable anger thus confronted the presenter of the outcome results. The team refused to discuss the results any further and a few of the team members undertook steps to register their objections to the procedure followed.

---

presenter attend the remainder of the meeting after the presentation of the outcomes? And is it important that the team and the presenter work together within the framework of management?

The presentation

The aim of the presentation of feedback is to make outcome results clear for each member of the team and motivate the team to undertake well based actions to improve the care process. The first step in the feedback process is therefore presentation of the attained results in the clearest manner possible. The form of presentation which may work best obviously depends on the nature of the process (e.g. technical versus organisational) and the relevant materials assembled (e.g. qualitative, quantitative or both). The feedback can be presented orally or in a written form and also possibly accompanied by a comparison to colleagues or an evaluation based on quality of care criteria or recommendations. A written visual presentation of the results also requires a clear and arresting verbal framework. The presenter can be expected to be qualified in the effective communication of information. And different presentation techniques may be used to provide a clear overview of quantitative results – graphs, numbers, percentages and so forth. However, the use of effective presentation techniques alone is not sufficient. The grouping of the results around objectives formulated by the team is also of critical importance.

1   Establish a fixed layout.
2   Present the most important results and their interrelations on the first page and as graphically as possible.
3   Provide a brief summary involving just a few sentences of the most important findings preferably formulated by the professional responsible for the care process or team leader.
4   Explain the first page systematically in the following pages with explicit reference to the relevant data and observed associations. Clear graphic presentation is again of importance. Use preferably one page per indicator and organise the different pages in a similar manner.
5   Present the report – with the aid of a Power Point presentation, overhead sheets and/or handouts – in a workshop with a duration of no more than a half-hour to two hours.

Where possible, underlying associations should be made as visible as possible. In the following example, for instance, a team has decided to map how patients are doing three months after the active phase of treatment. The objective is to make contact with the patients and use the information attained in such a manner to optimalise the treatment process and detect new problems in a timely manner. The presentation begins with a numerical overview of the patients contacted in graph form (Figure 10.2).

For the team receiving feedback, however, it is important that they know not only what numbers are involved but also the nature (inpatient or outpatient) of the treatment undergone. Which patient groups were sufficiently reached to provide representative figures and which patient groups were not reached sufficiently (see Table 10.3)?

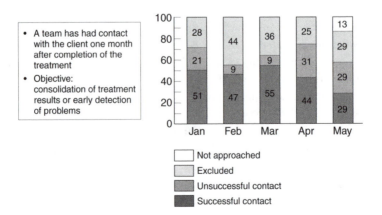

Figure 10.2 *Management: outcomes reached after discharge.*

Table 10.3 *Team: substantive explanation?*

	No success	Success	Total
Cluster a	37 (71%)	15 (29%)	52
Cluster b	38 (78%)	11 (22%)	49
Cluster c	7 (100%)	0	7
Total	82 (76%)	26 (24%)	108 (100%)

THE TEAM

While the presentation must certainly be clear, the members of the team also need a number of skills to be able to think about results together. Organisations within the field of health care can be construed as professional knowledge-intensive organisations (Weggeman 1997). Within such organisations, the qualities needed for permanent innovation are probably present. The professionals in such settings have, according to Weggeman, an intrinsic longing to attain new knowledge and integrate this knowledge into the conduct of their work. They are, not only as individuals but also as professional group, responsible for the best delivery of the most suitable treatment and care. And within the framework of performance management, the team can be considered an inquisitive group of professionals. The team is given feedback and, on the basis of this information, the quality of care processes can be improved in a manner which is understandable for the team. Quinn *et al.* (1996) argue that the professional intellect of a knowledge-intensive organisation should function at four different levels.

1   *Cognitive knowledge*: knowing what is the basic attitude which professionals must have to attain a suitable education, training and certification.
2   *Advanced skills*: knowing how means that the professional utilises the opportunity to apply professional standards in daily practice.
3   *System understanding*: knowing why means that the professional has insight into the theoretical concepts underlying the professional standards and is capable of answering very complex questions.
4   *Self-motivated creativity*: interested why means that the professional has the drive, motivation and adaptive power needed for innovation.

The professional with an intrinsic motivation to pursue a permanent education cycle will pass through the above four levels which can further the professionalisation of the discipline and the individual. In this light, innovation is an organically developing process although such innovation processes may not always run so smoothly. The concept of innovation within the field of health care encompasses all explicitly selected activities aimed at the realisation of changes in the treatment and care process with the goal of increasing the quality and/or efficiency of the care process irrespective of the manner in which this is accomplished.

What stands out in particular in the literature on innovation is the explicit attention paid to the implementation component of the innovation or improvement process (i.e. the active change phase). There are two assumptions in need of further clarification underlying the term implementation. First, implementation implies guided activity. There is apparently a situation where something, which does not occur on its own, is nevertheless expected to occur within the professional work environment. Second, implementation implies change. Something has apparently been thought up and designed for transfer to others. It can be described as being 'forced to leave' a particular state of being.

Basic team skills

A team that wants to get started on the improvement of its own care processes using the principles of performance improvement must meet a number of prerequisites. The team must have a certain degree of organisational stability (i.e. minimal absenteeism, limited turnover of personnel, no other large-scale change processes, team responsibility, adequate attendance of team meetings). The nature of the interactions of the team members with each other is also of considerable importance. The cooperation required for performance improvement means that team members must be able to effectively exchange information and ideas. But not all teams have sufficient skills within this domain. Insightful reflection upon outcomes and feedback requires a different form of communication than the purely informative exchange of facts. Chang and Kelly (1997) presented some tips for good communication (Table 10.4).

Active listening involves the receiver actively trying to understand the sender of a message and is an important communication skill. Active listening involves, for example, repetition of what the sender has said using one's own words, questioning, reflection on underlying feelings, recapitulation (i.e. summary) and the provision of feedback.

Table 10.4 *Tips for good communication*

■ Look for interesting aspects	■ Avoid distraction
■ Judge content, not packaging	■ Practise your thinking abilities
■ Wait to react	■ Be open to everyone
■ Practise listening	■ Benefit from thinking being faster than exploit

Source: Chang and Kelly 1997

Additional team skills

In addition to the basic team skills described above, attention can be devoted to three additional skills: the provision of feedback, the conduct of a discussion and the handling of conflict.

Provision of feedback

In discussions of the quality of care, feedback is often provided verbally. In that way it is supposed to be more challenging and thereby stimulating to the learning processes of a team. The feedback is aimed at the achievement of a change of behaviour, organisation or practice and based on a value judgement (Lombarts 1995). It is of critical importance that feedback regarding attained results be presented in a team context. The results then lead to a dialogue between the professionals who are involved. Feedback, positive or negative, provides inspiration and can motivate the members of a team to improve their functioning.

In order to provide good feedback it is important to formulate clear objectives. Clear and concise objectives can provide clear tasks for the members of a team. And a clear task description facilitates the provision of feedback. When the responsibilities of each member of the team are clear, objective and succinct feedback can be provided. Feedback needs to be descriptive and specific. When feedback is provided with regard to concrete, specific and clearly articulated achievements or behaviours, the team member can concretely go to work. He or she knows exactly what went well or not so well. General feedback can create obscurity as the members of the team do not know exactly what went well or not so well and thus where improvement is needed. When feedback is provided quickly, the team member can remember what he or she did well or less well and learn from this.

The provision of feedback is difficult. Despite attention to this skill in almost every training programme for health care professionals, there are actually very few professionals capable of giving feedback to colleagues or cooperating team members. The recommendations in Table 10.5 may provide a better grasp.

Conduct of a discussion

Outcomes can lead to different opinions at times, and a team obviously wants to reconcile these opinions to improve the care process. In addition to knowing how to provide understandable feedback, thus, one must also know how to conduct a discussion and handle conflict. The techniques in Table 10.6 hold for the conduct of a good discussion.

At the beginning of a discussion, it is important that the topic is explicitly mentioned and the objective of the discussion is clearly articulated. In the discussion

157

Table 10.5 Rules of thumb for feedback

Provision of feedback	Receipt of feedback
■ State first what went well and then what could go better	■ Stay open to feedback
■ Adjust feedback to recipient and provide in doses, if necessary	■ Do no get defensive
■ Provide concrete, descriptive feedback	■ Listen to both negative and positive feedback
■ Check to see that feedback has been understood	■ Ask for clarification if needs be
■ Give the recipient a chance to react	■ Make a distinction between performance and being
■ Realise that things may not sink in at once	

Source: Chang and Kelly (1997)

Table 10.6 Discussion techniques

■ Keep the discussion open	■ Provide summaries
■ Listen to each other's ideas	■ Limit digressions
■ Ask for clarification as needed	■ Look for agreement

Source: Lemmens *et al.* 2004

of care outcomes, the objective is often identification of the cause of the differences between the attained outcome and a set standard. The team members participating in a discussion should all be given sufficient background information.

The following questions may stand central in a team discussion. What do these results mean? What is the cause of the results? How can the results be improved? Via brainstorming, the team can attempt to answer the questions.

Handling of conflict

In every team, differences of opinion and conflicts are bound to occur sooner or later. It is important that conflict be adequately dealt with and not allowed to escalate. The defusion of conflict and avoidance of explosion can expand the involvement and productivity of team members. Responsibility for the handling of conflict lies with both the team leader and the members of the team. What are the causes of conflict? And how can impending conflict be detected? See Table 10.7.

Conflict can arise when two or more members of a team have different views or expectations on a particular matter or situation, with regard to what should

Table 10.7 *Causes and signs of conflict*

Causes of conflict	Signs of conflict
■ Inadequate communication	■ Emotional talk
■ Scarce resources	■ Interruption
■ Unclear distribution of tasks	■ Personal reproach
■ Personal disputes	■ Holding positions
■ Incompatible goals	

Source: Chang and Kelly 1997

happen. Conflict can also arise from miscommunication and/or misunderstandings. Conflicts cause the team to no longer function as a team; the members may operate next to each other but not as a team (i.e. in cooperation). It is therefore of utmost importance that impending conflict be quickly detected and addressed.

Stimulation of good communication and real cooperation among the members of a team and an organisation can certainly prevent many conflicts. When impending conflict is detected or a conflict actually manifests itself, the team needs to recognise and admit that a conflict exits. Acknowledgment of conflict is necessary to provide a solution to the conflict. In order to solve a conflict, the different parties must be able to state their positions. When all of the parties have expressed their opinions. Ideas can be formulated with regard to how to solve the conflict. The parties involved in a conflict should jointly search for a solution to the problem and discuss the alternatives. An open discussion can lead to a greater breadth of information and a greater number of alternatives. Open discussion can also result in people interacting in a more trusting and healthy manner. Compromise may also present a solution to the problem. In this case, both parties make concessions and thereby try to find a compromise acceptable to both. The other members of the team must also agree as much as possible with the solution (i.e. compromise).

The team dynamics

Earlier in this chapter, the distinction between R-profs or routine-oriented professionals and I-profs or improvisation-oriented professionals was introduced. The two groups can react very differently to the presentation of feedback. When the results are negative and thus imply a need for change, the R-profs will adopt a critical attitude. When the outcomes are very positive and thus supportive of the current manner of working, the I-profs will quickly search for a new challenge.

Within a single group of professionals, varying degrees of involvement and interest in improvement and change typically exist. Not every member has an intrinsic motivation to change ways of doing. Usually some are enthusiastic and some are not. Both groups need different sorts of encouragement and different styles of leadership.

The dynamics of the different forces within a team are of considerable importance for the success of the active learning process associated with the provision of feedback. Table 10.8 shows how five subgroups can be roughly distinguished within each team.

Inspection of the percentile distribution in Table 10.8 suggests that reaching the 'early majority' is of considerable importance. Once convinced, these individuals – together with the 'innovators' and the 'early adopters' – constitute the group majority. The 'early majority' is motivated particularly by the presentation of appealing examples and the opinions of colleagues whom they respect. This is in contrast to the individuals in the first two groups who are mostly convinced of the direction in which they are to move by rational consideration of clear and unambiguous figures. The leaders of innovators or the early adopters often serve as coach, role model and facilitator. Such leaders also actively establish room for discovery and experimentation. And this means that such leaders know how to give mistakes a place within the learning process. The attitude of such leaders is reflected in the following statement: 'The worst is doing nothing; better is doing something perhaps in err; and still better is doing something well.'

The 'later majority' and 'laggards' are, in closing, often convinced only in a top-down manner. They do not listen to arguments and are not impressed by facts and figures. If not voluntarily changing, their leaders need to give orders to make them accept changes. The role of the leaders is of inconsiderable importance to appeal to these groups on the basis of hierarchical principles. This may lead to job rotation for some of the laggards or transfer to another kind of work. Leaders must be aware of the necessity to handle different styles of leadership within the dynamics of a team. Understanding the different attitudes within a team to changes in the way they work was also explored in Chapter 4.

Table 10.8 Five subgroups of a team

Innovators (2.5%)	Early adopters (13.5%)	Early majority (34%)	Late majority (34%)	Laggards (16%)
Crave change and innovation; often seen as slightly radical; cope well with uncertainty	Gatekeepers of new ideas; opinion leaders	Adopt new ideas after deliberation	Adopt new ideas as a result of increased pressure from peers sceptical of change	Isolated from the social network; last to change; suspicious of change agents

Source: Rogers 1995

DISCUSSION QUESTIONS

1   How can you apply the principles from this chapter to ensure that feedback leads to improvement, rather than unhealthy conflict within your team?
2   How will you help develop the skills of your team to ensure this process is built into the way you work?
3   What is the best way to involve your patients and users in the feedback process?
4   How will you ensure that the feedback process has changed the way care is provided in future?

REFERENCES

Aarsse, R. (2003) *De betekenis van cliënttevredenheid als indicator voor kwaliteit van zorg (The signification of patients' satisfaction as an indicator for quality of care).* Dissertation, Faculteit Geneeskunde, Universiteit van Amsterdam.

Boonstra, J.J. (2000) *Lopen over water: over de dynamiek van organiseren, vernieuwen en leren (Walking upon the water, about the dynamics of organising, innovating and learning).* Oratie voor de Universiteit van Amsterdam: Vossiuspers.

Chang, R.A. and Kelly, K. (1997) *Stap voor stap problemen oplossen: een praktisch handboek om problemen op te lossen (Stepped problem solving: a practical manual to solve problems).* Zaltbommel: Thema.

Grol, R. and Wensing, M. (2001) *Implementatie, effectieve verandering in de patiëntenzorg (Implementation, effective change in health care).* Maarssen: Elsevier gezondheidszorg.

Lemmens, K.M.M., van Dijk, A.A. and Walburg, J.A. (2004) *Meer resultaat in het team, werkboek bij uitkomstenmanagement (More results in the team, manual for outcome management).* Maarssen: Elsevier gezondheidszorg.

Lombarts, M.J.M.H. (1995) *Dutch physicians using external peer review in implementing and evaluating clinical guidelines.* Utrecht: CBO.

Øvretveit, J. (1998) *Evaluating health interventions.* Buckingham and Philadelphia, PA: Open University Press.

Quinn, J.B.P., Anderson, S. and Finkelstein, S. (1996) Managing professional intellect: making the most of the best. *Harvard Business Review,* March–April: 71–80.

Rogers, E.M. (1995) Lessons for guidelines from the diffusion of innovations. *Joint Commission Journal on Quality Improvement,* 21: 324–328.

Van Beek, C.C. and Van Dorsten, T.C. (1997) *Veranderkundige instrumenten voor zorginnovatie (Instruments for change management in health care).* Houten: Bohn Stafleu Van Loghum.

Walburg, J.A. (2004) *Uitkomstenmanagement in de gezondheidszorg, het opbouwen van lerende teams in zorgorganisaties (Performance management in health care, the creation of learning teams in healthcare organizations)* Maarssen: Elsevier gezondheidszorg.

Weggeman, M. (1997) *Kennismanagement, inrichting en besturing van kennisintensieve organisaties (Knowledge management, framing and steering knowledge-intensive organizations).* Schiedam: Scriptum.

Chapter 11

Performance improvement and disease management

Karin Lemmens, Robbert Huijsman and Jan Walburg

KEY POINTS OF THIS CHAPTER

- Chronic disease management
- Outcome measurement
- Care continuum
- Implementation of guidelines
- Provider activities and patient interventions

INTRODUCTION

The care that a patient receives is seldom provided by a single organisation. For many clinical pictures and in cases of chronic illness in particular, the patient comes into contact with multiple care organisations. The quality of the care and the outcomes of the care are thus the sum of the efforts of many different parties. It is rarely the case that the outcome of an intervention depends upon just one process from a single organisation. The improvement of treatment and care outcomes must therefore occur through dialogue with other organisations.

In this chapter, the interrelations between different care providers and organisations are key. From an organisational perspective, the quality of integrated or transmural care is of importance. And from the perspective of the medical professional and patient, the quality of the care at the level of a particular clinical picture or so-called disease management will be very significant.

ELEMENTS OF CARE

Different individuals and organisations provide health care. And the situation has evolved in such a manner that the care is also organised according to separate 'silo's' (see Figure 11.1).

The different disciplines have their own structures, directorates, strategic policies and quality policies. Within such a discipline, people then attempt to provide the care in the most cost-effective manner possible and naturally everyone tries to coordinate the care to the greatest possible degree. Nevertheless, there is very little insight into the efficacy and costs of the care chain as a whole.

How, for example, should we evaluate cost effectiveness under the following circumstances?

CASE VIGNETTE

Cardiovascular disease

There is an emergency admission of a patient with acute heart complaints to a hospital. The patient's situation is life threatening and immediate intervention is successfully undertaken. Recovery proceeds smoothly. The patient is also satisfied with the course of things. And one can speak of excellent health care. Or perhaps not ...

A long period of arterial thickening with no attention from the family doctor preceded the heart attack. The patient was also, moreover, discharged without in-depth instructions regarding the prevention of cardiovascular disease. The acute medical intervention thus proceeded excellently while the care system as a whole clearly fell short. Doctors work as cost-effectively as possible and clearly address the complaints of a patient but have no time for preventive interventions. The hospital wants to make optimal use of beds; doctors discharge patients as soon as this is medically possible and see no place for behaviour-changing discussions of patient lifestyles.

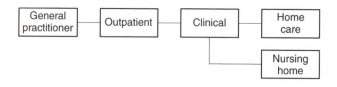

Figure 11.1 *Components of care.*

In a well-functioning cost-effective health care system in which all of the costs and outcomes for the entire chain of health care are considered, intervention would have occurred earlier and/or such a patient would have been labelled high risk with all of the associated implications for education and guidance. It is exactly the aforementioned patients who drive the costs of care up and repeatedly undergo expensive interventions, which often only leads to a declining quality of life.

The care efforts in the example above were not aimed at the prevention of illness or restriction of the dimensions of an illness but at the realisation of cost efficiency within one's own 'silo'. The optimalisation of one's own area of responsibility can thus be seen to actually increase the costs of the system as a whole at times. The fact that the care is provided in separate 'silo's' or components is not only a consequence of structure and financing; even when one can speak of delivery by a single organisation, the care within the organisation is typically broken down into separate units.

No matter how difficult it may be to integrate ambulant and clinical care within a single organisation, the following example shows this to be possible.

The increasing interest in evidence-based medicine and outcomes, on the one hand, and the involvement in the integration of general, specialist and community care sectors, on the other hand, are making the idea of 'disease management' an attractive one (Hunter and Fairfield 1997). And this is why we have decided to connect the notion of quality of integrated care to the notion of disease management.

CASE VIGNETTE

Mental health care in the Netherlands

In the 1990s in the Netherlands, a wave of mergers occurred for mental health care institutions. Up until that time, a distinction was made between institutions which provided outpatient care, and institutions which provided clinical care. In many cases and after a long period of development, the outpatient and clinical care have been integrated within a single organisational context. The aim of this integration is to have the care connect better and to organise the care in a better manner — from the perspective of the patient. Nevertheless, a number of 'care islands' have also emerged within this context. In other words, there are cases where the care professionals do their best and provide the best care possible but nevertheless fall short due to hitches in the fit of the different care components. Cost-effective care chains can be established for different clinical pictures only when care outcomes are considered in their totality across the entire care chain.

DISEASE MANAGEMENT

Disease management is the term used to refer to the total of the prevention, treatment and care for a patient with a particular disorder. We define disease management as follows: 'A multidisciplinary approach to care for chronic diseases which coordinates comprehensive care along the disease continuum and across health care delivery systems' (Ellrodt et al. 1997).

Disease management requires a proactive attitude with respect to an illness with preventive measures as an important component. For this reason, disease management is not only the responsibility of care providers but also equally the responsibility of the patient him/herself, the surrounding environment including the family and employers, insurance agencies/commissioners, pharmacists, pharmaceutical companies and other medical suppliers. The objective of disease management is to tackle the disorder in the most efficient and effective manner irrespective of individual care providers or their financial systems.

The reasoning underlying disease management is as follows. The quality of care can be improved by better regulation of the health condition of the patient via, among other things:

■   greater education of the patient;
■   better monitoring of the patient's health condition by the care provider;
■   use of evidence-based guidelines.

In such a manner, the patient learns to deal with his or her illness better, receives care which is in keeping with the recommended guidelines and has a more stable health condition as a result. Cost reductions will manifest themselves as a decline in the number of emergency care visits, decreased durations for hospital stays and the prevention of illness. However, a systematic evaluation of the disease management approach is needed to specify the extent to which the preceding goals are actually fulfilled (Villagra 2004).

Disease management distinguishes itself from traditional care via a shift of focus from the treatment of patients during separate care episodes to the delivery of high quality care across the entire care continuum (Ellrodt et al. 1997). Disease management also goes further than simply the connection of different care components to each other. Disease management requires the adoption of a different approach to care involving different underlying assumptions, and disease management is conducted via teams working across the boundaries of their own organisations. It is not so much the intention that care organisations become a single monolithic entity but, rather, that care is provided for the patient on the basis of a coherent vision of the patient and the overall clinical picture.

Disease management in Europe

The rising costs of health care and expectations with regard to the quality of care are placing tremendous pressure on the health care systems of Europe. The absence of care coordination, an unbalanced accent on acute care, disregard of preventive care and the delivery of inappropriate care constitute additional underlying problems (Hunter and Fairfield 1997). Disease management aims to improve the quality of care and reduce costs. Only if care outcomes are considered in their totality across the entire chain of care, can qualitatively good and cost-effective care chains be established around different clinical pictures. However, very little research has been conducted to date on the actual effects of disease management programmes.

Disease management does not match the manner in which the health care sector is organised in Europe. Given the differences in health care systems, moreover, disease management is developing differently in Europe than in the USA. Disease management was initially developed in the USA at micro level of the individual patient to limit liability costs. In Europe, disease management is generally conducted from a macro-economic perspective to develop an efficient and high quality health care system.

The establishment of disease management to its fullest extent is not as yet really possible. In the care systems in Europe, a number of interventions that are part of disease management are in place such as the use of guidelines and the gatekeeper function of family doctors. In order to speak of disease management, however, it is important that the other interventions such as patient education and outcome management be added to the chain and that the connections between the different disease management components be clear. The long-term development of disease management must also be accompanied by structural changes in the financing and organisation of care. Disease management is the ultimate form of integrated care and thus requires tremendous effort.

Important points of attention for the introduction of disease management in Europe are the presence of a good support infrastructure in the areas of financing and information processing and also attention to long-term planning and commissioning. The introduction of disease management does not produce direct cost reductions because the care itself must be organised differently which entails set-up costs. Also the outcomes which disease management claims to influence only become visible – as in the case of 'quality of life' – in the long run (Hunter and Fairfield 1997).

When we examine current care, a number of impediments to the provision of integrated care within a framework of disease management are encountered:

- the care system is aimed too much at the best treatment of the ill and too little at the prevention of illness;
- the care system is aimed too unilaterally at the development of extremely

expensive forms of treatment for the final stage of an illness often at the cost of a much less expensive intervention for an earlier stage;

■ the financial care structure is aimed too much at institutions and not at care partnerships and/or the whole clinical picture;

■ given that the care system does not operate as a whole, there is extensive and expensive attention to 'interface management' across departments and organisations;

■ certain cost-efficient interventions – such as lifestyle training in cases of high-risk patient behaviour – are not provided simply because the financing of such interventions is lacking.

Relative to integrated care and chain care, disease management thus goes one step further. The major differences between the traditional organisation of care and the organisation of care within a framework of disease management are summarised in Table 11.1.

PRINCIPLES OF DISEASE MANAGEMENT

In this section, the essential principles of disease management will be reviewed in order to later make the connection with outcome management.

Shared vision

One of the most essential features of disease management is that the nature and intensity of the interventions are based on the natural course of an illness. Detailed

Table 11.1 Differences between traditional care and disease management

Traditional care	Disease management
■ Reactive	■ Proactive
■ Aimed at treatment	■ Aimed at prevention and treatment
■ Optimalisation of total care chain	■ Optimalisation of specific care
■ Financing of institutions	■ Financing of clinical pictures
■ Improvement based on outcomes of own care process	■ Improvement based on outcomes of total care process
■ Based on monodisciplinary, institutional guidelines	■ Based on integrated multidisciplinary care protocols or critical paths
■ Care provider is responsible	■ Total patient system is responsible
■ Aimed at particular illness episode	■ Aimed at natural course of the illness
■ Passive patient role	■ Intensive patient involvement
■ Process oriented	■ Outcome oriented

insight into the causes of the illness and the manner in which the illness manifests itself is therefore required. Not only the course of the illness itself but also the costs associated with the illness are examined: where do the greatest health risks occur and where are the peaks with regard to costs?

Just how cardiovascular disease arises, for example, has been mapped: a gradual narrowing of the coronary arteries due to cholesterol. Those factors that appear to contribute further to the cause of an illness are then specified: a cholesterol-rich diet and often too little exercise with other factors such as heredity also play a limited role.

Disease management thus begins with insight into an illness. Then, all of those concerned with the illness develop a picture of those who are at risk, where the high-risk groups can be reached, using what information, and by whom as the starting points for the formulation of treatment guidelines.

Economic analyses

Disease management also takes economic trade-offs into consideration. Where are the highest costs incurred? By whom? And can the costs be reduced via other activities or interventions?

We know, for example, that 5% of chronically ill patients account for 60% of the health care budget, that 45% of these chronically ill patients account for 37% of the costs made, and that the remaining 50% account for no more than 3% of the care budget (Eichert et al. 1997). This situation is depicted in Figure 11.2.

The greatest cost reduction can thus be achieved with the smallest but most expensive group via – for example – prevention or early intervention.

It is generally assumed that disease management can produce greater cost-effectiveness: a better quality of care and reduced costs. However, systematic evaluations of the effects of disease management on costs are still missing as yet. The impulse to analyse the financial-economic aspects of the care trajectory will

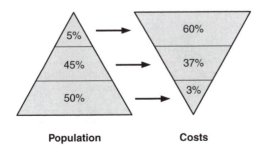

Figure 11.2 Economic analysis.

Source: Eichert et al. 1997.

presumably come mostly from insurance agencies or state funded health programmes in the future. But rather than taking institutions as the starting point for the evaluation of health care budgets, the illness constitutes the starting point for purposes of disease management. Possible savings are thus viewed from the perspective of the entire care chain – as illustrated in Table 11.2.

The implementation of a system of disease management also brings set up costs with it, and these costs must be weighed against any savings. The introduction of disease management will therefore most likely occur where it is clearly possible to quantify the costs of an illness and influence the associated costs. And the most obvious illnesses within this light are diabetes, cancer, cardiovascular disease, respiratory diseases, depression, alcohol addiction and AIDS.

Prevention orientation

Disease management is aimed at the prevention of illness and quick, effective treatment of acute illness episodes. This means that health care activities or interventions may be undertaken in stages when the illness has not yet presented itself or fully manifested itself. Examples are improving dietary habits to prevent cardiovascular disease, modifying smoking habits to prevent cancer, learning to handle social pressure to prevent drug abuse and encouraging condom use to prevent sexually transmitted diseases.

The relevant interventions will be aimed first and foremost at people with a particularly high risk for a particular illness. For cardiovascular disease and cancer, for example, people with a family history of the illness will be the target; for drug abuse and sexually transmitted diseases, adolescents will be the target. And when an illness begins to manifest itself in its earliest form and particularly when a potentially chronic illness with a long incubation period appears to be involved, screening and early intervention measures are clearly called for. When the illness actually manifests itself, immediate access to the necessary treatment and care must be provided. Disease management is also actively concerned with the prevention of relapse.

Table 11.2 *Economic analysis*

Care provider / Illness	General practitioner	Hospital	Nursing home	Outpatient	Pharmacist	Total
Diabetes						
Cancer						
COPD						
Total						

Strengthening of patient involvement

More than 50% of the causes of illness relate to individual lifestyle such as what someone consumes or the extent to which someone is physically active. For cardiovascular disease and cancer, the percentages are even higher. The behaviour of the patient is therefore one of the most critical aspects of health. In disease management programmes, a considerable investment is therefore made in the involvement of the patient. Stimulation of involvement concerns not only the patient but also the direct environment including the partner and other members of the family. And this can be done via educational support, motivational discussions and even forms of reinforcement.

Activities frequently used to enlarge the involvement of the patient within the framework of disease management are patient education and self-management. These two terms are closely related and refer to the process of improving the skills and trust of patients and thereby placing them in a position to better deal with their illness. Self-management may consist, for example, of a course on 'smoking cessation' or a fitness programme to improve the condition of a patient with cardiovascular disease. The rapid spread of the Internet also offers interesting possibilities for the personalised provision of information and education suited to the individual patient. In Table 11.3, a list of the different ways in which patient involvement can be enhanced and maintained is presented.

Continuity of care

Disease management concerns the total treatment and care for a patient with a particular disorder. The pursuit of continuity of care has two aspects: cooperation between care institutions in order to provide the most suitable care and the pur-

Table 11.3 *Means to enhance patient involvement*

- Increase knowledge of the illness: causes, course, prognosis
- Consult in formulation of treatment plan
- Increase knowledge of the treatment plan
- Increase confidence in the treatment plan
- Strengthen ability to follow treatment plan
- Emphasise importance of following treatment plan
- Increase confidence in the efficacy of the treatment plan
- Encourage adherence to treatment plan
- Involve in the conduct of the treatment plan
- Involve in monitoring of treatment progress
- Involve in evaluation of treatment and/or treatment plan

Source: Doyle 1997

suit of cost-effectiveness within the care chain via substituting one type of care for another.

In such a manner in the Netherlands, many hospitals have managed to greatly reduce the duration of stay. This has been through the increased substitution of less intensive and thus less expensive forms of treatment and care for more expensive forms. Examples are the substitution of outpatient care for inpatient care or transfer from hospital to nursing home. With regard to disease management, the sub-

CASE VIGNETTE

Stroke care project in the Netherlands

In the Netherlands, a stroke care project has been initiated within the framework of the so-called Breakthrough Series. The impulse for this breakthrough project was a study showing a regional stroke service to be more cost effective than traditional fragmented stroke care and also lead to greater satisfaction on the part of care recipients than traditional stroke care (Huijsman 2001a).

The regional stroke service is aimed at having both specialised and generalised care providers from all different echelons provide the most appropriate care for the right patient in the proper manner and in the most suitable place during all phases of an illness or disorder (Huijsman 2001b). The hospital stroke unit is concentrated on the acute phase while the units in nursing and rehabilitation centres are aimed at the revalidation phase. The different units work together with doctors, ambulance agencies and home-care organisations and, in such a manner, the regional stroke service involves ever more encompassing care chains (Van Splunteren *et al.* 2004). The main objective of the breakthrough programme for stroke service was drastic improvement of the care for stroke patients.

The focus of the project was on rapid turnover via, for example, the monitoring of hospital stay durations for stroke patients, sharpening of the discharge criteria, discussion of all patients within multidisciplinary consultations, agreements with partners in the 'care chain' and individual case management. The average hospital stay duration was cut drastically: from 19.2 days per patient at the start of the project to 12.0 days at the end of the project. This meant a reduction of 40% within the space of a year. The number of inappropriate bed days was cut by 50% from an average of 8 to 4 days per patient simply because the patients were more quickly transferred to the following link in the care chain.

In order to guarantee sufficient continuity of care, two elements appear to be of critical importance: clear agreements between the participating institutions with regard to the structure, processes and outcomes of the care chain and also the development of indicators to monitor the quality of the care chain and adjust it as needed.

stitution of care is pursued in the form of case management. A case manager who is typically a practice nurse or nurse practitioner takes over tasks from more expensive family doctors. They also oversee the whole episode of care with the patient.

The cooperation between institutions is also sometimes referred to as integrated or transmural cares, and a number of experiments, which fit the concept of disease management, have already been conducted in the Netherlands. The following example illustrates this for cardiovascular care.

Evidence-based guidelines and protocols

Guidelines and protocols play an important role in disease management. In order to provide qualitatively good and cost-effective care in an integrated setting, it is important that the care be based to the greatest extent possible upon the principles of evidence-based medicine. Guidelines and protocols should not only be patient oriented but also fit into the care organisation. The use of guidelines and protocols insures a certain degree of standardisation within the health care field and thereby improvement of clinical and financial outcomes (Ellrodt *et al.* 1997). However, many guidelines and protocols are still unidisciplinary and intended for application within a particular setting. For purposes of disease management, the care must be based on multidisciplinary guidelines, which thus encompass all of the individuals and organisations responsible for the treatment and care of patients with a particular illness.

The available literature must also therefore be analysed from a slightly different perspective. Simply combining the individual guidelines intended to regulate the different parts of the care chain is not true 'disease management'. For true disease management, a specific protocol should be aimed at not so much an organisation as a particular illness phase. Assuming that 'outcome management' is also embedded in the process, the outcomes of activities and interventions stemming from the care protocols can, in fact, be measured and evaluated – also at the level of the care chain in its entirety. And these results can, in turn, provide a stimulus for subsequent adjustment of the relevant guidelines and protocols.

CASE STUDY

Development of guidlines for COPD care in the Netherlands

A good example of this can be found in the development of guidelines in the Netherlands. The process of evidenced-based guideline development is now the norm in the Netherlands. Within this framework, problems were encountered with the achievement of a multidisciplinary guideline for the provision of high quality integrated care for cases of COPD. The general aim of the guideline was and is to make the outcomes of scientific research applicable to actual practice or so-called knowledge synthesis (CBO 2004).

The guideline contains concrete recommendations with regard to both the content of the care and just how this should be organised. The guideline contains evidence-based recommendations with respect to such topics as detection, diagnosis and follow-up; smoking cessation; breathing exercises; education and information; and self-management. Patients are involved in the development of the guideline in various manners.

The guideline constitutes an important part of an actual integrated care system. Other activities within the system include:

- implementation of new care processes for COPD within the care chain via the breakthrough method;
- taking an inventory of best practices for the organisation of the chain of care for COPD;
- development of guideline-related indicators to measure the quality of the COPD care provided within a chain and adjust it accordingly;
- training of change agents (i.e. family doctors) to support fellow family doctors in the optimalisation of COPD care;
- formulation of a vision document on the basis of an inventory of the information and communication technology (ICT) possibilities for the chain of care.

In addition to stimulating of the use of guidelines and protocols, there are other components of disease management which can help care providers consistently deliver cost-effective and qualitatively good care. Among the other components are education, consultation between care providers, feedback, rewards and reminders.

Case management

Proactive case management is the shortest definition of disease management (Ward and Rieve 1996). Case management involves one person taking responsibility for the organisation, coordination and integration of the care for a patient.

The ultimate form of case management within the context of disease management is consideration and coordination of the entire care continuum for people with the same illness. This goes one step further than the forms of individual case management which we now know in the Netherlands.

Case managers keep track of the care provided to patients and thus form a type of mini-centre of knowledge around the patient. On the basis of their knowledge, case managers coordinate the care and solve any bottlenecks related to the transfer of a patient from one organisation to another. This type of care management does not simply combine the elements of care but, rather, plays a proactive role. The case manager can support the patient in the adjustment of his or her lifestyle, diet and pattern of exercise, support the patient in adherence to medical regimes and also play a role in the provision of information and education for the entire patient system including the family and neighbours of the patient.

The role of the case manager within the context of disease management can be quite varied (Ward and Rieve 1997). Among other things, the case manager may:

- identify individuals at high risk or patients in an acute illness phase and therefore in a position to benefit from support in the form of case management;
- help promote the health, lifestyle and quality of life for the relevant patients;
- ensure access to necessary treatment and care;
- translate evidence-based guidelines into individual care protocols;
- support the implementation of the treatment and care plan for purposes of disease management;
- provide information and education;
- monitor and stimulate patient involvement;
- measure and evaluate care outcomes;
- evaluate and adjust the care plan in consultation with those responsible;
- serve as a point of contact for patient, family and those responsible for treatment.

Case management in this form is thus more far-reaching than traditional case management. In Table 11.4, the differences between traditional case management and case management within a framework of disease management are summarised in the terms of Ward and Rieve (1997).

Norris *et al.* (2003) published a systematic review of the effectiveness of case management conducted within the framework of disease management. For diabetes care, the case manager is in many instances a nurse and case management is found to positively contribute to the control of blood sugar levels and monitoring of blood sugar levels by the care recipient.

Other possible activities that relate to case management within the framework of disease management involve multidisciplinary teams and the nurse specialist. Multidisciplinary teams are quite common for the organisation of the care around a patient with one person usually serving as the contact or case manager. The nurse specialist or practice nurse are newly emerging functions within the framework of disease management, and this person functions as a case manager in many instances.

Integrated data processing systems

Disease management clearly depends on effective and efficient information processing and communication. The computer processing of data thus goes much further than the sending of bills to patients or insurers. A data processing system is

Table 11.4 *Traditional case management versus case management for purposes of disease management*

Traditional case management	Disease management
■ Focus on individual patient	■ Focus on population
■ Intervention in clinical episode	■ Education, prevention and lifestyle-oriented interventions
■ Uses care system	■ Develops care system
■ Patient-oriented care outcomes	■ Population-oriented care system
■ Prevention of hospitalisation	■ Prevention of illness
■ Information and education around illness	■ More general health information and education
■ Short-term and intensive case management relation with patient	■ Long term and not very intensive case management relation with patient
■ Cost savings per patient	■ Cost savings per population
■ Care management in certain domains	■ Case management for entire care continuum

required to do the following among other things: keep track of what care is provided where, the costs incurred and how the patient reacts to interventions in terms of not just illness but also quality of life. The relevant data thus come from the different segments of the care chain and must be integrated and made available within the data processing system. The electronic patient file and computer-based questionnaires are also components of such a data management system.

The relevant data must be available in such a format that at least the following are apparent:

■ whether there has been appropriate utilisation of care institutions;
■ what costs are incurred, and where;
■ what medication is prescribed and/or whether the patient adheres to medical regimens;
■ what the outcomes of specific interventions are;
■ where the patient is at any particular moment;
■ which regulation applies for which sector.

In addition to the aforementioned types of data at the level of the patient, a databank should be constructed in such a manner that meta-analyses are possible for other purposes such as:

■ justification of treatment choices;
■ ongoing improvement of the system;
■ research on the effectiveness of particular guidelines and protocols.

In many countries, the unavailability of data management systems constitutes an important obstacle to the complete implementation of disease management (Todd and Nash 1997). The next example shows that the United States already has come a long way using electronic management systems.

CASE STUDY

Washington State Diabetes Collective

In 1999 the Breakthrough Series started the Washington State Diabetes Collaborative, the first state-level collaborative on chronic disease. Participating teams were responsible for maintaining a registry of the patients in its pilot population. Registries enabled teams to extract summary statistics and to track their progress on clinical measures. Any team without an existing electronic system was encouraged to begin building a registry. Teams were offered and trained to use a public-domain diabetes registry known as the Diabetes Electronic Management System (DEMS), developed by the Washington State Department of Health Diabetes Prevention and Control Program (Daniel *et al.* 2004a). The provider uses the DEMS in real time during the clinical visit; data is aggregated according to clinical assessment and administrative tasks (Smith *et al.* 1998).

The Olympic Physicians team, in rural Western Washington, participated in the first collaborative. The clinic team used the DEMS to analyse one year of medical history data (n = 221 patients with diabetes) and selected eight measures of care standards along with corresponding goals at which to aim their efforts. The team developed innovations like creating a communications process to inform physicians of patients' self-management goals and using the DEMS registry to indicate which patients had not had recent visits. A lack of resources and trouble running DEMS posed challenges for the team, however, they met or exceeded their goals for four measures and made progress on the other four (Daniel *et al.* 2004b).

Involvement of the pharmaceutical industry

The pharmaceutical industry has the image of being interested only in increased turnover and thereby greater profits from the sale of medicines. However, there is an immense amount of knowledge and experience with regard to specific disorders and illnesses within the pharmaceutical industry. An increasing number of the industries are, moreover, seeking a new role defined by not only the marketing of pills but also joint responsibility for health care.

The activities of the pharmaceutical industry within the domain of disease management are twofold: first, optimalisation of medication; second, identification and location of risk groups.

Optimising the value of medication means including of medication within the evidence-based guidelines and thereby possible advantages for both patient care *and* the pharmaceutical industry. When one is oriented towards the reduction of pharmaceutical costs but *not* optimalisation of medication, this can actually increase the total costs of care. A New Hampshire study (Bernard 1997), for example, showed a reduction of 5% in the use of medication to be followed by a 50% increase in the number of elderly people admitted to nursing homes. There are many more examples suggesting that the pharmaceutical industry can best position medication within the total disease management process and not just as an isolated aspect of treatment. And for this reason, many pharmaceutical companies are getting involved in disease management via educational activities for doctors, the formulation of guidelines, the conduct of economic analyses, provision of patient education and information, use of the sales organisation for the distribution of public relations materials, the development of programmes to increase the involvement of the patient in treatment and the development of methods for early detection. The illnesses that have received attention to date are asthma, depression and diabetes in particular. Decisive in each case was the company being able to show the economic and clinical advantages of medication within a disease management programme. The pharmaceutical industry can also help promote the development of good disease management by making the data from clinical trials available.

Further considerations relevant to the principles of disease management

With the rise of disease management programmes, there is a growing need for a thorough method of evaluation to make both clinical and economic outcomes clearly visible is presenting itself. The lack of a systematic framework of analysis makes it impossible to compare evaluations with each other and also makes many evaluations unreliable (Villagra 2004). Determination of a clear and unambiguous definition for the concept of 'disease management' and specification of the interventions, which constitute disease management, thus form the first steps in the development of such an analytic framework.

In the area of disease management for diabetes, for example, considerable heterogeneity in the various interventions to be undertaken by the care providers and the structure of the care provided has been ascertained. This heterogeneity limits the extent to which the results can be combined and compared. In a systematic review by Renders *et al.* (2004), moreover, the studies were found to vary from patient education to audit to feedback for care providers. At a time when health care resources are limited, it is important that the most suitable interventions be identified in order to promote both efficiency and improved patient outcomes (Norris *et al.* 2003).

Most evaluation studies or systematic reviews are still aimed at the individual interventions which constitute disease management. The meta-analyses conducted

178

by Weingarten *et al.* (2002) and the systematic review by Ofman *et al.* (2004) are examples. In these studies, thus, the interactions between various interventions and activities are ignored. In many cases, the economic effects of the various interventions and activities are also not included in the evaluations. Once again, the need for a thorough analytic framework for the conduct of evaluation research for purposes of disease management is thus demonstrated.

HEALTH MANAGEMENT

In the following, we go one step further than disease management and consider the development of health management in general. Disease management is primarily aimed at individuals who are sick or at risk. When we apply the principles of disease management to healthy populations, we can speak of health management. And according to Peterson and Kane (1997), health care management involves the following:

- optimalisation of health and well-being;
- minimalisation of health risks;
- prevention of particular illnesses in populations at risk;
- promotion of early illness detection;
- maximalisation of clinical efficacy and efficiency;
- prevention of illness-related complications;
- elimination of ineffective and unnecessary care;
- measurement of outcomes and continual improvement of outcomes.

For purposes of health management, our attention thus shifts from the small part of the population with illnesses to the larger healthy part of the population. A health management programme thus invests in keeping a large group of people healthy because this is considerably cheaper in terms of cost-effectiveness in the long run.

The World Health Organisation (WHO) defines health as involving more than simply the absence of illness. Health involves 'a state of complete physical, mental and spiritual well-being'. At present, the health care system is concerned with primarily symptoms, illness and disability. In the future, considerable gains stand to be made in the areas of health promotion, increased awareness and knowledge and particularly increased responsibility for one's own personal health.

As already mentioned, the majority of the illnesses which currently lead to death – such as cardiovascular disease and cancer – heavily depend on individual lifestyle factors which can clearly be manipulated and modified. Those chronic illnesses which emerge after a period of anywhere from five to thirty years affect large groups of people and thus constitute a tremendous financial burden. Some two-thirds of all the life years which we lose before we are 65 are caused by lifestyle factors with 75% pertaining to smoking, high blood pressure and obesity. We thus know many of the causes of illness and should use this knowledge to modify risky behaviour.

Among the possibilities available to us to modify behaviour are the following (Walburg 2001):

- promotion of health at work and school based on recognition of the fact that many health care costs are caused by such risky behaviour as smoking, poor diet and too little exercise;
- early detection and screening either aimed at high-risk groups or not;
- the conduct of lifestyle analyses in order to determine which aspects place at risk and which aspects facilitate;
- motivation and support of people with the modification of their lifestyles;
- supply of financial and other rewards for people with a healthy lifestyle such as the differentiation of insurance premiums for smokers versus non-smokers;
- promotion of knowledge of illnesses and the interventions associated with such illnesses based on recognition of the fact that many of the illnesses which people report in the field of health care today can be handled quite well by the individuals themselves with internet possibly playing a good supportive role.

On the basis of such activities, the concept of disease management can be developed to achieve a better quality of treatment and care for certain illnesses and into a concept which maintains and promotes the health of the population as a whole. Investment in health is thus a good investment not from an ideological perspective but simply because the economic trade-offs aimed at optimalisation of cost-effectiveness and maximalisation of care outcomes can produce considerable gains in the long run.

PERFORMANCE MANAGEMENT AND DISEASE MANAGEMENT

The measurement and management of outcomes is one of the key aspects of disease management. For purposes of disease management, key outcomes for patients and populations must be defined, measured and managed. The outcome quadrant described in Chapter 7 offers a clear starting point for identification of the domains in which outcomes should be measured. However, disease management goes one step further as it encompasses the entire care continuum. The complexity of disease management is thus greater and, in the following sections, the expansion of outcome management for purposes of disease management and as depicted in Figure 11.3 will be discussed.

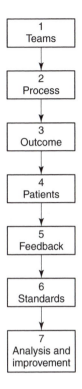

Figure 11.3 *Build-up of disease management.*

Team

All of the stakeholders involved in disease management constitute the team here with, in practice, the disease management team organised around a clinical or team leader. In the different literatures concerned with disease management, the role of multidisciplinary disease management teams is also discussed (Villagra 2004; WHO 2002).

The mission of the disease management team receives support via the development of a shared vision of the care process. Just how the disease management system should look must be formulated. And the time axis should also be included in the vision of the care process as the establishment of such an integrated system of disease management requires time.

The vision of the disease management team must next be translated into what it means for the different components of the care continuum, as depicted Figure 11.4.

Important components for the vision of the care process are as follows (Todd and Nash 1997):

- identification of high-risk populations;
- knowledge of the natural course of the illness;
- determination of necessary care and information services;
- build-up of patient information system;
- utilisation of evidence-based guidelines;
- recognition that disease management crosses institutional boundaries;
- continual measurement and feedback;
- establishment of a system of care financing and patient reward, financial reward or some other reward system.

Process

The process phase of building a system of disease management includes the following:

- depiction of the current care process in a flow chart;
- identification of which costs are incurred where in order to determine the total cost;
- description of best practices;
- formulation of the most explicit evidence-based guidelines possible.

The extent to which existing activities must be adjusted or changed should also be made clear. One can decide to start from the existing activities and gradually

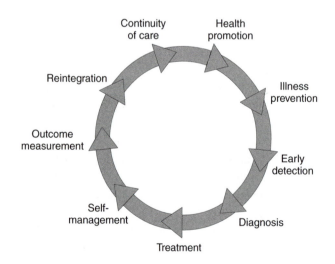

Figure 11.4 *Care continuum.*

Source: Todd and Nash 1997.

modify these in the direction of disease management. Or one can decide to redesign or adjust the activities first. Various process indicators – such as indicators of whether the cooperation is developing adequately or not – must then be identified.

The description of the care process within the framework of disease management can be given much of its form via the identification of clinical paths. Given that clinical paths rely upon evidence-based protocols and often encompass multiple components of the care continuum, clinical paths constitute a good starting point for disease management. The role of the case manager within this process is, moreover, critical as the case manager fulfils a leading role in the development, implementation and adjustment of clinical paths (Rohrbach 1999).

Another important characteristic of clinical paths which flawlessly fits the principles of disease management is the use of process and outcome indicators. An important component of disease management is continual evaluation of outcomes and the comparison of such to a standard for purposes of improving (clinical) results and optimalisation of care processes.

CASE STUDY

An asthma management programme

Mr Cooper is 25 years old with a history of asthma. He has been referred to a disease management programme for treatment and management of his condition. The programme starts with a screening examination which includes a detailed health history and diagnostic tests as outlined by the clinical practice guidelines. These results of the screening examination are used to determine the severity of Mr Cooper's illness and position him along the critical pathway which probably resembles a decision tree for treatment in this case. The critical pathway includes those elements of the clinical practice guidelines which apply to the case of Mr Cooper and the severity of his condition. Various clinical outcomes – such as the number of nocturnal awakenings, inhaled beta antonist usage and inhaled corticosteroid usage – are evaluated. The case manager in cooperation with the primary care physician examines Mr Cooper's current treatment regimen and initiates changes in his medication after consultation of the clinical practice guidelines. The clinical path also includes educational components to be conducted by the case manager and appropriate staff. Mr Cooper is further evaluated to ensure the proper use of inhaled medicines and identify any lifestyle changes needed to promote the treatment of his asthma. The clinical path also calls for evaluation of the effectiveness of Mr Cooper's treatment via documentation of any deviations from the path. Which portions of the treatment plan are ineffective is determined. By tracking deviations and outcomes, the clinical path can also assist the disease management programme with the identification of areas which are less effective and thus in need of revision. As a result of new treatment, Mr Cooper has had fewer hospitalisations and fewer emergency visits. The overall cost of Mr Cooper's care is thus reduced and his disease is also managed more effectively (Rohrbach 1999).

An important aspect of disease management is the interaction between provider and patients. When informed patients take an active role in managing their health and providers feel prepared and supported with time and resources, their interaction is likely to be much more productive. This active role does not really appear from this case study, it would have been better if there was a big emphasis on involving Mr Cooper in designing and agreeing a care process which suited him.

Outcomes

An important aspect of disease management is the ability to measure and report health outcomes (Epstein & Sherwood 1996). Once again, the outcome quadrant provides an excellent starting point with indicators of clinical outcomes, quality of life, patient satisfaction and costs. In the disease management literature, clinical outcomes, financial outcomes (i.e. cost comparisons) and humanistic outcomes (i.e. quality of life, patient satisfaction) are similarly highlighted. The measuring of outcomes might differ, depending on the priorities of those examining the data. A clinician is likely to be primarily interested in clinical or humanistic outcomes, whereas a health insurer may be interested in economic ones. Patients are interested in humanistic outcomes and have trouble interpreting clinical outcomes (Epstein and Sherwood 1996). Disease management programmes include mixtures of all measures.

In order to attain the relevant outcome information, the data-processing systems from the different organisations must be made compatible and integrated. And this, of course, constitutes a major undertaking.

Patients

The patient information which one wants to collect at the beginning of the treatment and care process and during the remainder of the care process must also be determined for purposes of disease management. An electronic patient file is essential for the integration of information regarding the care process, outcomes and patients.

It is also important that the severity of the illness be estimated in addition to other variables related to the risk of becoming ill, such as heredity and lifestyle. The usual variables, such as biographical factors and comorbid conditions, should also be registered.

CASE VIGNETTE

A COPD management programme

A disease management programme for COPD patients involves the following interventions: patient education, self-management means and support, case management and follow-up of COPD patients by the care provider. In order to measure the effectiveness and efficiency of the care, the following information is collected:

- reduction of functional limitations;
- quality of life according to the St George's Respiratory Questionnaire (SGRQ);
- knowledge of self-management on the part of the COPD patient;
- compliance with medication regimens;
- patient satisfaction with the accessibility of care.

The patients are followed for a few years, with measurement initiated one year after treatment. The target group was patients 65 years of age and older in stage 2 according to the guidelines of the Global initiative for chronic Obstructive Lung Disease (GOLD).

Feedback

As previously indicated, a fairly refined and complicated form of feedback must be established for purposes of disease management. Not only the teams responsible for the various components of the care process and the team responsible for the care process as a whole but also the patient and the financiers must be given feedback.

O'Brien *et al.* (2002) conclude in their systematic review of the effects of audit and feedback that these interventions can effectively improve the skills of the professional. However, the effect is usually quite limited and larger when combined with other interventions aimed at the care professional such as education. Given a combination of different activities, feedback from the perspective of disease management can be expected to be more effective than feedback for purposes of outcome management alone.

Standardisation

In principle, standardisation within the framework of disease management is nothing more than standardisation within the framework of outcome management where outcomes are evaluated with respect to professional standards, self-formulated standard and benchmarks (i.e., best practices). In the case of disease management, the benchmark is identified by comparing different disease management programmes with each other. The programmes must be based on the same definition of disease management and similar interventions, however.

Analysis and improvement

At this point, various analytic tools can be applied and the PDSA cycle followed. Such analysis is essential for identification of what should be adjusted. Decisions can sometimes be painful when, for example, a particular component of the care chain is found to be less than cost effective. At such a point, institutional interests can come to the fore.

The introduction of disease management is complicated at every step. Considerable resistance must be overcome, but very promising results are appearing from experiments with chain formation. Disease management requires the utmost of the system (i.e. data processing networks, logistics, organisation) and also the people involved. And for this reason, such a form of organisation for health care can be established only with enthusiastic professionals and managers facilitated in the development of such a system by government and financiers.

CASE STUDY

As we saw in the earlier case study, the aim of the diabetes project is to establish cooperative ties between care providers in the state of Washington to help realise demonstrably better care for patients. Diabetes care is complex and depends on a number of care providers and organisations, which clearly hampers the introduction and implementation of effective improvements. In the relevant project, attention is thus explicitly devoted to the guarantee of results. And this occurs via the use of, among other things, indicators to monitor the results, steer the implementation process and promote further innovation.

The teams test and implement individual changes in the care system in order – in the end – to incorporate all of the interventions from the Chronic Care Model (CCM), which is a form of disease management. Most of the teams showed improvement in the process and outcome measures relevant to blood sugar levels, control of blood sugar levels, control of blood pressure, foot examinations, eye examinations and self-management goals (Daniel *et al.* 2004a). In this research, a number of factors of essential importance for further analysis and possible improvement stood out: good administrative support, presence of a data-processing system, and clarity and transparency of the relevant figures.

CONCLUSIONS

Applying the principles of 'outcome management' by care providers has led to efforts to establish more general disease management programmes (Epstein and Sherwood 1996). In contrast to the traditional programmes of care providers, disease management programmes are organised, proactive and integrated. Disease management relates to the delivery of care which is evidence based, entails multiple interventions and applies to a group of patients with a specific illness. The interventions are designed for the benefit of the patient, the professional and the organisation with the delivery of optimal quality *and* efficient care as the objectives. In doing this, the measurement of outcomes and use of data processing systems play an important role.

It should be clear that outcome management fits into a disease management framework and therefore constitutes a component of disease management. However, disease management involves a much more complicated playing field with multiple teams and organisations. For outcome management, the first feedback loop concerns (in principle) only a single process; for disease management, the first feedback loop concerns multiple processes. As depicted in Figure 11.5, teams which receive feedback with respect to their component of the care continuum, and a group of teams which is jointly given feedback within the framework of disease management.

Disease management implies a paradigm shift from the individual professional who cares for the patient in a reactive, monodisciplinary and treatment-oriented manner to a proactive and systematic approach to the delivery of care in which individuals at risk are identified, intervention occurs, outcomes are measured and continual quality improvement takes place. Central to disease management is the knowledge base used to identify patients, determine interventions and evaluate outcomes. An important component is the involvement of the patient in determining, and in some cases co-providing, the package of care.

Disease management is a very promising concept. The results of different studies have already shown that the individual interventions which constitute disease management can clearly enhance the quality of care (Ofman *et al.* 2004;

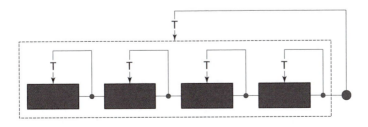

Figure 11.5 *Outcome measurement for purposes of disease management.*

Weingarten *et al.* 2002). The effectiveness of disease management programmes as a whole nevertheless has yet to be examined. This is because, among other things, there is an absence of an unequivocal definition of disease management and the interventions which constitute disease management. This does not, however, mean that such research should not be quickly initiated in order to fully explore the potential of disease management.

DISCUSSION QUESTIONS

1 What incentives can be identified for patients, clinicians and institutions to adopt 'disease management' instead of more traditional models?
2 What are the constraints to the introduction of disease management, and how might they be overcome?
3 How can resources (including staff) be moved from traditional care settings to provide more joined-up systems of care?
4 What 'performance measures' should be applied to disease management processes, covering the perspective of patients and other stakeholders?

REFERENCES

Bernard, S. (1997) The role of pharmaceutical companies in disease management, in W.E. Todd and D. Nash (eds) *Disease management.* Chicago, IL: American Hospital Publishing.

CBO (2004) www.cbo.nl

Daniel, D.M., Norman, J., Davis, C., Lee, H., Hindmarsh, M.F., McCulloch, D.K., Wagner, E.H. and Sugarman, J.R. (2004a) A state-level application of the chronic illness breakthrough series: results from two collaboratives on diabetes in Washington State. *Joint Commission Journal on Quality and Safety,* 30(2): 69–79.

Daniel, D.M., Norman, J., Davis, C., Lee, H., Hindmarsh, M.F., McCulloch, D.K., Wagner, E.H. and Sugarman, J.R. (2004b) Case studies from two collaboratives on diabetes in Washington State. *Joint Commission Journal on Quality and Safety,* 30(2): 103–108.

Doyle, J.B. (1997) Health outcomes: measuring and maximising value in disease management, in W.E. Todd and D. Nash (eds) *Disease management.* Chicago, IL: American Hospital Publishing.

Eichert, J.H., Wong, H. and Smith, D. (1997) The disease management development process, in W.E. Todd and D. Nash (eds) *Disease management.* Chicago, IL: American Hospital Publishing.

Ellrodt, G., Cook, D.J., Lee, J., Cho, M., Hunt, D. and Weingarten, S. (1997) Evidence-based disease management. *JAMA*, 278: 1687–1692.

Epstein, R.S. and Sherwood, L.M. (1996) From outcomes research to disease management: a guide for the perplexed. *Annals of Internal Medicine*, 124: 832–837.

Huijsman, R. (2001a) From elements to chain care – Stroke Service provides better care for CVA-patients (Van *units naar ketenzorg – Stroke service biedt betere zorg voor CVA-patiënten*). *Medical Contact (Medisch Contact)*, 56: 1765–1768.

Huijsman, R. (2001b) *Edisse: evaluation Dutch integrated stroke service experiments*. Den Haag: ZonMW.

Hunter, H. and Fairfield, G. (1997) Managed care: disease management. *British Medical Journal*, 315: 50–53.

Norris, S., Glasgow, R.E., Engelgau, M.M., O'Connor, P.J. and McCulloch, D. (2003) Chronic disease management: a definition and systematic approach to component interventions. *Disease Management and Health Outcomes*, 11: 477–488.

O'Brien, T., Oxman, A.D., Davis, D.A., Haynes, R.B., Freemantle, N. and Harvey, E.L. (2002) Audit and feedback: effects on professional practice and health care outcomes. *The Cochrane Library*, 3. Oxford: Update Software.

Ofman, J., Badamgarav, E., Henning, J.M., Knight, K., Gano, A.D., Levan, R.K., Gur-Arieb, S., Richards, M.S., Hasselblad, V. and Weingarten, S.R. (2004) Does disease management improve clinical and economic outcomes in patients with chronic diseases? A systematic review. *American Journal of Medicine*, 117: 182–192.

Peterson, K.M. and Kane, D.P. (1996) Beyond disease management: population-based health management, in W.E. Todd and D. Nash (eds) *Disease management*. Chicago, IL: American Hospital Publishing.

Renders, C.M., Valk, G.D., Wagner, E.H., Van Eijk, J.T.M. and Assendelft, W.J.J. (2004) Interventions to improve the management of diabetes mellitus in primary care, outpatient and community settings (Cochrane Review). *The Cochrane Library*. Chichester: John Wiley.

Rohrbach, J.I. (1999) Critical pathways as an essential part of a disease management program. *Journal of Nursing Care Quality*, 14(1): 11–15.

Smith, S.A., Murphy, M.E., Huschka, T.R. *et al.* (1998) Impact of a diabetes electronic management system on the care of patients seen in a subspecialty diabetes clinic. *Diabetes Care*, 21(6): 972–976.

Todd, W.E. and Nash, D. (eds) (1997) Disease management: a systems approach to improving patient outcomes. Chicago, IL: American Hospital Publishing.

Van Splunteren, P., Minkman, M. and Huijsman, R. (2004) Breakthrough in chain care – significantly better care for CVA-patients (Doorbraak in ketenzorg – zorg voor CVA-patiënten kan aantoonbaar beter). *Medical Contact (Medisch Contact)*, 59: 557–560.

Villagra, V. (2004) Strategies to control costs and quality: a focus on outcomes research for disease management. *Medical Care*, 42(4): III24–III30.

Walburg, J.A. (2001) *Actively healthy (Actief gezond)*. Utrecht: Kosmos-Z&K.

Ward, M.C. and Rieve, J.A. (1997) The role of case management in disease management, in W.E. Todd and D. Nash (eds) *Disease management*. Chicago, IL: American Hospital Publishing.

Weingarten, S.R., Henning, J.M., Badamgarav, E., Knight, K., Hasselblad, V., Gano, A. Jr and Ofman, J.J. (2002) Interventions used in disease management programmes for patients with chronic illness—which ones work? Meta-analysis of published reports. *British Medical Journal*, 325: 925–932.

WHO (2002) *Innovative care for chronic conditions*. Geneva: World Health Organisation.

Part III

Performance management and society

Chapter 12

Public disclosure of outcome data

Wim Schellekens

KEY POINTS OF THIS CHAPTER

- Objectives of external indicators
- Difference between internal and external indicators
- International external disclosure of performance data
- Conflicting interests

INTRODUCTION

Parallel to the development of indicators which can be used by care providers to steer and improve the care process (i.e., internal indicators), there is interest in indicators which can be used by care organisations for purposes of external accountability. The call for public performance indicators with regard to care providers, in fact, is getting louder. The question, however, is whether public disclosure of care outcomes is useful or even makes sense. This question stands central in this chapter. More specifically, does public disclosure of performance outcomes work to the advantage of the consumer and are such outcomes of importance for the care system?

Most organisations have set up a system of outcome measurement to improve and strengthen the relevant teams. And the primary objective of outcome measurement is indeed quality control and improvement. But can such information also be of more general societal interest?

OBJECTIVES OF EXTERNAL INDICATORS

External indicators can serve different objectives. The first objective is to provide confidence in the care system and help consumers choose care providers. In the

USA, stimulation of the choice behaviour of the care consumer is the most important reason for external disclosure of outcome information. The assumption underlying this is that the informed consumer can, in turn, influence the market. But the question is whether performance or outcome indicators are really suited for use by the care consumer. Indicators have a signal function and do not necessarily represent the full reality. Furthermore, a judgement based exclusively on indicators can quickly lead to mistaken conclusions (Schellekens *et al.* 2003).

A second objective of the use of external indicators is to expand the transparency of care. The health care sector has always been very opaque. Public disclosure of performance results is intended to give external parties – such as the government and health insurance companies – and also the patient greater insight into the quality and efficiency of an organisation.

In order to be able to compare figures across health care institutions and care providers in a responsible manner, considerable attention must be paid to the comparability, validity and reliability of the relevant figures. A variety of statistical methods, including risk adjustment, are available for this purpose. The paradox, however, is that the use of statistical methods only decreases the intended increase in transparency (Schellekens *et al.* 2003).

According to Marshall *et al.* (2000), the most frequently mentioned reason for public disclosure of outcomes in the USA is to support consumer freedom of choice. This is based on the assumption that an informed consumer can influence the market and thereby the quality of the services provided. In the past, financial outcomes in particular have been published, which suggests that consumer health care choices are currently based upon mostly financial considerations. Public disclosure of information regarding quality of care should, in theory, produce a shift from competition based on financial considerations to quality of care considerations.

Societal parties

The modern *care consumer* is increasingly better educated and increasingly critical of companies and social institutions including the health care system. This holds for not only the individual consumer but also and most certainly for consumer groups organised in the form of patient associations or regional and national platforms. Such consumers demand good care, good service and want to be thoroughly informed.

The care consumer now considers receipt of information regarding the quality of care in relation to the cost of the care quite normal. That is, health care information is the same as other types of consumer information (e.g. the information which one receives when entering into an insurance contract or taking out a mortgage). The consumer thus wants comparable information with regard to the individual care provider and care institution.

In addition to production demands, *health care insurers* are imposing quality demands on care institutions to an increasing extent. The quality demands are very process oriented and pertain to not only certification and accreditation but also – to an increasing extent – cost-effectiveness. In the future, it will thus be possible for insurers to make higher production agreements with the most cost-effective care institutions and presumably at the cost of other institutions.

The purchase of care is made transparent only when the insurer has access to information regarding results and costs. In such a manner, the insurer is placed in a position to provide the consumer with a competitive offer as the price–quality relation per component of the package is clear. And such a situation also has advantages for the care providers themselves as they are then evaluated on the basis of quality and not only price as now threatens to be the case.

The *government* strongly stimulates benchmarking activities under the rubric of heightened effectiveness. The trend on the part of the government is certainly in the direction of steering at a distance, but figures are at least demanded in return. By gaining insight into the results of care, moreover, the government can evaluate the results of various care investments and innovations in relation to costs.

The *care providers* obviously have a considerable interest in evaluation of the results of the care processes provided by them because this information can help them improve the quality of their work. An external interest is that insight into results can indicate which means are needed to attain which results and thereby limit the probability of 'dumb' cutbacks.

Care institutions are increasingly being placed in a position of competition with respect to commercial care providers, foreign care providers and each other. Insight into results gives care institutions an opportunity to demonstrate what they are good at.

The *media* also play a large role in the demand for transparency of health care. The availability of information via predominantly the internet has increased greatly, and media interest in health care in general has also increased.

Application of external indicators in different countries

In the USA, outcome figures are published via brochures and the internet and often take the form of report cards. Many different organisations have contributed to the development of report cards in the USA, including national and local governments organisations, employers, consumer organisations, interest groups and the media. The report cards typically contain information with regard to both the structure and process of care but also outcome indicators. However, the scientific soundness of the report cards strongly varies (Marshall *et al.* 2000).

The government in Great Britain also actively supports the public disclosure of comparative information with regard to the quality of the care within the National Health Service. The underlying objective is to expand accountability and stimulate quality improvement. A systematic and comprehensive external system of reporting has been developed in the form of a national performance framework for this purpose. Given that the public disclosure of performance data is only a very recent event, however, little has been published with regard to the effects of such for the NHS (Marshall 2002).

In the Netherlands, interest groups such as consumer platforms are also paying greater attention to care results. Elsevier publishes the results of a survey containing an evaluation of hospitals on an annual basis, for example. The hospitals grouped as academic, large and medium are assigned a general report mark and specialist expertise, nursing expertise, patient friendliness and cooperation with primary and supplementary health care providers are evaluated. All of the specialisations are evaluated, and an inventory of both the strong and weak points is created. In such a manner, a rank ordering of the best and the poorest scoring hospitals can be established. The scores are created on the basis of surveys of doctors, nurses and directorates (Hen 2000).

One of the newest developments in the area of performance indicators in the Netherlands is a basic set of hospital performance indicators. In order to better fulfil its supervisory task, the Inspectie voor de Gezondheidszorg (IGZ) or National Dutch Health Inspectorate has started to make use of the performance indicators supplied by care institutions. All hospitals have been asked to disclose their performance in terms of the basic set of hospital performance indicators for the past year. Public disclosure of the indicators improves the transparency of the care and also enables better supervision (Meijerink *et al.* 2003). There are also possible counterproductive effects of public disclosure of performance indicators, but the Health Inspectorate attempts to prevent any such effects with a focus on feasibility and focus on internal quality improvement.

The basic set of hospital performance indicators was formed via selection from the many international examples of indicator sets using the following criteria:

- preference for outcome indicators;
- quality improvement desired and possible;
- no or minimal and responsible increase of registration pressure;
- translation into hospital care possible;
- careful treatment of particularly sensitive indicators.

(Berg *et al.* 2003)

The basic set of hospital performance indicators contains indicators in the areas of patient safety and efficiency. In addition, a number of parameters considered to be of importance for the accountability, steering and benchmarking of hospitals by the three branch organisations are included (www.igz.nl).

It is clear from the foregoing that the first steps have been taken in Europe towards the comparison of organisations and that the use of outcome indicators is being given an increasingly larger role within this process. In the USA, outcome indicators have been used for purposes of external accountability for quite some time already.

This overview also makes it clear that care institutions are increasingly being followed with respect to their performance and that the care institutions, themselves, are developing a more proactive policy with regard to the public disclosure of information. The consumer does not, as yet, make much use of the outcomes as the following example shows.

CASE VIGNETTE

Open heart surgery waiting times

In a recent experiment patients awaiting open heart surgery were given the choice between a longer waiting time with treatment in a nearby Dutch hospital or faster treatment, in this case by Dutch surgeons working in an academic care institution in Germany. The experiment was halted due to a lack of interest on the part of patients who almost all opted for a longer waiting time.

QUALITY AND OPENNESS

Institutions with quality of care policy attend to more than just patients and care providers. The frequently used EFQM model has as one of its result criteria, for example, appreciation or satisfaction on the part of corporate social responsibility. The term 'socially responsible entrepreneurship' will be used to refer to this criterion here.

Socially responsible entrepreneurship implies a business consciously and structurally giving content to its role in society in a manner which goes further than what is obligated by law and a manner which provides added value for both the business *and* society (Cooymans and Hintzen 2000). This involves a careful balancing of business and social interests which are, of course, largely intertwined within care organisations. The social environment may also be quite varied, as depicted in Figure 12.1.

The various parties involved in care organisations can be more generally grouped as follows: those primarily involved, which includes the patients, families, referrers and employees; those secondarily involved, which includes the insurers and chain partners; and those with a tertiary involvement – that is, other parties. The management concerned with the social environment determines the

Figure 12.1 *Different parties involved in care organisations.*

extent to which it wants to involve and inform the various representatives of the social environment.

The accountability associated with quality of care policy and the various social partners is aimed at not only production and costs but also what is called the triple bottom line: result aspects, social aspects and ecological aspects (see Figure 12.2). Responsibility for care outcomes falls under 'result aspects'.

Figure 12.2 *Triple bottom line.*
Source: after Cooymans and Hintzen 2000.

Predominantly in the USA, experience has been gained with the public disclosure of health care outcomes. As an example, we can take bypass operations in the state of New Jersey (Cardiovascular Health Advisory Panel, 1998). In the USA, some 14 million people suffer from coronary heart diseases. A frequent treatment for this is bypass surgery and, in the state of New Jersey in 1994–1995, some 14,510 people underwent such surgery. For purposes of this intervention, information was gathered on demographic variables, preoperative risk factors, complications both during and after surgery and discharge status. It was thus attempted to obtain an indication of the preoperative severity of each patient's heart problems. In Table 12.1 the data are presented as originally published.

The public disclosure of the information shown in Table 12.1 led to a number of quality improvement measures and to a significant decline in the mortality figures. An evaluation of the publication of outcomes in a comparable quasi-experimental study also revealed large improvements in post-bypass mortalities (Hannan *et al.* 1994).

THE PUBLICATION OF OUTCOMES

The publication of health care outcomes has led to heated debate. The proponents see the following advantages of publication.

- Publication stimulates competition in health care. The informed consumer opts for better hospitals, and those hospitals scoring lower will thus do their best to close the performance gap.
- It is better for discussions of the quality of health care to be concerned with outcomes than with costs as is usually now the case.

Table 12.1 *Outcome indicators for bypass surgery*

Hospital	Cases	Deaths	OMR	EMR	RAMR	95% CI for RAMR
Cooper Hospital/University MC	797	29	3.64	4.36	3.13	(2.09, 4.49)
Deborah Heart and Lung Center	1.676	51	3.04	2.80	4.08	(3.04, 5.36)
General Hospital Center at Passiac	838	36	4.30	3.90	4.13	(2.89, 5.72)
Hackensack University Medical Center	1.554	45	2.90	4.08	2.66	−(1.94, 3.56)
Jersey Shore Medical Center	835	40	4.79	4.04	4.45	(3.18, 6.05)
Morristown Memorial Hospital	1.860	47	2.53	3.47	2.73	−(2.01, 3.63)
Newark Beth Israel Medical Center	938	66	7.04	5.03	5.24	+(4.05, 6.67
Our Lady of Lourdes Medical Center	1.672	65	3.89	3.97	3.67	(2.83, 4.68)
Robert Wood Johnson University Hospital	1.400	42	3.00	2.99	3.67	(2.71, 5.09)
St Joseph's Hospital/ Medical Center	945	41	4.34	4.21	3.87	(2.77, 5.25)
St Michael's Medical Center	874	34	3.89	3.94	3.71	(2.57, 5.18)
The Valley Hospital	998	42	4.21	3.51	4.50	(3.24, 6.08)
UMDNJ/University Hospital	123	6	4.88	2.74	6.67	(2.43, 14.51)
Statewide total	**14510**	**544**	**3.75**	**3.75**		

Notes: OMR: observed mortality rate
EMR: expected mortality rate
RAMR: risk-adjusted mortality rate; RAMR = (OMR/EMR) *Statewide OMR
+ Risk-adjusted mortality rate significantly higher than statewide rate based on 96 per cent confidence interval.
− Risk-adjusted mortality rate significantly lower than statewide rate based on 95 per cent confidence interval.

- Outcomes constitute the best starting point for government inspections and government involvement.
- If the institutions do not publish their own outcomes, others will.
- When outcome figures are known, the patient has a right to inspect the figures.
- Professionals can adopt successful methods from each other.

The opponents see the following disadvantages of publication (Davies and Lampel 1998).

- Performance is influenced only in part by the professionals involved. Other factors such as the lifestyle of the patient or access to particular equipment or facilities strongly influence treatment and care outcomes.
- Outcomes strongly relate to the end of the treatment process where adjustment is often too late. For this reason, there is more to be said for the use of process indicators.
- There are severe methodological shortcomings associated with the routine collection of data, and these shortcomings severely limit the interpretability of the data. It is not possible to deduce cause–effect relations on the basis of such data.
- An overemphasis on outcomes can lead to defensive behaviour and further damage the quality of care as a result.
- The media will provide simplistic reports of results and thereby damage reputations.

The opponents further argue that the spectacular results produced in New Jersey would also have occurred had the outcome data been made available for internal use only. Observed improvements may also have to do with selection, it is argued that people at particularly high risk may go to other states; people at particularly high risk may be refused treatment (i.e. surgery in this case); the recording of the data may be unreliable; inadequate risk adjustment may have occurred; and many risk factors may be over-reported (Marshall *et al.* 2000).

The opponents also frequently suggest that the costs of recording outcomes may be higher than the benefits as the establishment of an outcome measurement system requires an enormous bureaucratic effort, outcomes can lead to prolonged discussions and outcomes can simply call for the collection of additional data.

Given the magnitude of the debate to date, it is surprising that not more studies have been done on the effects of public disclosure. An overview of the publications in this area (Marshall *et al.* 2000) revealed the following. Consumers and financers ask many but often opposite questions in response to the disclosure of outcome information. Only a small number of people actually read the outcome information. And the relevant reports are understood only to a limited extent. Nevertheless, the available evidence suggests that the reporting of outcomes exerts a small but increasing influence on the choices of consumers and financers.

It is also surprising that doctors have been found to make relatively little use of outcome information and to be very critical of this information. Doctors read the reports, but rarely discuss what they have read with patients. A confirmation of this is the fact that little or no change in bed occupation emerged after the publication of relevant outcomes.

The fact that a large number of hospitals rarely react to the published outcomes also comes as a surprise. And if hospitals react, it is often defensively. Some hospitals do, however, consider the information to be of value and integrate the outcome information into their quality of care policy.

Despite all of the misgivings mentioned above, there is evidence suggesting that the publication of outcome data improves care outcomes. An example is the already mentioned decrease in bypass mortality rates for hospitals in New Jersey.

THE HANDLING OF OUTCOMES

It is important that a distinction be made between internal versus external indicators. Internal indicators have a clear quality improvement function while external indicators have more to do with control. In Table 12.2, the major differences between internal versus external indicators are summarised (Berg and Schellekens 2002).

The public disclosure of outcome results is probably unavoidable for care organisations in the most developed countries in the world (Marshall *et al.* 2000). An organisation which introduces outcome management – including the benchmarking of outcomes – for purposes of quality improvement can best do this in an anticipatory and proactive manner, moreover, as the unwilling leakage of outcome results can be fatal. When an outcome management system is being established for purposes of learning and quality improvement, outcome results which fall into the

Table 12.2 Differences between internal and external indicators

Internal indicators	External indicators
For internal use	*For external accountability*
■ aimed at self-steering and improvement	■ aimed at minimum quality and comparison
■ relevant for professionals and management within care institutions	■ relevant for government, inspection, health care insurers, patient organisations
■ specific, detailed	■ nonspecific, global
■ thorough validation not needed	■ exhaustive validation necessary
■ simple registration at the source	■ registration requires separate infrastructure
■ irrelevant or useless to the public	■ public in nature
■ intended to learn (and not control)	■ intended for comparison and control
■ quick, 'fun', instructive	■ difficult, long term, potentially threatening
■ 'good–better' quality paradigm is typical	■ 'poor–good' quality paradigm is typical

hands of external parties without a suitable interpretive framework can be particularly damaging. Without sufficient contextual information, outcome indicators can present a completely mistaken image of the quality of care provided by an organisation. Outcomes indicators cannot be viewed separate from their initial purpose. And only on very rare occasions can a single indicator fulfil both internal and external functions as in the case of unplanned hospital readmission. In many cases, furthermore, the confidential internal use of indicators may actually be the most obvious means to bring about acceptance and use as in cases of avoidable death.

It is better to handle the public disclosure of care outcomes from the same learning attitude. However, the adoption of such an attitude has a number of consequences. Given that the use of care outcomes for external accountability has disclosure and comparison as its objective, the relevant information must be accurate, reliable and valid (Solberg *et al.* 1997). The comparisons must be realistic, which means that sufficiently large population must be sampled. A large amount of data preferably across a longer period of time must be collected. And differences in the care contexts must also be considered. Unfortunately, many potentially relevant indicators appear to be unusable due to no guarantee of their comparability (Berg and Schellekens 2002).

As already mentioned, the external publication of internal indicators can also be counterproductive at times. And in this light, it is better that indicators used for purposes of internal improvement be protected from external control unless it has been decided within the organisation in advance to supply the figures to a third party. The thoughtless external use of data collected for internal purposes can clearly damage the enthusiasm of those working on improvement.

On a different front, patients should be involved in the design and set up of a system of outcome measurement. What do they see as outcomes? What has priority for them? Experience to date shows patient satisfaction and quality of life to be important outcomes for patients. Patients can thus be involved in the measurement of outcomes as the most important source of information, play a role in the interpretation of the data and – more than this – play a role in the implementation of improvements. The same holds for health care insurers. Their focus on price can be influenced when the care provider and financer jointly define the desired outcomes.

In sum, the reporting of health care outcomes must occur with utmost care. A communication plan for the attained outcomes can be formulated using the guidelines outlined in Table 12.3.

CONCLUSION

After reflection upon the debate concerning the publication of health care outcomes, we can conclude that the measurement of outcomes is of primary

Table 12.3 *Formulation of a communication plan for outcome results*

1 After identification of outcomes to be measured, specify which information is of importance to which stakeholders

2 Consult the stakeholders with regard to this information and the context for the publication of the information including any confidentiality requirements

3 Provide stakeholders with the relevant data for a particular period of time, information regarding the significance of the data and information regarding the conclusions which can be attached to the data

4 Monitor how the stakeholders handle the information provided and formulate the remainder of the communication plan on the basis of this information.

importance within the framework of policy aimed at quality improvement. The confidence which the participating individuals and teams have in such measurement largely depends upon the confidentiality of the discussions surrounding such outcomes. And in this light, the external publication of outcomes has little to offer.

When the disclosure of outcomes constitutes part of a more general and integrated quality of care policy, in contrast, external publication can certainly be considered. The outcomes to be disclosed must be carefully selected. The disclosure of the outcomes must be judged useful by not only the financers and patients but also the institution (e.g. medical personnel and managers). And exactly what the findings mean must be clearly and carefully communicated. Only then can the publication of outcomes be effective and actually strengthen the efforts of an organisation to provide increasingly better care and maintain good relations with the different social partners.

DISCUSSION QUESTIONS

1 What role does leadership play in the discussion on public disclosure of outcome data?

2 What effects could public disclosure have on team learning?

3 Which outcome indicators could be used internally and externally, under which conditions?

4 What conditions should be demanded for external use of outcome indicators?

5 Who could really benefit from external presentation of outcome indicators and why?

REFERENCES

Berg, M. and Schelleken, W. (2002) Quality paradigms: differences between internal and external quality indicators (Paradigma's van kwaliteit: De verschillen tussen externe en interne kwaliteitsindicatoren). *Medical Contact (Medisch Contact)*, 57(34): 1203–1205.

Berg, M., Gras, M., Meijerink, Y., Eland, A., Kallewaard, M., Haeck, J. and Kingma H. (2003) Learning from measures: public publication of performance (Leren van cijfers: ziekenhuizen gaan prestaties openbaar maken (2)). *Medical Contact (Medisch Contact)*, 58(40): 1535–1539.

Cardiovascular Health Advisory Panel (1998) *The outcome symposium.* Harvard University, Cambridge, MA.

Cooymans, M.P.M. and Hintzen, E.F.M. (2000) *Winst en Waarden.* Deventer and Den Bosch: Samson.

Davies, N.T.O. and Lampel, J. (1998) Trust in performance indicators? *Quality in Health Care,* 7: 159–162.

Hannan, E.L., Kilburn, H. and Raaz, M. (1994) Improving the outcomes of coronary artery bypass surgery in New York State. *JAMA,* 271: 761–767.

Hen, P. de (2000) The best hospitals (De beste ziekenhuizen). *Elsevier,* 56(39).

Marshall, M.N., Shekele, P.G., Leatherman, S. and Brook, R.N (2000) Public disclosure of performance data: learning from the US experience. *Journal for Health Services Research and Policy,* 5: 1–2.

Marshall, M.N. (2002) *The publication of performance data in the National Health Service: a review of the implications for policy and practice.* Discussion paper.

Meijerink, Y., Gras, M., Eland, A., Kallewaard, M., Haeck, J., Berg M. and Kingma, H. (2003) Working on improvement: publication of hospitals' performance (Werken aan verbetering: ziekenhuizen gaan prestaties openbaar maken (1)). *Medical Contact (Medisch Contact)*, 58(40): 1531–1534.

Schellekens, W., Berg, M. and Klazinga, N. (2003) Flying and being flown: myths and possibilities of performance indicators (Vliegen en gevlogen worden: Mythen en mogelijkheden van prestatie indicatoren van zorgaanbieders). *Medical Contact (Medisch Contact)*, 58(8): 291–294.

Solberg, L.I., Mosser, G. and MacDonald, S. (1997) The three faces of performance measurement: improvement, accountability and research. *Joint Commission Journal on Quality Improvement,* 23(3): 135–147.

Chapter 13

Outcome measurement and scientific development of the field

Jan Walburg

KEY POINTS OF THIS CHAPTER

■ Evaluation research
■ Experimental designs
■ Scientific aspects of outcome measurement

INTRODUCTION

Should the measurement of outcomes – either using a benchmark or not – be considered scientific? This question is of importance for, when one can speak of a scientific status, the results of research into outcomes can have consequences which go far beyond the specific care process which constitutes the topic of outcome measurement. Does outcome measurement have scientific value? If so, what is the value and how can we use the results for the development of the medical field? The discussion below draws heavily upon the outstanding overview entitled *Evaluating health interventions* by John Øvretveit (1998).

OUTCOME RESEARCH AS EVALUATION RESEARCH

Scientific research can be defined as 'committed, systematic inquiry or investigation in order to validate and refine existing knowledge and generate new knowledge' (Schmele 1993). In the measurement of outcomes, it is attempted to answer such questions as what is the best treatment process? Which patients are most satisfied? It is also attempted to test hypotheses as 'we attain better outcomes when we apply this or no intervention.' This investigative process requires the careful collection and processing of data with the aid of specially developed statistical methods. The objective is to expand our knowledge of the care process or gain new insights. And in this sense, one can certainly construe outcome research as science.

Outcome measurement is not fundamental scientific research to assemble valid and generalisable knowledge of a phenomenon in order to promote further scientific knowledge of a topic (Øvretveit 1998). Outcome measurement is much more applied research intended to achieve better decisions with regard to the treatment of people. And in this sense, outcome research constitutes a form of evaluation research: 'a comparative of value to an intervention, in relation to criteria and using systematically collected and analysed data, in order to decide how to act' (Øvretveit 1998: 50).

Evaluation research into interventions may pertain to individuals, a particular population or an entire population. That is, the treatment of individual patients, health promotion in the form of disease management for a group of patients or health promotion with the care system constituting the intervention for an entire population may be of interest. In the case of outcome research, the individual patient is of primary concern followed by groups of patients.

Given the use of scientific methods, outcome research is a form of evaluation research which differs from audits or popular science writing. Outcome research also differs from fundamental research because it is aimed primarily at the support of clinical practice.

PURPOSE, USE AND PERSPECTIVE OF EVALUATIONS

The design and perspective of an evaluation is basically determined by the purpose of the evaluation. In order to achieve usable and valid forms of evaluation, at least the following must be made clear: the target audience, the questions to be answered, what decisions and procedures must proceed in a better informed manner and how much time and what means are available (Øvretveit 1998).

The aims of evaluation research can vary. The interested parties can also have different perspectives.

■ *Financers*. Given that health care does not function within a free market, the market cannot determine whether a particular intervention or medical procedure is conducted or not. Interventions may thus be motivated by the different interests of the care provider, a financer or other interest groups. Evaluation research concerned with the outcomes of interventions can thus provide support for a particular rationale and enable a well-reasoned choice of interventions to apply and to cover or not.

- *Patients.* Yet another motive to evaluate an intervention may lie in the interests of the patients themselves. Patients may want more information with regard to the consequences of different interventions for a particular pathology in terms of costs and quality of life, for example. Radiotherapy or surgery in cases of cancer? Bypass or angioplasty in cases of coronary heart disease? Psychotherapy, pills or electroshock in cases of depression?
- *Professionals.* A third interest motivating evaluation of an intervention may stem from professionals and the question of the cost-effectiveness of certain interventions. This question is certainly justified as not all interventions are really effective. An estimated 25% of all health care interventions has undergone evaluation, and some of the interventions which have undergone evaluation have been found to be ineffective or probably ineffective.
- *Managers.* Another motive for the conduct of evaluation research is to gather support for the decisions of managers. Armed with the results of evaluation research, the manager is in a position to implement changes which actually lead to a better provision of care and not just changes based on management ideology.
- *Policymakers.* The government or insurer may also welcome a particular evaluation in order to facilitate political decision-making.

Within the context of this book, the evaluation of outcomes is aimed predominantly at health care professionals and the managers of health care organisations. These people can decide to make their evaluation results available to patients, insurers, and government bodies, but the learning of the care providers stands central.

THE DESIGN OF AN EVALUATION STUDY

Øvretveit (1998) distinguishes the following six evaluation designs: a descriptive design, an audit design, a before-after comparison, a comparative-experimentalist design, a randomised controlled experimental design and intervention to a health organisation design. The different designs are now briefly considered further.

Descriptive design

This type of evaluation research involves the systematic observation and description of an intervention. Such descriptions can be enlightening and signal problems, but they are not scientific because their quality heavily depends upon the observer who can be biased by observing from a particular theoretical perspective, for example (see Figure 13.1).

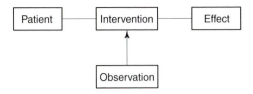

Figure 13.1 *Descriptive design.*

Audit design

In this type of evaluation research, the investigator judges the extent to which the intervention fulfils written standards, procedures or objectives. This is what occurs during a site visit or a certification or accreditation process. When the standard or guideline is based upon scientific evidence, audit provides a cost-effective manner to achieve improvement (see Figure 13.2).

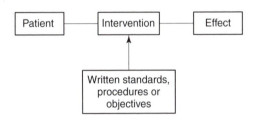

Figure 13.2 *Audit design.*

Before-after comparison

In this type of research, measurement occurs both before and after an intervention in order to evaluate the effect of the intervention. Causal relations cannot be established in such a manner because the change can also be caused by other factors which have not been controlled for. Nevertheless, comparison of pre-test with post-test can provide a 'quick and dirty' impression of the effects of an intervention. When outcome research is conducted without benchmarking, such a design is followed: measurements prior and measurements following intervention are conducted with no further comparison (see Figure 13.3).

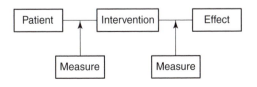

Figure 13.3 *The before–after comparison.*

Comparative-experimentalist design

In this case, the effects of two interventions are compared using before and after outcome measurement. Due to the absence of a control group, it is difficult to causally connect the outcomes to the intervention. But such research can establish which of two interventions exerts more of an effect and thereby avoid the ethical problems associated with the use of placebo (no treatment) control groups.

This is the design of the outcome model with benchmarking and thus comparison of several interventions. Different experimental principles are applied such as the formulation and testing of hypotheses and compensation for influences other than that of the intervention via description of the patient groups in terms of sex or severity of the problems. One can speak of matching to a certain extent: the patient groups are composed to correspond to each other (see Figure 13.4).

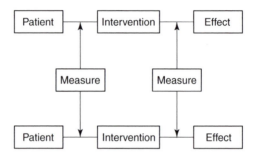

Figure 13.4 *Comparative-experimentalist design.*

Randomised controlled experimental design

Patients are randomly assigned to an experimental intervention and to a placebo. The difference between the conditions indicates the extent to which the experimental intervention has worked. This is the classic, most frequent and most valued research design. One creates two virtually identical groups but with only one subjected to the experimental intervention. Via the elimination of alternative explanations, evidence emerges for the causal relation between the intervention and effect (see Figure 13.5).

The randomised control study is unmistakably most convincing when it comes to demonstration of the effects of an intervention. The randomised control study is also extremely expensive which means that no more than 10% to 20% of all clinical interventions are evaluated in such a manner. In the actual practice of a non-academic hospital, it is difficult to conduct randomised research not only due to the costs but also because of ethical considerations. In addition to these

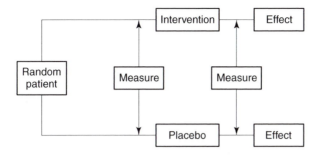

Figure 13.5 *Randomised controlled experimental design.*

problems, there are numerous methodological problems associated with the conduct of such research (Sperry *et al.* 1996).

- The research setting often deviates much too much from the normal care setting for patients.
- In order to control for innumerable variables and be absolutely certain of the
  causal connection, the dimensions of the research must be immense.
- Some patients react differently to the same treatment.
- Patients are randomly distributed across study interventions but the health
  care professionals rarely or never.
- The statistical differences are never so strong that there is absolutely no overlap between the experimental and control groups. There are always patients
  in the control group with outcomes, which are better than or equal to the
  outcomes for patients in the experimental group and vice versa.
- There are always patients who drop out and, when the amount of missing data
  is too large, the research loses its power.
- The application of the inclusion and exclusion criteria used in such research
  to actual patients is often very difficult.

Øvretveit (1998) adds the following problems to those listed above:

- It is difficult to describe the intervention precisely.
- Important differences can still exist between the experimental and control
  groups despite random assignment of patients.
- Important outcomes such as quality of life are sometimes not measured.
- Some outcomes become clear only with the passage of time.

All of the foregoing criticisms do not undermine the strength of randomised control study. The many problems simply indicate the relative value of such research

and that less expensive alternatives can be seriously considered under the condition that the collection of the relevant data be conducted with utmost care.

Intervention to a health organisation design

This type of research measures whether a change in the care system influences the effects of the interventions or not. Examples are the introduction of a training, quality policy or a form of certification. Not only the influences of the organisational change upon the personnel – in the form of satisfaction or knowledge and skills – but also the influences of the change upon patients – because the care process now unfolds differently, the context of the care process has changed or the attitudes of the personnel have changed – are examined (see Figure 13.6).

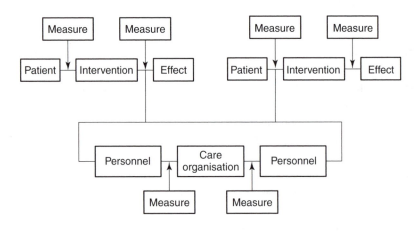

Figure 13.6 *Intervention to a service.*

CONCLUSION: STRENGTHENING THE SCIENTIFIC VALUE OF OUTCOME MEASUREMENT

We think that health care teams should not only conduct treatment and care but also evaluate these for purposes of improvement of care. Such evaluation obviously has greater significance and power when the relevant data has been collected in a precise and scientific manner. Only then will professionals be convinced that a good reason exists for modification of existing procedures and methods. Scientific evidence is thus gathered during the conduct of research on care outcomes.

In the hierarchy of scientific evidence, three basic levels of evidence can be distinguished (Øvretveit, 1998):

- ■ *Level 1*   Evidence attained from at least one well-designed randomised clinical trial.
- ■ *Level 2.1*   Evidence from well-designed controlled studies without randomisation.
- ■ *Level 2.2*   Evidence from well-designed cohort or case-control analytic studies preferably conducted by more than one centre or research group.
- ■ *Level 2.3*   Evidence from comparisons across time or place with or without intervention and dramatic results within such uncontrolled experiments.
- ■ *Level 3*   Opinions of respected authorities thus based upon clinical experience, descriptive studies and reports of expert panels.

The research conducted for purposes of outcome management using benchmarking provides evidence between levels 2.2 and 2.1.

With the aid of outcome research, we are in a position to learn from daily medical practice. Different care processes can be compared, and the effects of particular interventions or particular client populations upon the care outcomes can be derived in such a manner. This form of research strengthens external validity and generalisability because it involves large numbers of patients who undergo a particular treatment. The internal validity of the findings of such research is guaranteed because the intervention process is conducted in keeping with recommended guidelines or some other standards. When indications of important differences in the daily care process reveal themselves, further randomised study may be called for. The situation of outcome management as we have sketched it to date provides an initial feedback loop in which information regarding the outcomes of a care process is supplied to the responsible health care team. A second feedback loop is provided when teams compare outcomes with other health care teams and thereby strengthen the first feedback loop.

With the use of care outcomes for scientific purposes, a third feedback loop is established. Data regarding different care processes is collected from different institutions. A medical knowledge bank thus emerges with respect to these care processes and, in order to complete the third feedback loop, the information in the knowledge bank must be analyzed with some regularity by experts within the field. Among other things, the following should regularly be determined: the nature of the outcome differences; relative cost-effectiveness of the different interventions; how the outcome differences can best be explained in terms of process, structure and patient characteristics; and the implications of the observed outcome differences and their explanations for guidelines and protocols.

The pharmaceutical industry also stands to benefit from outcome management research if only, for example, because the time for product development is shortened. Steps may be more quickly taken towards the supply of either very promising or, of course, already tested medicines for evaluation of their added value within the framework of outcome management. Non-medicinal interventions which may potentially contribute to the improvement of care outcomes may similarly be more quickly introduced and tested with the more rapid innovation of care as a result. Those experts who analyse the knowledge banks can then advise the government and institutions with regard to promising new interventions. Outcome management can, then, under particular conditions contribute to further scientific development. Drawing upon Pronovost and Kazandjian (1999), the conditions for further scientific learning are:

1 specification of hypotheses;
2 careful securing of the care process;
3 use of valid measures;
4 sufficient sample size;
5 study of interactions with patient variables;
6 application of appropriate statistical tests;
7 carefully drawn and valid conclusions.

Outcome management is in a position not only to contribute to the policy of an organisation with respect to the quality of care but also to contribute to the development of its own scientific field of study.

DISCUSSION QUESTIONS

1 What are the purposes of evaluation research for which parties?
2 What are the problems with randomised controlled experimental designs?
3 Under what conditions can outcome management contribute to the development of our scientific knowledge?

REFERENCES

Øvretveit, J. (1998) *Evaluating health interventions.* Buckingham and Philidelphia, PA: Open University Press.

Pronovost, P.J. and VKazandjian, A. (1999) A new learning environment: combining clinical research with quality improvement. *Journal of Evaluation in Clinical Practice* 5: 33–40.

Schmele, J.A. (1993) *The textbook of total quality in healthcare*. Delray Beach, FL: St Lucie Press.

Sperry, L., Brill, P.L., Howard, K.I. and Guissom, G.R. (1996) *Treatment outcomes in psychotherapy and psychiatric interventions*. New York: Brunner/Mazel.

Chapter 14

Outcome management and performance improvement
Reflections and future directions

John Wilderspin and Helen Bevan

KEY POINTS OF THIS CHAPTER

- Summary of main learning points from preceding chapters
- Possible ways in which the 'discipline' of performance improvement may develop in future
- Asks readers to think about how they can apply the learning points in the book to their own day-to-day work
- Encourages readers to contribute to the future development of performance improvement within health care

THE OBJECTIVES OF THE BOOK

This book has described the development, and application, of outcome management and performance improvement within the field of healthcare. Our purpose has been to share learning on the subject with practitioners and students and to help fellow professionals in their work in healthcare improvement. The book is written for the benefit of leaders and managers at every point in the organisation, clinical leaders working directly with patients, as well as executives taking responsibility for healthcare within or across whole organisations.

Our other purpose is to encourage further the development of the performance improvement 'discipline' within healthcare across national boundaries. The authors work in different countries, in very different roles, but it is clear to us that there are lessons about defining and enhancing performance improvement, which are applicable to healthcare leaders across the globe. However, the discipline is still relatively young in the healthcare field, and important lessons are not always widely disseminated. We hope that this book will help to generate further debate, and further spreading of good practice.

THE BACKGROUND TO PERFORMANCE IMPROVEMENT IN HEALTH CARE

We began the book with concepts of performance management and learning organisations which are largely drawn from the business world. We traced the origins of outcome management in healthcare. We observed the similarities and differences between the 'business' model of performance management and that which has been applied in healthcare. In particular we have focussed on the importance of 'outcome management' using the generic disciplines of performance improvement to improve clinical outcomes for individual patients and whole populations.

We also considered the synergies and links between outcome management and other approaches to quality improvement such as the European Foundation for Quality Management Excellence Model, projects using Plan-Do-Study-Act cycles and accreditation and certification processes. We concluded, that in order to maximise success we need to apply quality improvement methods in an integrated way directly to care processes. Outcome management is an effective mechanism for integration.

THE PRINCIPLES OF PERFORMANCE IMPROVEMENT IN HEALTH CARE

Despite our difference in backgrounds and experiences we have common understanding about how performance improvement can be applied for the benefit of healthcare users. These underlying principles run throughout the book.

Performance management and performance improvement

Although the term 'performance management' has wide usage, particularly in British healthcare, our real passion is for 'performance improvement'. What is the difference?

For us, performance management is associated with the more traditional application of methods from industry, focussing on financial performance and organisational parameters, not always necessarily related to outcomes for patients. Performance improvement, by contrast, is a blend of the best features of performance management (measurement, clarity etc) with a major focus on learning and support for improvement. The following factors are central to this approach.

Focusing on improved outcomes for patients

According to the World Health Organisation, healthcare exists to provide high quality treatment to patients, and to prevent ill health in individuals and whole populations. Central to this is the outcome of care: improved health status, increased well-being, the absence or reduction of symptoms of ill health. It goes without saying therefore that any reference to 'performance' in health care needs to reflect primarily on the outcomes of the health care process.

As demonstrated in Chapters 3, 6 and 10, effective processes of care are instrumental to effective outcomes. Poor processes lead to poor or unmeasurable outcomes. As Paul Batalden tells us, 'Every system is perfectly designed to achieve the results it gets' (Institute of Medicine 2001: 23). If we want to get better outcomes, we have to change the system. However, a *process* improvement focus on its own is insufficient. It has to be seen as an implementation strategy to achieve specific outcome goals. Too many efforts in the history of healthcare quality improvement have focussed on process improvement or process standardisation without the underpinning outcome improvement goal. Consequently the results for patients have been disappointing or poor.

In order to develop outcome goals, 'outcomes' have to be defined. As Chapter 7 demonstrated, it is possible to apply a multidimensional framework of outcomes. This takes account of clinical outcomes, patient experience of care, functional outcomes linked to patient quality of life and cost of treatment. These categories form the basis of a powerful approach to outcome goal setting and outcome delivery. This can be applied at the level of the individual patient and at the level of the organisation as whole.

Adapting and testing methods from other fields

The discipline of 'performance management' has been borrowed and adapted from non-health-care organisations. A pragmatic philosophy of not reinventing the wheel runs throughout the book. Our approach to performance improvement draws from other sources including the following:

- Scientific methods used widely within clinical practice. Many of the practitioners of healthcare performance improvement are from a clinical background, or have spent their working lives in a clinical organisation. As we have said before, 'performance' needs to be defined in clinical terms, focussed on the outcome of clinical care. It is necessary therefore to use methods which are familiar to both practitioners and users, where they have relevance. Examples of this include the use of qualitative research and the linkage of cause and effect.

- Methods drawn from manufacturing, and other service organisations outside of healthcare. Healthcare is different from other industries but it also has many similarities. It is built on the application of complex processes, relying on the contributions of many individuals. It comprises a series of processes that can be measured and improved. It is typically provided by teams which need to work closely with other teams and other organisations to be successful. It is a service organisation requiring long-term support for its users. As such, learning from other organisations about human resource management, service orientation, process control and productivity improvement can be adapted and applied to the healthcare field.

- A key theme we can take from performance improvement in other sectors is reducing unnecessary 'variation' in the system. Chapter 6 introduced the concepts of 'natural' and 'artificial' variation. In order to improve performance, we need to take steps to reduce the artificial variation which is created by the way that we organise our healthcare delivery system. Variables created by different patient characteristics, as described in Chapter 8, are examples of natural variation, which needs to be taken account of and managed. Chapter 8 sets out a range of techniques for managing and alleviating the risks in outcome management associated with patient variables.

Utilising measurement and feedback

Central to the notion of outcome management is the notion of measurement. 'Improvement' is by definition concerned with relativities: are we 'better' than we were before? Better than other teams? Better than the standards we set ourselves? Being able to measure our progress against goals, both in tangible terms but also in the eyes of our 'customers', is fundamental. We have explored this not only from the point of view of the healthcare process (Chapter 6) but also from the perspectives of patients and other key stakeholders (Chapter 11). Measurement is a critical component of outcome management but is insufficient on its own. As Chapter 3 reminded us, measurement is one component of a wider system of improvement. The measurement process must be linked to the achievement of clear goals and a tangible improvement process. It also must be connected to mechanisms for feeding results back to clinical teams so that performance can be reflected on and further changes to the care process planned. This was explored in detail in Chapter 10.

Employing performance tools

Performance management and improvement are intensely practical. Its practitioners are busy people, with limited time for study or reflection. Methods or techniques which will bring the greatest benefit in the shortest time for the least effort or complexity are therefore referred to throughout the book. This includes case studies of where these tools have been shown to work.

Managing performance in a multilayered system

We recognise that 'improved performance' can mean different things at different points of the healthcare system. For whole organisations, regions or even countries, it will be focussed on the impact for whole populations. For clinical teams, individual practitioners and of course patients, it will focus on the outcome of specific care processes and treatments. An effective outcome management strategy must align improvement needs at all levels. The aim is to bring about tangible improvements in the quality of care. Therefore the focus in this book is naturally at the level of the clinical microsystem (Chapter 3), the point of interaction with the patient where care is actually delivered.

Developing different perspectives on improving performance

We have acknowledged that performance is not always a completely objective process in relation to healthcare. At a patient level, differences between the views of patients and clinicians are crucial just as are those between healthcare executives and their local populations. Trying to capture those differences and ideally to reconcile them into a set of common objectives, measures and agreed outcomes is a huge challenge. Developing our skills in this area is fundamental to the development of the whole discipline. Some of the challenges inherent in this process are explored in Chapter 12.

ESSENTIAL INGREDIENTS FOR EFFECTIVE PERFORMANCE IMPROVEMENT

If the principles set out above are to be applied effectively, certain prerequisites have to be in place to support their application.

Sustained leadership

Delivering and sustaining high performance in healthcare is a demanding job. Although healthcare staff and users are intrinsically supportive of the task of improving the outcomes of care, turning that intrinsic support into delivery is challenging. This is especially the case when performance improvement or outcome management is still a relatively new discipline in the healthcare field.

Developing an environment where high performance can flourish and then systematically applying the principles to achieve sustainable change, require high levels of skill. Recruiting or identifying good leaders at every level, then training and supporting them is a foundation stone for performance improvement.

Creating a 'receptive context'

In Chapter 4, we described the necessary steps to create an environment where high performance can flourish. These included clarity of objectives, focus on priorities and 'whole system' support for the 'case for change'. This process is essential if key stakeholders (staff, users, funders) are to be receptive to the necessary changes which are going to take place.

It also helps build an understanding about the process of improvement; what success should look like, how individuals can make their contribution, what are the milestones we need to achieve. This is important as a means of bringing about a change in the way the organisation/team/individual works, but critical if that change is to be sustained and built upon.

Sharing knowledge and facilitating learning

Chapter 2 focussed on the development of the 'learning organisation' and this theme runs throughout the book. It is vital to the principle of 'performance improvement'; excellence based on enabling staff to do their very best, rather than on imposing sanctions for poor performance. Central to this is the need for knowledge. Knowledge about best clinical practise, about the views of users, about better ways of organising care for patients. Underpinning this is a systematic approach which creates a 'thirst' for knowledge and ensures that knowledge is shared quickly and well.

Developing effective teamwork

High performance (defined as good outcomes of care) is founded on effective teamworking. Although individuals make an important personal contribution, the outcome of the care process is reliant on the effectiveness of the team. At its most fundamental level this is the multidisciplinary term which pools collective knowledge and diverse skills to deliver improved outcomes for individual patients. At its widest, it is the web of relationships between departments and whole organisations which underpins the modern healthcare system. Linked to this is the emerging thinking about teams and organisations as complex adaptive systems: Chapter 5 explores this issue in detail.

Utilising information, measurement and analysis

It is said that 'information is power' and this is certainly true in the field of performance improvement. Whether you are measuring improvements in the condition of a diabetic patient or the health status of a whole city, good information is critical. However, this is more than simply a question of collecting data, useful though that is. It is about establishing a culture where clear objectives, open to measurement and comparison, combined with a desire to analyse critically, leads to sustained changes in outcome. It is worthy of a book in itself, and features heavily throughout the preceding chapters. Of particular importance for the emerging discipline of performance improvement in healthcare is the way that well established processes from clinical medicine and manufacturing systems are now being combined into a new healthcare 'improvement science'. This is explored in more detail in Chapter 6.

Engaging stakeholders

Perhaps the most exciting aspect of performance improvement in healthcare is the way in which 'consumers' are being involved in the improvement process. Traditionally in healthcare, consumers have been 'done to'; exercising influence over the way healthcare is provided only through elected politicians, and then at a very high level. In so far as 'performance' was judged from the standpoint of the consumer, it was in terms of coldly clinical changes such as reductions in morbidity.

In line with changes in the rest of society, this is changing fast. 'Outcomes' are now seen to relate as much to patients own perceptions and well being as to changes in clinical status. Importantly, we also see that individual patients and society as a whole are 'partners' in the improvement process. This is not simply a question of bowing to societal pressure; in few other industries do consumers have such insight into the way services are organised, or such a stake in the outcome. We cannot afford for that insight, and commitment to be wasted.

DEVELOPING THE DISCIPLINE

Performance improvement in healthcare is here to stay. Whatever negative views one might have about some of its manifestations, it is too useful to patients, politicians, taxpayers/insurers and practitioners to be abandoned. Chapter 13 explores the scientific basis for the discipline, but practitioners also need to consider issues such as the following:

- Can results be shared between practitioners and internationally to allow the development of better practice?
- How can we encourage greater sharing and debate about learning in this field?
- What will ensure that practitioners adopt a more systematic approach to their work?

- How can we enable patients and other stakeholders to participate in and enrich the process of performance improvement?
- What are the new challenges to which performance management will need to be applied?

Throughout the book we have posed questions of the reader to help them focus on the learning points from the preceding chapter. The questions above are issues for all of us, including the authors. We have summarised the 'learning so far' on the application of a performance management approach within healthcare. Our specific focus has been on the applications of a performance management approach at a clinical level, so that the outcomes for individual patients can be optimised. However, we know that this 'discipline' is still at a very early stage of development. We hope, therefore, that our book will stimulate readers not only to try new approaches in their own work, but also to share their experiences, to take the development of the discipline onto a new level.

REFERENCE

Institute of Medicine (2001) *Crossing the quality chasm*. Washington, DC: National Academy Press.

Index